PRAISE FOR *THE AMERICAN COVENANT*

I highly recommend Marshall Foster's book *The American Covenant* to every freedom-loving individual. Marshall Foster is a premier historian who has the unique gift of making history truly come alive. His passion to teach the Biblical source of America's freedoms inspires all who hear him. "Covenant keepers win, and covenant breakers lose." His writings open the door to personalities and events of the past in vivid color. He connects dots that make sense of current events, and he stirs the hearts of his readers to engage in the struggle to pass our liberties on to a promising future generation! Marshall personally inspired me many years ago. I purchased and devoured his books and tapes and can unequivocally say that he is significantly responsible for my career in writing and teaching American history.

— William J. Federer, President of Amerisearch Inc. and best-selling author

A friend laid a copy of *The American Covenant* on the table between a group of us, put her hand firmly on the cover, looked us square in the eye, and said, "This is exactly what America needs right now. The American people have to have this book." She's exactly right. We need the American Covenant right now. There is no better study suited to provide answers for the challenges we are facing today. Don't miss the opportunity to own a book that will thrill your heart, bolster your courage, and inspire your thinking.

— Charcie Russell, Radio Talk Show Host; Cofounder and Director of Development, MOPS International

Marshall Foster has crisscrossed America and the British Isles for decades, teaching the truths of Providential history, covenantal understanding, and Christian self-government. All three are emphasized and articulated in a fresh way to a new generation in his book *The American Covenant: The Untold Story*. This book is truly a tool to give you a passion and deeper understanding of the prayer that Jesus taught: "Thy kingdom come, Thy will be done, on earth as it is in heaven."

— Dr. Paul Jehle, President, Plymouth Rock Foundation; Senior Pastor, The New Testament Church, Plymouth

The American Covenant: The Untold Story has changed the lives of so many people. I was one of the first people to read it. I started a school as part of our church ministry. Marshall's book became the primary textbook for the students in U.S. History. It opens the reader's eyes to the reality of America's greatness and the reason for it: God!

— Pastor Rob Scribner, Pro-football running back, Los Angeles Rams; Pastor, Lighthouse Church, Santa Monica

I am honored to recommend Marshall Foster's book *The American Covenant: The Untold Story*. Marshall has a passion to teach Americans about our rich Christian legacy, including our own nation's background, but also the incredible impact of Christianity on Western civilization.

— Jerry Newcombe, D.Min., Senior Producer, D. James Kennedy Ministries and best-selling author

THE
AMERICAN
COVENANT

THE UNTOLD STORY

American Campfire Revival Edition

MARSHALL FOSTER

Nordskog Publishing inc.

VENTURA, CALIFORNIA

The American Covenant: The Untold Story
American Campfire Revival Edition
by Marshall Foster • © 2021 Marshall Foster
ISBN: 978-0-9903774-0-5
Library of Congress Control Number: 2021935520

Editing and Production:
Mary-Elaine Swanson, Inaugural 1981 Editor
Cody Duck Designs, Cover Design
Michelle Shelfer (benediction.biz), Managing Editor and Typesetting
Nikola Dimitrov, Proofreader
Cover Painting: "Mayflower in Plymouth Harbor," (detail) by William Halsall, 1882
Thank you Wikimedia Commons for art {{PD-US}}

Published by

Nordskog Publishing, Inc.
2716 Sailor Avenue, Ventura, California 93001
805-642-2070 • 805-276-5129
NordskogPublishing.com

Christian
Indie Publishing
Association

Dedicated to
my beloved family

Table of Contents

Foreword
by Kirk Cameron

*M*ost history books I read as a kid specialized in long, boring sentences and loads of dates, destinations, and dead guys. Marshall Foster changed all that. He made me realize that I'd been reading history through the wrong set of glasses. History is truly "His Story" of the forming of the cosmos, the spark of the miracle of life, a war in the heavens, a monstrous betrayal resulting in generational disaster, true global climate change, a worldwide rescue mission, the forming of nations, the beginning of religious and civil government, wars and famines, tyranny and miracles, fulfilled prophecies, the war to end all wars, and the spread of freedom across the earth!

I met Marshall in LAX airport after reading another one of his excellent books, *The Battle for the 21st Century*. To be honest, I was wrestling with whether or not to invoke a permanent surgical solution to having too many kids (we had six wonderful children already!).

Marshall's storytelling about God giving generational blessings and the gift of children to the faithful stopped me in my tracks and caused me to question my motives for turning off the fruitful faucet. We agreed to talk further…

Morning coffees led to afternoon meals, discussing everything from the kids to communism, pyramids to Plato, and the apostle Paul to the Pilgrims. I had never heard history told from what Marshall called the "Providential Perspective." That is, explaining and understanding the stories of the past—including their heroes and villains, main and supporting characters, exciting plots, and surprise endings—as an unfolding narrative told by God, demonstrating His power, character, and faithfulness to His people. And I don't mean just the stories in the Bible. I'm also talking about Chinese history, African history, European history, American history, and all the history of all the world—all demonstrating God's goodness and the power of the Gospel to transform hearts, homes, communities, and nations! Now *that's* not how I was taught to read history in eighth-grade civics. If Marshall Foster had been my history teacher in high school, I wouldn't have had so many notes sent home from the principal asking my mom why I was always falling asleep in class.

In 2011, Marshall and I made a documentary movie together called *Monumental: In Search of America's National Treasure*. In it, we retraced the escape route of the Pilgrims from England to Holland to the New World to learn about the people, the places, and the principles that created the greatest nation the world has ever known.

The American Covenant: The Untold Story has become the study guide for millions of people gathering (virtually) around a campfire in my backyard as part of the *American Campfire Revival: A 100-Day Plan*. Marshall Foster served as our faithful "Gandalf," whose knowledge and wisdom led us as the "fellowship of the faithful" through the land of America—explaining its miraculous beginnings, revealing life-giving secrets, forgotten covenants, and a road map for defeating darkness, and stirring up our passion to see liberty not only for "the land of the free and the home of the brave," but for every nation on earth!

My prayer is that this book will become a source of light and life to you and your family as it has been for me and mine, and that as a result, the fires of revival will so burn within our hearts that the eyes of the whole world will be upon us and say, "May God do for us in our nation as He has done again in America."

— KIRK CAMERON

"THE SIGNING OF THE MAYFLOWER COMPACT" (1620)
BY PERCY MORAN

MAYFLOWER COMPACT 1620

GOVERNOR BRADFORD'S COPY OF THE MAYFLOWER COMPACT
Preserved in his handwriting in his History of Plymouth Plantation.

OVER 400 YEARS AGO!

Introduction

$\mathcal{M}$any people in America today feel trapped in a slowly sinking ship. They see crushing taxation, despotic regulations, and shutdowns eating their incomes and future dreams. Most Americans still share a Judeo-Christian view of life, yet they are seeing their traditional values driven from the public square. For centuries, these values have been understood as the foundation of America's freedom and prosperity. But in recent decades, a small elite appears to be imposing a destructive secularization on our nation,

To understand our present condition, we need to come to grips with the fact that for the last 150 years, we have fallen away from the original American Covenant of our Founders. Most of us are so far away from it that we are unable to remember that it existed and formed the foundation of our nation.

Layer upon layer of secularized misinterpretations have obscured the true meaning and culturally regenerating nature of the covenants and compacts of our early settlers. As often happens when generations pass and prosperity comes, the deeply religious foundation for our national blessings has been forgotten. In the early nineteenth century, the Christian community, which had been the dominant cultural force for two hundred years, began to ignore its responsibilities. Compromising voices came forth to explain the greatness of America as a "manifest destiny." We were born to rule, some postulated. Others said we were a "chosen people." The voices of Christians, needed to expose such blatant error, were muffled by a growing ignorance of our heritage.

Establishment politicians and others have tried for decades to rally the American patriot under the banner of a "secular democracy," the "Great Society," or the call to "fundamentally change America." But all these attempts have failed or will fail to unite our people and restore the nation, for they are built upon the shifting sands of secular humanism or cultural Marxism. They are leading us into a potentially violent division and the collapse of our civilization.

We as a people have forgotten that our foundations were laid upon the Rock of Ages. Daniel Webster acknowledged this truth. Speaking at Plymouth, Massachusetts, on December 22, 1820, at the bicentennial of the founding of Plymouth, he ended his address with the vital importance of remembering what makes the "happiest society":

> *Finally, let us not forget the religious character of our origin. Our fathers were brought hither by their high veneration for the Christian religion. They journeyed by its light and labored in its hope. They sought to incorporate its principles with the elements of their society, and to diffuse its influence through all their institutions, civil, political, or literary. Let us cherish these sentiments and extend this influence still more widely; in the full conviction, that that is the happiest society which partakes in the highest degree of the mild and peaceful spirit of Christianity.*[1]

What is a Covenant?

The word *covenant* is not in common usage today as it was at the time of our founding. A covenant is a solemn agreement, or sacred promise, signed or not, between God and an individual, or individuals, a church, or a nation.

Our Founders understood the power of covenants because they were Biblicists. They knew that God would inevitably act in accordance with His Word if the human covenanter would obey His Word. They also knew that this truth of blessing was applicable to a nation as well as to an individual. Deuteronomy 7:9 says: "Know therefore that the LORD your God is God, the faithful God who keeps covenant and steadfast love with those who love Him and keep His commandments, to a thousand generations."

The America Covenant

The covenants of our colonists and Founders reveal the fundamental reason America has been blessed. The self-governing Christians known as Pilgrims who wrote the Mayflower Compact were aboard the *Mayflower* at the time of its writing, surveying a desolate wilderness in the dead of winter. Persecuted in England for their religious convictions, they had spent twelve difficult years of exile in Holland and had at last arrived on the wild New England coast to begin a colony for the "glory of God."

But even as the *Mayflower* rode at anchor, they knew that before setting foot in the New World, they had to draw up this covenant before God. They knew that they could not launch their colony until there was a recognition of God's sovereignty and the need to obey Him. They wrote the Mayflower Compact in the captain's cabin on board the *Mayflower*. The Mayflower Compact is America's first great constitutional document.

The Mayflower Compact

In the name of God, Amen. We whose names are underwritten, the loyal subjects of our dread sovereign Lord, King James, by the grace of God, of Great Britain, France, & Ireland king, defender of the faith, etc., having undertaken, for the glory of God, and advancement of the Christian faith, and honor of our king & country, a voyage to plant the first colony in the Northern parts of Virginia, do by these presents solemnly & mutually in the presence of God, and one of another, covenant & combine ourselves together into a civil body politic, for our better ordering & preservation & furtherance of the ends aforesaid; and by virtue hereof to enact, constitute, and frame such just & equal laws, ordinances, acts, constitutions, & offices, from time to time, as shall be thought most meet & convenient for the general good of the colony, unto which we promise all due submission and obedience. In witness whereof we have hereunder subscribed our names at Cape Cod the 11. of November, in the year of the reign of our sovereign lord, King James, of England, France, & Ireland the eighteenth, and by Scotland the fifty-fourth. Ano:Dom. 1620.[2]

These serious vows were echoed by colony after colony, church after church, as we moved toward nationhood.

According to Professor Andrew McLaughlin's *Foundations of American Constitutionalism*, "The word 'covenant' and its significance will appear over and over again as we trace the development of American constitutional theory."[3]

Our Declaration of Independence ends with the acknowledgment of the sovereignty of God, in which the Founders covenanted together to form a nation: "And for the support of this Declaration, with a firm reliance on the protection of divine Providence, we mutually pledge to each other our lives, our fortunes, and our sacred honor."

Political scientist Daniel J. Elazar, director of the Center for the Study of Federalism, Temple University, Philadelphia, and associated with Bar Ilan University, Israel, writes:

> *Just as the heart of the covenant of ancient Israel consists of two parts—the Decalogue or Ten Commandments with its electrifying statement of fundamental principles and the Book of the Covenant with its more detailed framework of basic laws of the Israelite Commonwealth, so too does that of the American covenant consist of two basic documents serving the same purposes—the Declaration of Independence and the Constitution.[4]*

The Hope of America

If there is to be a real American renewal, it can only begin through a repentant reaffirmation of our American Covenant. God blessed our forebears because they covenanted, agreed, and contracted with God to obey His Son.[5] God has not changed His purpose for America, but we as Americans have forgotten our covenant—that is, our response to His purpose.

The real hope of America is in the return of God's people to their corporate as well as individual covenant with their God. The following chapters will detail the untold story of how this covenant came about and how it can be renewed so that America can be a light to the world—a shining "city on a hill," for the spreading of the Gospel and liberty to the world.

The Hope of All Nations

The unchanging lesson of history is that long-term, voluntary obedience to the Bible and its liberating truths is the only way that lasting liberty and justice has ever been brought to the world. We in America, like the people of other nations who are experiencing God's hand of judgment, must *Remember* from what heights we have fallen, *Repent*, and *Repeat* the deeds we did at first.[6] Then we can reverse our present downward spiral and become once again a shining light to the nations.

> *Now therefore, O kings, be wise; be warned, O rulers of the earth. Serve the LORD with fear, and rejoice with trembling. Kiss the Son, lest He be angry, and you perish in the way, for His wrath is quickly kindled. Blessed are all who take refuge in Him.*[7]

Great Concept, But Can We Win?

Most Christians claim liberty from within through faith in Christ.[8] We are told in the Scriptures that we have internal dominion over sin,[9] yet we still find that in the reality of the external world, our lives are out of control in a climate of economic uncertainty and growing political tyranny. Is there a Biblical and historically proven method of dealing with this dilemma engulfing us and our children, without accepting tyranny or resorting to violence?

The answer is emphatically—yes! Two thousand years ago, the Almighty unleashed upon the world the most powerful world-changing force ever known to man—*the self-governing Christian.* This new individual freed from the shackles of sin and guilt was armed with the only weapon that can subdue the earth and its institutions—the Word of God. He became the bulwark of a movement that was begun by God Himself and about which Jesus said, "The gates of hell shall not prevail against it."[10]

Historically, whenever this new creation (a true believer) has understood God's instructions and has applied them to all spheres of life, he has gained dominion over his circumstances. He has progressively proven that "whoever is born of God overcomes the world."[11] He is not dominated by history; he shapes it according to God's will.

J. C. Ryle, nineteenth-century theologian, summarizes the impact Christianity has had upon the world. He says that we

> cannot deny the effect that [Christianity] produced on mankind. The world before and the world after the introduction of Christianity were as different worlds as light and darkness, night and day. It was Christianity that starved idolatry, and emptied the heathen temples, that stopped gladiatorial combats, elevated the position of women, raised the whole tone of morality, and improved the condition of children and the poor. These are facts which we may safely challenge all other enemies of revealed religion to gainsay [try to deny].[12]

Leading historians are also realizing the central, positive impact of Christian civilization. Award-winning historian Tom Holland says:

> To live in a Western country is to live in a society still utterly saturated by Christian concepts and assumptions. This is no less true for Jews and Muslims than it is for Catholics or Protestants. Two thousand years on from the birth of Christ, it does not require a belief that He rose from the dead to be stamped by the formidable—indeed the inescapable—influence of Christianity.[13]

This self-governing Christian, who received his greatest liberty in America, was not from any one denomination, race, or nationality. As the apostle Paul said of these Christians, "There is neither Jew nor Greek, there is neither slave nor free, there is no male and female, for you are all one in Christ Jesus."[14] Nor do the covenants with God of our forebears put them in a "special-nation" category impervious to divine judgment—and they certainly were not perfect, as no humans have ever been without fault.

Also, our reference to the American Covenant is no allusion to the theology of any particular denomination but is an attempt to highlight the historical significance of the various Colonial covenants with God, which, when taken as a whole, became a great motivating, unifying, and preserving influence upon our nation.

In the following chapters, we shall see how all of us—students, parents, and individuals in all walks of life—can be self-governing through God's power and His Word in every area of life. These chapters are placed in the context of America's Christian history because, as Americans, we have received the greatest heritage and example of Christian self-government ever known. Our Founders built a nation based upon the premise that self-governing Christians will produce the finest society for believer and unbeliever alike. God blessed them as they trained their children in *the art of self-government*. Samuel Adams, October 4, 1790, summarized the kind of training that produced the people who formed our nation:

> *Let divines and philosophers, statesmen and patriots, unite their endeavors to renovate the age, by impressing the minds of men with the importance of educating their little boys and girls, of inculcating in the minds of youth the fear and love of the Deity and universal philanthropy, and, in subordination to these great principles, the love of their country; of instructing them in* THE ART OF SELF-GOVERNMENT *without which they never can act a wise part in the government of societies, great or small; in short, of leading them in the study and practice of the exalted virtues of the Christian system.*[15]

The Battle of ideas

It is essential that the vital nature and nation-changing capacity of our task be emphasized. The battle for leadership and control of any nation has always been waged most effectively at the idea level, not on the battlefield. An idea, whether right or wrong, that captures the minds of a nation's youth will soon work its way into every area of society, especially in our social-media age. *Ideas determine consequences.*

Through the study of this book and others, individuals throughout our nation are discovering the missing links, the untold stories, and the forgotten principles that, if studied and applied, will result in a new reformation in our country. To illustrate the importance of ideas and the study of them for the changing of nations, let us briefly survey the rise of socialism in America. Over the last century, the ideas of a small minority have become the dominant philosophy in America's educational institutions and its political structure.

Socialism in America

In September of 1905, a group of five young socialists met in lower Manhattan to plan to replace and suppress the predominantly Christian worldview that still pervaded America. Their organization was called the Intercollegiate Socialist Society. Their purpose was to "promote an intelligent interest in socialism among college men and women."[16]

These men were ready to become the exponents of an idea passed on to them by an obscure writer named Karl Marx[17]—a man who never tried to be self-supporting but was financed by a wealthy industrialist who, inexplicably, believed in his theory of "the dictatorship of the proletariat." Although a small group in the beginning, these adherents to socialism more than succeeded in their task.

By using the proven method of *gradualism*, taken from the Roman General Quintus Fabius Maximus, these men and others who joined them slowly infiltrated their ideas onto the college campuses and into the public schools of our nation. By 1912, there were chapters in forty-four colleges. By 1917, there were sixty-one chapters in schools and twelve in graduate schools.

In 1921, they changed their name to the League for Industrial Democracy and entered the mainstream of America's education elite. By the mid-1930s, there were 125 chapters of student study groups of the League for Industrial Democracy. At that time, John Dewey, the godfather of progressive education, was the vice-president of the League. By 1941, Dewey had become president, and Reinhold Niebuhr, the liberal socialist theologian, was the treasurer.[18]

Today, as a result of the efforts of a small minority of men who dared to study and propagate their ideas (which were indisputably abhorrent to the character of a predominantly Christian nation), their philosophy has become dominant in America's major cultural spheres.

Now we, as American Christians, are fighting a counteroffensive to recapture the heart of our nation. But the reason we find ourselves in this defensive position is that we have abandoned our covenant with God as a nation, our Biblical dominion mandate, and the legacy given to us by our American ancestors. Armed with the truths of Scripture and the examples of our Founders, we can offer a peaceful reformation led by the Army of Compassion. Let us lovingly lead our nation back to the covenant of our Founders and the blessings we are promised in God's Word. "Blessed is the nation whose God is the LORD."[19]

Introduction Notes

1. Verna M. Hall, *The Christian History of the Constitution of the United States of America: Christian Self-Government* (San Francisco: Foundation for American Christian Education, 1975), 248.

2. Ibid., 204–5.

3. Andrew D. McLaughlin, *The Foundations of American Constitutionalism* (New York: New York University, 1932; Fawcett World Library, 1961), 19.

4. Daniel J. Elazar, "From Biblical Covenant to Modern Federalism: The Federal Theology Bridge," in *Workshop on Covenant and Politics* (Philadelphia: Center for the Study of Federalism, Temple University, 1980), 17.

5. Psalm 2:12.

6. Revelation 2:5.

7. Psalm 2:10–12.

8. John 8:36.

9. Romans 6:11.

10. Matthew 16:18.

11. First John 5:4.

12. J. C. Ryle, *The Upper Room: Biblical Truths for Modern Times* (New Kensington, PA: Whitaker House, 2015).

13. Tom Holland, *Dominion: How the Christian Revolution Made the World* (New York: Basic Books, 2019), 13.

14. Galatians 3:28.

15. Hall, *The Christian History of the Constitution*, xiv.

16. Paul W. Schafer and John Howland Snow, *The Turning of the Tides* (New Canaan, CT: The Long House, Inc., 1962), 1.

17. See Robert Payne, *Marx, A Biography* (New York: Simon and Schuster, 1968).

18. Schafer and Snow, *The Turning of the Tides*, 2–3.

19. Psalm 33:12.

Chapter 1

Clearing the Smokescreens

For the weapons of our warfare are not of the flesh but have divine power to destroy strongholds. We destroy arguments and every lofty opinion raised against the knowledge of God, and take every thought captive to obey Christ.

Second Corinthians 10:4–5

GEORGE WASHINGTON ADDRESSING THE
CONSTITUTIONAL CONVENTION (1787)
(DETAIL) BY JUNIUS B. STEARNS

*Let us raise a standard to which the wise and honest can repair; the
event is in the hand of God.*

— George Washington

Chapter 1

Clearing the Smokescreens

*T*he untold story of America's covenant relationship with God is once again being unveiled to the American people. This book is part of a renewal in understanding what God did in the founding of our nation. Decades of historical research of primary-source documents have uncovered conclusive evidence of this truth: our nation, its republican institutions, economic prosperity, and individual liberty can only be attributed to the hand of God and the covenant between our Founders and their Creator.

For several generations, we have been assured that the American experience is just the chance accumulation of adventurers, deists, and religious outcasts who came here seeking their own economic gain and stumbled into assured prosperity because of abundant natural resources. The above distortions are perpetrated, in varying degrees, through history textbooks, films, and every media platform.

Because the Providential perspective of this book is new to our generation—although certainly not to our Founders—it is important to address common questions that hang as shadows over the possibility of restoring the American Covenant. In seminars throughout America, I have found that people consistently ask certain important questions. Let us begin to clear away the smokescreens of falsehood and myths that stand between us and the restoration of our republic.

Why Is Our History So Important?

The story of the hand of God in the founding and preservation of our nation must be given great priority if there is to be hope for a cultural and spiritual restoration. The Bible clearly teaches that reformation cannot occur in a vacuum without historical reference. In the book of Deuteronomy, a pattern is laid down for the renewal of a nation and its people. The pattern is repeated in the Old and New Testaments (see the sermons of the apostles in the book of Acts) with variations, but it begins with the concept of *remembering* God's deeds in history. *Remember* is the key word in Deuteronomy, repeated frequently throughout the book as a command that was to begin the repentant process of rebuilding. Deuteronomy ("Second Law") was the second statement of the Law to a new generation about to enter the Promised Land. Their fathers had died in the wilderness, having forgotten God's Law and their covenant. Now, a new generation needed to be reminded of why they had fallen. God had graciously prepared their deliverance from Egypt, and they were commanded to remember it and give God the glory.

Deuteronomy 5:15 says: "You shall remember that you were a slave in the land of Egypt, and the LORD your God brought you out from there with a mighty hand and an outstretched arm." But the generation that Joshua led into the Promised Land soon forgot this admonition. In Judges 2:10, we read that after the death of Joshua and the elders, "There arose another generation after them who did not know the LORD or the work that He had done for Israel." As a result, the Bible goes on to say that they went off and worshipped the Baals and debased their faith in godless idolatry. Does this sound familiar?

Repeated addresses by the prophets, apostles, and our Lord admonish God's people to remember His deeds, and to recognize how they have abandoned His way. The major sermons of the apostles recorded in the book of Acts begin with a historical treatise on how God's people had fallen away from His blessing.[1] In Revelation 2:4–5, Jesus says to the church at Ephesus: "But I have this against you, that you have abandoned the love you had at first. Remember therefore from where you have fallen; repent, and do the works you did at first." Notice that they had to *remember* before they could *repent*.

We in the United States today have forgotten what God has done for us. Many Americans would say that they do remember and acknowledge Christ as their personal Liberator from the bondage of sin. But how many of us celebrate God's work in liberating us from 2,700 years of domination, under the totalitarian rule of the "divine right of kings"? From the time of Samuel the prophet in 1120 B.C. until the founding of our nation, the pagan idea of man and government dominated the world scene. But since the American Christian today does not know what God has done for him, is it any wonder that his personal repentance only works a personal reformation? For there to be a national reformation, there must also be repentance for sins of omission and commission by the Christians who have forgotten the covenant of their fathers and the hand of God in their history.

Our Christian foundation and all of the godly institutions that were products of the Biblical faith of our forefathers are to be passed on as a legacy, and we, as Christians, are held accountable for what we do with this unprecedented heritage. Jesus said that to whom much is given, much is required. We had better remember and recount God's history—His story—to our children and to a perishing generation or be prepared to lose our freedom.

Rev. S. W. Foljambe summarized the importance of our history on January 5, 1876, saying:

> *The more thoroughly a nation deals with its history, the more decidedly will it recognize and own an overruling Providence therein, and the more religious a nation will it become; while the more superficially it deals with its history, seeing only secondary causes and agencies, the more irreligious will it be.[2]*

Verna M. Hall, a pioneering educator and scholar of American history, says, regarding the way of restoration and its roots in historical remembrance:

> *America from the days of creation has been for God's glory and for His people, and if His people will be willing to learn what He has done for them in the days past, repent, and ask God's forgiveness for forgetting what He has done in bringing America into being, God will deal with her enemies within and without.[3]*

Is the study of history important? It is so significant that the future of our republic may well be determined by what we do with our great legacy.

Why Is America's Christian History Relevant Today?

A knowledge of America's Christian history makes it possible to discern fundamental answers to current problems in our nation. Many politically active Christians and media personalities today are addressing the issues of the day, but most, unfortunately, have little knowledge of our history. Because of this lack of knowledge, many leaders and people become easy prey for well-trained humanist journalists who know all of the clichés about "witch hunts," "bigoted Puritans," and the "blessings" of pluralism. When Christian leaders call for a return to a God-centered America, the secularist undermines the message by equating it with the ambitions of extremists and demagogues. If Christians do not know their true history, a false sense of guilt will set in, and they will be on the defensive concerning their God and their country. Once in a defensive, reactionary position, the Christian community is one of the easiest groups in America to immobilize, because Christians who know the Bible know they cannot and should not force their beliefs on others. They do not want a Church-run society, and if they think this is the only option other than a secular, "do-your-own-thing" State, they will complacently opt for the latter. The beauty of America's heritage is that our Founders provided a third alternative: a nation with true liberty and justice for all, including both the believer and the unbeliever.

Here are some specific examples of how the knowledge of America's Christian history clarifies issues and answers current dilemmas.

What Is the Separation of Church and State?

For decades, the debate over the meaning of the "separation of Church and State" has burned hot in the courts and legislative halls of our land. The expression "separation of Church and State" has been used as a catchall phrase to attempt to eliminate religious influence upon anything involving the State or civil affairs. The history of the First Amendment to the Constitution gives us quite a different perspective. Our Founders came from European lands ruled by monarchs, who used official State churches to control the people. They'd had enough of the supposed divine right of kings. So, according to James Madison, the First Amendment was drawn up because "the people feared one sect might obtain a preeminence, or two combine together, and establish a religion to which they would compel others to conform."[4] The First Amendment was intended to shield the churches from the encroachment of the federal government, specifically the Congress. But the framers of the Bill of Rights never intended that the Church (speaking of the Christians and their various denominations) should have no influence in the State or that religion should be separated from our national life by an impregnable wall of separation.

Our Founding Fathers presupposed Christianity as the moral foundation of governmental action. George Washington said: "True religion offers the government its surest support."[5] Supreme Court Justice Joseph Story, writing in the early days of the republic, said of the period when the First Amendment was adopted: "An attempt to level all religions and to make it a matter of State policy to hold all in utter indifference, would have created universal disapprobation [strong disapproval], if not universal indignation."[6] He explained further that the real object of the First Amendment was "to prevent any national ecclesiastical [church] establishment which should give to a hierarchy the exclusive patronage of the national government."[7]

In 1849, Robert C. Winthrop expressed the common understanding of the constitutional period well when he said:

> It may do for other countries, and other governments, to talk about the State supporting religion. Here, under our own free institutions, it is religion which must support the State.[8]

In fact, the term "separation of Church and State" is not in the First Amendment or, indeed, anywhere in the Constitution. It appears in a personal letter Thomas Jefferson wrote in 1802, replying to one from a group of Baptists and Congregationalists in Danbury, Connecticut, questioning his religious position. Jefferson was neither a member of the Constitutional Convention of 1787, nor of the first Congress under the Constitution, which passed the Bill of Rights. Yet the Supreme Court has consistently relied on this personal statement, by a man who had nothing to do with writing the Bill of Rights, to uphold their rulings that public schools may not hold devotional exercises or Bible readings, that the Ten Commandments may not be posted on the walls of schoolrooms, and many other antireligious decisions.

Let us remember what the First Amendment actually says: "Congress shall make no law respecting an establishment of religion or prohibiting the free exercise thereof." John W. Whitehead, a respected constitutional lawyer and author, gives the following excellent paraphrase of the amendment into modern English: "The federal government shall make no law having anything to do with supporting a national denominational Church, or prohibiting the free exercise of religion."[9]

When we examine the evidence from history, it becomes clear that "separation of Church and State" is a non-Constitutional phrase now used as a battle cry by those who would frighten godly Americans away from involvement in civil affairs.

Education in the Light of History

No issue looms larger in the minds of American parents than the failure of the American educational system. We can best understand this failure and its remedy within the framework of America's Christian history, focusing on the long-term reasons for the downfall of education in America. Otherwise, the debate becomes an exercise in assigning blame among teachers, parents, and bureaucrats rather than a search for a solution.

A comparison of the educational philosophy of early America and the modern, progressive methodology and content used in most schools today is helpful as a reference point, as a standard by which to understand and reform the present educational mainstream.

Early American Education

Early education in America was unique. The norm was private education in the home, churches, and schools, with the Bible as the foundation for character development as well as intellectual insight. The Pilgrims and other colonists were greatly interested in education, but they saw it as a personal, family, and church responsibility.

Communities sometimes offered formal education at the township level, but always under parental control and always Biblically based. These early Founders, knowing the importance of education, founded hundreds of private schools and colleges during the Colonial period. Most of the colleges were started for the purpose of training men for the ministry. Educator Rosalie J. Slater gives this account of the success of our Founders' educational efforts:

> At the time of the Declaration of Independence, the quality of education had enabled the colonies to achieve a degree of literacy from 70% to virtually 100%. This was not education restricted to the few. Modern scholarship reports "the prevalence of schooling and its accessibility to all segments of the population." Moses Coit Tyler, historian of American literature, indicates the colonists' "familiarity with history,… extensive legal learning,… lucid exposition of constitutional principles, showing, indeed, that somehow, out into the American wilderness had been carried the very accent of cosmopolitan thought and speech." When the American State Papers arrived in Europe,… they were found to contain "nearly every quality indicative of personal and national greatness."

If we seek the sources of our nation's greatness, we will find none more central than the 150 years of instruction in Christian schools and the self-governed, principled study and reasoning undertaken in Christian homes. Noah Webster, the father of American education, made the development of Christian character the centerpiece of his educational philosophy. Because all education built upon the foundation of the Bible, children grew up knowing how to find guidance for all human endeavor through reasoning from its principles. The Bible was the political and economic textbook of the Founders. The Rev. J. Wingate Thornton's *Pulpit of the American Revolution* notes that in 1777, the Continental Congress wrote "directing the Committee of Commerce to import twenty thousand copies of the Bible, the great political textbook of the patriots."

Modern Progressive Education

In 1838, Horace Mann became the secretary of the Massachusetts Board of Education. During the following years, Mann promoted a philosophy of education diametrically opposed to that of the Founding Fathers' generation. He is known as the father of the progressive public-school movement.

He supported forced taxation for state schools, which undermined parental control and was detrimental to the private schools. Mann and those who followed him deemphasized the Biblical doctrine of salvation as the basis of character development, replacing it with a humanistic view of the perfectibility of man through education and environment. He encouraged group thinking and study rather than individual initiative and creativity. He standardized teacher training, textbooks, and accreditation, beginning the transition away from the principles of the Christian philosophy of education taught by the great Founder of America's educational system, Noah Webster.[10]

As the twentieth century dawned, John Dewey, with his progressive method of education derived partially from his exposure to the communist educational system in Russia, carried on the march toward federal secularism. By 1935, a humanistic curriculum had become the dominant influence in most fields of scholarship in this country. Since then, the American public-school bureaucracy, the largest in the history of the world, has *vaccinated* the vast majority of America's youth against what it considers to be the infectious disease of absolute moral values. Obscured are our Christian heritage and the Christian history of our republic.

Today, as progressive public education collapses before our eyes, damaging millions of young lives in the process, we now witness the inevitable consequence of 150 years. We cannot correct the bad fruit of bad education by simply permitting voluntary prayer in schools. Success requires a complete change of philosophy and leadership. Criticizing the status quo is an American pastime, but the real question is: How many of us will be willing to sacrifice our time and private funds to rebuild and not tear down? Learning the deeds of our fathers will not only cause us to repent but will give us the wisdom needed to restore the broken walls of our culture.

Other questions, such as the reason for the rise in crime, the failure of the government control of welfare, the failure of the jurisprudence system, and the failure of evangelical activity to transform society, can all be understood only when placed against the backdrop of our history and an examination of Scripture. Let us not lose our future by failing to come to grips with our past. We, like the church at Ephesus, need to repent and do the deeds we did at first; but first we must learn what those deeds were!

Is There Time to Restore America? Isn't Evangelism More Urgent?

But, some would object, isn't the spread of the Gospel our most important duty? Shouldn't it take precedence over repairing our cultural institutions? First, there is no greater priority than world evangelism. Our Colonial ancestors and the Founders would agree, and, in fact, many of them were fundamentally motivated by this goal as they came to America. William Bradford, the Pilgrim historian and governor, clearly stated that the Pilgrims came with a desire to spread the Gospel worldwide when they covenanted with God to found their colony:

> *A great hope and inward zeal [passion] they had of laying some good foundation, or at least to make some way therunto, for the propagating and advancing the Gospel of the kingdom of Christ in those remote parts of the world; yea, though they should be but even as stepping-stones unto others for the performing of so great a work.*

Given this priority to "disciple the nations"[11] and to "proclaim the Gospel to the whole creation,"[12] it is important to keep in mind that God is glorified and people reached not only through words but by His children showing the practical application of Christianity to all of life. Nowhere has the balance between evangelism and the manifestation of Christianity in culture been so clearly illustrated as in America. Our nation came into being through the obedience of millions of Christians who took God's Gospel and its application into *every sphere of life.* When we were caring for "our own vineyard," we were likened to a "city on a hill" and a "light to the nations," showing forth the power of Christ in the life of individuals, manifested across our nation.

Is There Time to Occupy?

Our attention to the maintenance of our culture has waned, however, and we have pursued other diversions. Over the past 150 years or so, a growing trend among many religious groups speculates on the exact date of the end of the world and the second coming of Christ. Many people have been led to faith in Christ as a result of studying the coming of Christ in judgment at the end of time. But the setting of dates concerning His return and overspeculation as to the significance of current events in relation to this subject sometimes have caused many to lose all hope of reforming our government and society.

The purpose of this book is not to focus on eschatological issues. But one point should be clearly made concerning our attitude toward Christ's return, regardless of what millennial view we have. We, as Christians, will not be judged on how well we guessed the exact time of Christ's coming but concerning the deeds we have done to build His Kingdom while He is not physically present.[13] Regardless of when Jesus Christ comes again—and only the Father knows the time[14]—Christians cannot ignore their duty to "occupy till I come."[15] Who and whose ideas will govern our nation and its administration as well as our homes, churches, and schools? The Christian or the unbeliever? Who has taken leadership in our society—Christians or unbelievers? Will Biblical principles prevail only in our Christian homes, churches, and missionary endeavors and not the civil, economic, and cultural spheres of life in America? A knowledge of God's hand in history assures us that God gives His people the time needed to accomplish what He has called them to do. "Righteousness exalts a nation, but sin is a reproach to any people."[16]

God's Power in Building a Nation

Not only are we called to tend to our affairs, but to share with other people and other nations the Biblical principles that built our nation. Christ and His Word offer liberty, not only from the burden of personal sin, but also from external tyranny, when the people of a nation acknowledge His sovereignty and heed His Word.[17] The people of the world need to know that the principles and institutions of our world-changing God are without equal in all of history. They need to see a model of those principles and institutions in a reformed America. We cannot separate the Gospel message from its external manifestations. The message of Isaiah 58:12 is vital today: "Your ancient ruins shall be rebuilt; you shall raise up the foundations of many generations; you shall be called the repairer of the breach, the restorer of streets to dwell in."

Don't Spiritual Activities Take Priority over Secular Pursuits?

Why have Christians failed to rise up and restore our institutions as a testimony to the world? We Americans have accepted in the last few generations that a real distinction exists between the spiritual and secular pursuits of life. The 1950s defined religion as a personal thing, with the implication: "Don't talk about it or try to push it into other 'nonreligious' areas of life." But the question must be asked: Are there any nonreligious areas of life?

Some time ago, I spoke to a large audience of pastors concerning the strategic need to rebuild our nation to the glory of God. After my speech, a pastor from Southern California came up to me and said, "What you are attempting to do is a worthy effort. But, ultimately, you know, if God wants to restore our nation, He will do it. All we can do is pray." I paused and asked him if he had any farmers in his church, and he said he did. I asked, "Why don't we go back to our churches and tell our farmers not to plant their spring crops, but to simply pray and believe; if it is God's will, we will have a great harvest in the fall." The pastor understood. Prayer is important, but if we do not sow our seeds into every area of life, we will have no harvest to reap but the destruction of our liberty and the rise of totalitarianism.

The practice of distinguishing between and separating spiritual and practical pursuits can be traced back to the Greek philosophers, who separated physical life from the aesthetic or spiritual life. Thomas Aquinas, the Catholic theologian, expounded the view that an area of life called "grace" in the realm of the spiritual coexists with a separate, autonomous area called "nature" in the realm of natural activities or worldly pursuits.[18] The implication of this philosophy is that we need God to understand the spiritual, but that our human reason adequately directs most human activities. The philosophers of the Enlightenment expanded this concept. In the last century, many people have attempted to apply human reason to spiritual matters, with predictably confused results. During the same period, many Christians have abdicated any involvement in "earthly affairs," since they view all but religious activity as "secular."

In recent years, a great revival of Biblical Christianity has grown. Some good results from the development have occurred, including an emphasis on the need for a personal relationship with Jesus Christ. But, unfortunately, this movement's classification of certain activities as "spiritual" and others as "secular" has produced a very negative effect.

Preaching Politics?

Circumstances confronted a great Colonial pastor with this same attitude prior to the War of Independence, although in those days that attitude was held only by a small minority. When Jonathan Mayhew, a Congregational minister at West Church, Boston, heard of the English Parliament's plan to impose the Episcopal Church on America as its State Church, he was aroused to vigorous opposition. Around him, men's hearts were filled with consternation. Had not their forefathers fled to New England to escape persecution by the State Church, which had thrown ministers and laymen alike into foul prisons to rot and die? What could they do? Some Colonial ministers preached blind submission to the higher powers, but Mayhew was outraged at such teaching. Feelings in Boston ran high when he mounted his pulpit and preached the sermon that became famous throughout the colonies. Even folks in far-off London read the sermon with anger.

In this sermon, "Concerning Unlimited Submission to the Higher Powers," he attacks such submission:

> It is evident that the affairs of civil government may properly
> fall under a moral and religious consideration.... For, although
> there be a sense, and a very plain and important sense, in which
> Christ's Kingdom is not of this world, His inspired apostles have,
> nevertheless, laid down some general principles concerning the

office of civil rulers, and the duty of subjects, together with the reason and obligation of that duty. And...it is proper for all who acknowledge the authority of Jesus Christ, and the inspiration of His apostles, to endeavor to understand what is in fact the doctrine which they have delivered concerning this matter.

And not only this matter. When published later by popular demand, Mayhew commented in his preface to the sermon that he hoped few people would think the subject an improper one.

Under a notion that this is preaching politics instead of Christ,... I beg it may be remembered that "all Scripture is profitable for doctrine, for reproof, for correction, for instruction in righteousness." Why, then, should not those parts of Scripture which relate to civil government be examined and explained from the desk, as well as others?

Why not, indeed? Why not take the Scriptures and apply them to all areas of our lives? Mayhew's words are an eloquent answer today to the false division that would split our lives into two mutually exclusive areas: the religious and the secular.

No Neutrality

At last, it appears that millions of Americans are remembering the great truths of the Reformation, such as the priesthood of all believers (emphasizing the importance of the individual as opposed to a priestly class in authority over the many) and the sovereignty of God over every sphere of life. There is no neutral—or secular—area of life. When we set up an area or institution that does not acknowledge God's sovereignty, we become enemies of God and are in rebellion. The public-school system in America is a good example. It is not neutral religiously. It has simply exchanged the Christian religion for that of humanism.

It should be noted that in 1961 in the *Torasco v. Watkins* case, the Supreme Court recognized secular humanism as a religion. In delivering the unanimous opinion, justice Hugo Black stated: "Among religions in this country which do not teach what would generally be considered a belief in the existence of God are Buddhism, Taoism, Ethical Culture, Secular Humanism, and others."

The Biblical Worldview

The Biblical worldview requires that all human endeavor be in service to God, whether praying or riveting together a plane. Vocations are holy callings just as much as are church work or missionary activity. In Genesis, when the descendants of Adam are named, their occupations are also named.[19] When we view all of life in this context, then important "spiritual" exercises, such as prayer, Bible study, and fellowship with other believers, take on greater importance in our commission to replenish the earth, both physical and spiritual. We have purpose in life beyond ourselves! In light of our current crisis, nothing could be more spiritual than saving our children from socialism, our economy from deprivation, and our liberty from extinction.

Weren't We Founded by Deists, Unruly Adventurers, and Religious Castaways?

Is America really a Christian nation? It is said by some that deists, unruly adventurers, and religious castaways founded our nation. This stereotype of our Founders is frequently presented in films, documentaries, and history classrooms throughout the nation. It is one of the greatest defamations of national character ever perpetrated upon a people.

The influence of deism in America remained minimal until the nineteenth century, when inroads through the Unitarian Church made the atheistic philosophy of the French Revolution mainstream. During our founding period, however, it had little influence. According to historian Perry Miller, deism was strictly "an exotic plant" imported from Europe that did not flourish here. This distinguished historian also makes the point that the Colonial clergy presented to the people a religious rationale for the American Revolution, which united them behind its goals.[20] Deism could not have produced such a phenomenon. It professed a belief in one God but denied the divine origin of Scripture. Its weak philosophy of an inactive, spectator God, leaving all affairs of the world to human whim, could not match the powerful Biblical faith of the majority of our people in the founding generation.

Even Jefferson and Franklin, the two men most often cited as deists, give little credence to the view in their writings. Undoubtedly, both of these men entertained a number of European religious heresies, but the predominant influence upon their world continued to be Christian.

Franklin's Plea for Public Prayer

In the summer of 1787, a feeling of desperation and deadlock had descended upon the Constitutional Convention. Men from various states were planning to leave, and it would be years before they could gather again for another try at bringing the loosely knit confederated colonies together to form a republic.

On June 28, 1787, as the Convention was ready to adjourn in dissension, a wise old man addressed its president, George Washington, with quiet simplicity:

> How has it happened, Sir, that we have not hitherto once thought of humbly appealing to the Father of lights to illuminate our understandings? In the beginning of the contest with Great Britain, when we were sensible to danger, we had daily prayers in this room for divine protection. Our prayers, Sir, were heard, and they were graciously answered.... I have lived, Sir, a long time, and the longer I live, the more convincing proofs I see of this truth—that God governs in the affairs of men. And if a sparrow cannot fall to the ground without His notice, is it probable that an empire can rise without His aid? We have been assured, Sir, in the sacred writings that "except the LORD build the house, they labor in vain that build it."... I firmly believe this.

God heeded Benjamin Franklin's plea, and the Convention went on to compete its task. Although often considered a deist, it is clear from this statement that Franklin was deeply influenced by the Christian worldview.

It could well be argued that many Christians today act more like deists than the few men among the Founders linked to this heresy. Today, we often give lip service to the Lord Jesus Christ over all things, but then act as though He were an absentee, distant monarch just biding His time to claim His throne.

Don't Believe All You See

Of the claim that wild adventurers and womanizers roamed the land in early America, there is little need for refutation. On the frontier, *some* scouts and settlers did precede the churches and families, and there were *some* atrocities perpetrated on *some* Native Americans. *Some* rowdy settlements did develop for a while. But as soon as settlers established themselves and formed churches, the immoral and rowdy would submit to the rule of law. The Christian women of the communities, especially, demanded it. Perhaps our media generation has seen too many violent westerns, most of them fictitious distortions of true life in early America. *U.S. News & World Report* reported that the American people receive most of their knowledge of history from watching TV docudramas. And most of these docudramas bear little resemblance to the true story of our history. Honest history paints a starkly different picture.

Marcus and Narcissa Whitman, World Changers

By the 1790s, America had lost its passion for God that had once been kindled in the Great Awakening (1734–70). A young minister from Kentucky, James McGready, and his congregation began to pray for revival. Revival soon came in 1789, sweeping through Kentucky, the Carolinas, and up to New England.

Dr. Marcus Whitman and Narcissa Prentiss, both from New York's high society, were deeply touched by the Awakening. They both individually committed their lives to celibacy to better serve as missionaries. But, as Providence planned it, they met and shared a common bond and love for reaching the First Nation peoples of the Northwest. They were married and almost immediately set out across America out of love for the two hundred thousand Natives in the Columbia River Valley, whom they had never seen.

No one but mountain men and Natives had dared to take a wagon across America. They were the first to cross the Rocky Mountains to Canistoga. Narcissa was the first non-Native woman—and possibly the first woman— ever to cross America. They arrived in Washington State near the Columbia River and began their eleven-year medical mission to the Natives at Waiilatpu, near the Cayuse Indians.

In 1843, Marcus undertook the perilous trip back to Washington, D.C., to meet with President Tyler to plead for the settlement of Washington and Oregon, since the British were planning to annex the territory in trade for Nova Scotia.

He beseeched the president: "All I ask is that you will not barter away Oregon or allow English interference until I can lead a bank [group] of stalwart American settlers across the plains. For this I shall try to do." He was granted his wish and led the first train back on the Oregon Trail.

President Warren Harding wrote of this momentous meeting:

Never in the history of the world has there been a finer example of civilization following Christianity. The missionaries led under the banner of the cross, and the settlers moved close behind under the star-spangled symbol of the nation.

Tragically, four years later, Marcus and Narcissa, along with most of the converted First Nation people at their medical mission and school, were brutally maimed and martyred by a violent uprising incited by a renegade Native man, Jo Lewis, who spread lies among the Natives that Dr. Whitman had poisoned them. In fact, there had been a measles outbreak because of Native vulnerability to Western disease, and the Whitmans' treatment had been their only hope.

What was the fruit of this family dynasty? Their only baby died, their mission (in the world's eyes) was a failure, and the American board of foreign missions did not renew the outreach. They lived hard and died young. But today, in the great cloud of witnesses, Marcus and Narcissa see the fruit of their work. Twenty thousand prairie schooners followed the Whitmans' lead across the Oregon Trail. Thousands of Nez Perce and Cayuse were reached for Christ because of their faith. And the West Coast of America was reserved for the United

States, where even today, a great number of foreign missions and finances for evangelizing the world are headquartered.

The truth is that those who saved their money and possessed the fortitude to settle this country were, for the most part, Christians of great character. It took two years' living expenses just to cross and settle America. Families established in the Christian work ethic and faith constituted the vast majority of those who settled our country. These godly men and women, due to their family orientation, free-enterprise spirit, and Christian discipline, restrained the wild inclinations of the reprobates that we read so much about. Our history evidences the fact that, in the long run, nothing can thwart an individual with an understanding of his commission from God to subdue the earth—one who believes God for the victory.

Was America Founded as a Christian Nation?

Christians founded America, but is America therefore a Christian nation? The question of whether this nation was founded on Biblical principles has been debated for many decades. The concept of a Christian nation is often written off because of misconceptions as to what this means. A Christian nation is not one in which all people in a society are Christians, just as in an Islamic country not all people are necessarily Muslims. But in a Christian nation, as our Founders would have defined it, the principles and institutional foundations are Biblically based, and the people in general share a Biblical worldview.

It would be dangerous to confuse the term "Christian nation" with a Christian State. Since the word *State* refers to a political body or the body politic of the nation, the term "Christian State" would mean one in which the government ruled in religious matters through a State Church. A State Church would make religious liberty impossible.

All Laws Are a Codification of a Religious System

It is imperative to understand that all laws of a nation are the codification of a presupposed worldview. That is, the laws of the United States have presupposed the Bible as the foundation of our system from the beginning. Consider the words of President John Quincy Adams's 1837 oration:

> *Is it not that, in the chain of events, the birthday of the nation is indissolubly linked with the birthday of the Savior? That it forms a leading event in the progress of the Gospel dispensation? Is it not that the Declaration of Independence first organized the social compact on the foundation of the Redeemer's mission? That it laid the cornerstone of human government upon the first precepts of Christianity and gave to the world the first irrevocable pledge of the fulfillment of the prophecies announced directly from Heaven at the birth of the Savior and predicted by the greatest of the Hebrew prophets 600 years before.*

Such convictions as these concerning the Christian foundations of our nation persisted into comparatively recent times. John W. Whitehead analyzes the Supreme Court's historic understanding of the relationship between Christianity and government in the United States:

> *In 1892 the United States Supreme Court made an exhaustive study of the supposed connection between Christianity and the government of the United States. After researching hundreds of volumes of historical documents, the Court asserted, "These references add a volume of unofficial declarations to the mass of organic utterances that this is a religious people,… a Christian nation." Likewise, in 1931, Supreme Court Justice George Sutherland reviewed the 1892 decision in relation to another case and reiterated that Americans are a "Christian people," and in 1952, Justice William O. Douglas affirmed that "we are a religious people, and our institutions presuppose a Supreme Being."*[21]

Christianity the Dominant Influence in America

Christianity dominated cultural influence in America from 1620 until well into the nineteenth century. Many, in their desire to lay claim to the great accomplishments of that era, have tried to minimize the Christian influence and take the credit for themselves and their parties. But only God deserves the glory for what He did in the founding of this great nation.

While people from many denominations came to America in the early years, the vast majority of them shared a common faith in the basic tenets of Christianity. Whitehead's research reveals that:

> *When the Constitution was adopted and sent to the states for ratification, the population of America numbered only about 3 1/4 million. The Christian population numbered at least 2 million. James C. Hefley has commented that about 900,000 were Scotch or Scotch-Irish Presbyterians, with another million also holding to basic Calvinistic beliefs.*[22]

Today, although we are still essentially a Christian nation in form (the Constitution, legal structure, church affiliation), we are not one in conduct. For the first 250 years of our existence, Christian character determined self-governing conduct in homes, churches, and civil society. But today, too many of us have forgotten our heritage, and only the skeleton remains. Even so, deep within the American character there lingers a Christian conscience ready to be revived by the Spirit of God through awakened American Christian patriots.

It should be noted that in claiming America as a Christian nation, we are not saying that we were the "New Israel" or a special race that God must bless. Quite the contrary, God blessed America because our forebears built their nation with reliance on Him and His Word, and because God had a Gospel purpose for our nation. If we turn from His purpose, we can expect His judgment—perhaps greater judgment than other nations because "everyone to whom much was given, of him much will be required."[23] We will discuss this further in Chapter 3.

Every nation can be a nation under God if it chooses to follow Jesus Christ.[24] Our history is unique in that God allowed us to express a full flowering of Christian civilization and government. This fact should give us cause to ponder the price we have paid for not maintaining our Christian heritage of liberty. Will we be the generation that loses our liberty?

A Pluralistic Society or a Christian Nation?

Many Christians today believe the common teaching that it is good to live in a "do-your-own-thing" society where anything goes, because that protects their liberty to worship and preach the Gospel. The argument goes like this: I'll protect your right to flood the Internet with pornography and control the government, as long as you will let me preach Jesus.

Barbara Morris, in her book, *Change Agents in the Schools*, points to the fact that the public schools are becoming values changers. Students learn in their classes that there are no absolutes in our "evolutionary," pluralistic world. For example, our children may learn that while we might not think it is right to kill grandmothers "by cultural consensus" (at least not yet), it may be a fine practice for some cultures who have done so as a way of life for centuries.

Oftentimes, the Christian who finds the philosophy of relativism personally offensive gives in to it culturally because his education has conditioned him to accept the non-Christian culture as the norm. To complicate the problem, churches have taught many Christians today that the world (God's created world) is evil and under the control of Satan. We, as Christians, must accept assignment as misfits who can only hope to be a counterculture. As a result of this attitude, many Christians presuppose the impossibility of a Christian nation because they believe the above distortions. The Bible teaches the opposite to be true. Every nation is called upon to obey Jesus Christ:

> *Now therefore ,O kings, be wise; be warned, O rulers of the earth. Serve the LORD with fear, and rejoice with trembling. Kiss the Son, lest He be angry, and you perish in the way, for His wrath is quickly kindled. Blessed are all who take refuge in Him.*[25]

This is not a call to build pluralistic societies but godly ones, which become disciples of our Lord—in other words, Christian nations. In fact, Jesus, in the Great Commission of Matthew 28:18–20, gives us our marching orders to teach *the nations* to obey all that He has commanded.

There is no neutrality with God. Either a nation will build itself upon a foundation of God's Word or create for itself destruction by kindling the Son's wrath. A pluralistic society is just another term for a Christian nation on its way to becoming a humanistic society devoted to war with the Gospel. English historian E. R. Norman has observed: "*Pluralism* is a word society employs during the transition from one orthodoxy [worldview] to another."[26]

If we abandon our Biblical roots in favor of pluralism, we will soon lose all the attending benefits of Christian civilization, such as the rule of law, absolute moral standards, a sound economy, a limited government, and any vestige of liberty that we still maintain.

The restoration of our land will not be accomplished by bartering with the devil for equal time. We must lead our society through the strength of our character, our Biblical reasoning and action, and our financial resources if there is to be liberty for either the righteous or the unrighteous. Proverbs 29:2 says that "when the righteous increase, the people rejoice, but when the wicked rule, the people groan." As Christians, we cannot hide behind the excuse that Satan rules the day, because he does not. We must work to restore our republic, which rightly belongs to God, not the devil. Unbelievers also should come to grips with the facts of history that show that only in a Christian republic will their liberty of conscience and freedom to prosper be guaranteed. Pluralism, on the other hand, will lead us to tyranny. For, its chaos of relative values leading to anarchy will ultimately succumb to some form of tyranny.

Some will say, "Don't we have greater liberty today under pluralism?" No! Our Founders would stand on another Lexington Green if, like us, they had to submit to confiscation of 40 percent of their property through government taxes to sanction the murder of more than sixty million babies through abortion—if they had to endure the State propagandizing the youth of our nation in the religion of secular humanism, while removing the Bible and prayer from our schools. We are not truly free today. Worse is coming if we do not restore our Christian nation by remembering and renewing our American Covenant.

The decision we face today is between freedom and tyranny, as Dr. Jedediah Morse said on April 25, 1799:

To the kindly influence of Christianity, we owe that degree of civil freedom and political and social happiness which mankind now enjoys. In proportion as the genuine effects of Christianity are diminished in any nation, either through unbelief, or the corruption of its doctrines, or the neglect of its institutions; in the same proportion will the people of that nation recede from the blessings of genuine FREEDOM and approximate the miseries of complete DESPOTISM.[27]

The following statement in 1876 by the eminent professor and theologian Charles Hodge, of Princeton Seminary, illustrates the cogent and balanced thinking that once prevailed concerning our nation and its purpose. If we are to restore our nation, we must learn from the words of men such as Rev. Hodge, who wisely saw the dilemma that was approaching in America:

The proposition that the United States of America [is] a Christian and Protestant nation is not so much the assertion of a principle as the statement of a fact. That fact is not simply that the great majority of the people are Christians and Protestants, but that the organic life, the institutions, laws, and official action of the government, whether that action be legislative, judicial, or executive, is, and of right should be, and in fact must be, in accordance with the principles of Protestant Christianity.

When Protestant Christians came to this country, they possessed and subdued the land. They worshipped God, and His Son, Jesus Christ, as the Savior of the World and acknowledged the Scriptures to be the rule of their faith and practice. They introduced their religion into their families, their schools, and their colleges. They abstained from all ordinary business on the Lord's Day and devoted it to religion.

They built churches, erected school-houses, and taught their children to read the Bible and to receive and obey it as the Word of God. They formed themselves as Christians into municipal and state organizations. They acknowledged God in their legislative assemblies. They prescribed oaths to be taken in His name. They closed their courts, their places of business, their legislatures, and all places under the public control on the Lord's Day. They declared Christianity to be part of the common law of the land.

In the process of time, thousands have come among us, who are neither Protestants nor Christians.... All are welcomed; all are admitted to equal rights and privileges. All are allowed to acquire property, and to vote in every election, made eligible to all offices, and invested with equal influence in all public affairs. All are allowed to worship as they please, or not to worship at all, if they see fit. No man is molested for his religion or for his want of religion. No man is required to profess any form of faith, or to join any religious association. More than this cannot reasonably be demanded. More, however, is demanded. The infidel demands that the government should be conducted on the principle that Christianity is false. The atheist demands that it should be conducted on the assumption that there is no God, and the positivist on the principle that men are not free agents. The sufficient answer to all this is that it cannot possibly be done.[28]

Chapter 1 Study Questions

1. Why is remembering our past important to our future?

2. Why does God hold us accountable for what we do with our heritage of liberty?

3. Did the Founding Fathers intend to separate religion from the State?

4. What was the foundation stone of our educational system in America until 1838?

5. What is the nature of the educational system that supplanted it?

6. Why is "progressive" education really retrogressive?

7. Why are Christian schools of vital importance for our children and the nation?

8. Shouldn't transformed Christians also transform the society around them?

9. Is it wrong to apply Christianity to "nonreligious" areas of life?

10. Why did Colonial ministers preach on political as well as personal questions?

11. What traits of Christian character were vital in settling America?

12. What three elements are essential in order to restore America?

13. Why is it impossible to build a neutral nation without religious roots?

Chapter 1 Notes

1. Acts 7.

2. Verna M. Hall, *The Christian History of the Constitution of the United States of America: Christian Self-Government* (San Francisco: Foundation for American Christian Education, 1975), i.

3. Verna M. Hall, *The Christian History of the American Revolution: Consider and Ponder* (San Francisco: Foundation for American Christian Education, 1976), xxxv.

4. Jonathan Elliot, *The Debates of the Several State Conventions on the Adoption of the Federal Constitution*, vol. 3, p. 45, quoted in John W. Whitehead, *The Second American Revolution* (Elgin, IL: David C. Cook, 1982), 96.

5. Hall, *The Christian History of the Constitution*, 68.

6. Joseph Story, *Commentaries on the Constitution of the United States*, vol. 2, quoted in Whitehead, *The Second American Revolution*, 98.

7. Ibid.

8. Hall, *American Revolution*, 20.

9. John W. Whitehead, *The Separation Illusion* (Milford, MI: Mott Media, 1977), 90.

10. For further information on Horace Mann's approach to education, read his *Education of Free Men*.

11. Matthew 28:18–20.

12. Mark 16:15.

13. Luke 19:11–27; Second Corinthians 5:10.

14. Acts 1:7.

15. Luke 19:13 KJV.

16. Proverbs 14:34.

17. Proverbs 29:2.

18. See Francis Schaeffer's *Escape From Reason*.

19. Genesis 4:20–22.

20. See Perry Miller quotation from *Nature's God* in Francis A. Schaeffer, *A Christian Manifesto* (Westchester, IL: Crossway Books, 1981), 128–29.

21. Foundation for Christian Self-Government, *Newsletter* (April

1981).

22. Ibid.

23. Luke 12:48.

24. Psalm 2:10–12.

25. Ibid.

26. James Hitchcock, "Competing Ethical Systems," *Imprimis* 10:4 (April 1981).

27. Hall, *The Christian History of the Constitution*, v, emphasis added.

28. Charles Hodge, *Systematic Theology*, 1871, quoted in Hall, *American Revolution*, 156–57.

Chapter 2

What Your History Books Never Told You

He established a testimony in Jacob and appointed a law in Israel, which He commanded our fathers to teach to their children, that the next generation might know them, the children yet unborn, and arise and tell them to their children, so that they should set their hope in God and not forget the works of God, but keep His commandments; and that they should not be like their fathers, a stubborn and rebellious generation, a generation whose heart was not steadfast, whose spirit was not faithful to God.

Psalm 78:5–8

"A SPECIAL INSTRUMENT SENT OF GOD"

About the 16th of March [1621], a certain Indian came boldly amongst them and spoke to them in broken English…. His name was Samoset. He told them also of another Indian whose name was Squanto, a native of this place, who had been in England and could speak better English than himself…. About four or five days after, came… the aforesaid Squanto…. [He] continued with them and was their interpreter and was a special instrument sent of God for their good beyond their expectation.

— William Bradford

Of Plymouth Plantation

Chapter 2

What Your History Books Never Told You

A study of the authentic documents of our Colonial ancestors reveals consistent references to their faith in the Providential hand of God in the founding of their nation. Yet in the vast majority of modern textbooks, this central truth goes unacknowledged. This omission has had a profound impact upon the American republic and its youth. Walter Karp, writing in *Harper's Magazine*, states:

> *From the new textbooks, the children of the American republic will never gain knowledge of, or the slightest incentive to partici-pate in, public affairs.... No reader of these degraded texts will ever learn from them how to "judge for themselves what will secure or endanger their freedom." The new textbooks have snuffed out the very idea of human freedom, for that freedom at bottom is pre-cisely the human capacity for action that political history records and that the textbooks are at such pains to conceal....*
>
> *What the political history of the textbooks reveals is that a pow-erful few, gaining control of public education, have been depriv-ing the American republic of citizens, and popular government of a people to defend it. And the American history textbook, so innocent seeming and inconsequential, has been their well-chosen instrument.[1]*

The interpretation of history advocated in this book presupposes that the God of the Bible controls history, acts in history through Providential events, and is bringing all events to a conclusion to show forth His glory.

Acting from Presuppositions

Most modern educators deny the Providential view of history. They would have us believe that their promotion of one of several *secular* views of history is simply the recounting of brute facts. They fail to tell their students that their own ideological presuppositions and humanistic doctrines pervade their selection and interpretation of the people, places, ideas, and events of history. They fail to communicate that it is impossible to be neutral in the teaching of history, since the historian's worldview will dictate his perspective. Here again, Walter Karp's insight is of interest:

> *Writing American history is a harmless occupation, but teaching it to American schoolchildren is a political act with far-reaching consequences. The reason for this is clear. You cannot recount the past without making fundamental political judgments, and you cannot deliver those judgments without impressing them deeply on the minds of future citizens.*

With these observations in mind, it should be clear that one of the most significant political acts parents will ever make is deciding who will teach their children history. A closer look at some of the historical worldviews that have been advocated in America at different times will help us analyze their continuing significance in changing our world and our children today.

Grab Bag of Historical Theories

Most Americans, including most Christians, are products of our progressive public-education system. Sadly, every day, bored and hopeless youth drag through their social studies classes learning only a sanitized, secular version of history. The separation of Church and State means that they cannot be taught history from the inspiring perspective of God's Providence. The views now presented in many schools are no less religious than the Biblical view of history; they are simply not founded on the religion of the Bible.

As a result of this educational tragedy, humanistic views of history are all that we have been taught for generations. The humanist sees man as the decisive mover in history rather than God. These views vary greatly, and we are not suggesting that all teachers and students have absorbed them. But the religion of secular humanism has been a powerful controlling force since John Dewey and his allies gained control of the educational establishment.

In the *Humanist Manifestos I* and *II*, an influential group of humanists, including John Dewey, who signed the first, gives its own definition of its theological and historical presuppositions:

> *Religious humanists regard the universe as self-existing and not created.... We find insufficient evidence for the belief in the existence of a supernatural; it is either meaningless or irrelevant to the question of the survival and fulfillment of the human race. As non-theists, we begin with humans, not God, nature not deity. Nature may indeed be broader and deeper than we now know; any new discoveries, however, will but enlarge our knowledge of the natural.... But we can discover no divine purpose or Providence for the human species. While there is much that we do not know, humans are responsible for what we are or will become. No deity will save us; we must save ourselves.*[2]

Because this religious presupposition leaves its faithful devotees with no absolute standard or purpose with which to judge history, a grab bag of historical theories competes for public acceptance. These theories are religious ideologies posing as views of history. They deeply influence the life choices of all those who believe them.

The Cyclical View of History

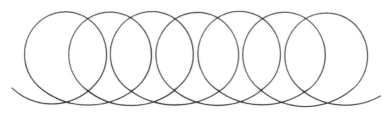

Repeating historical cycles with no ultimate purpose or goal

The Cyclical View of History

The cyclical view of history is as old as antiquity and sees the same pattern in the events of men that exists in the seasons and the life cycle. This interpretive scheme was commonly held in China, India, the Middle East, Greece, and Rome, and in the 1960s, it gained wide acceptance on the American college campus. Its byproducts, as seen in the works of such men as Friedrich Nietzsche and Arnold Toynbee, are often pessimism and determinism, since all of life and culture is seen as just an endless repetition of birth and death, mimicking the rhythm of the universe. Many college students, influenced by eastern religions and cyclical philosophies of history, find themselves saying, "It doesn't matter what I do. There is no meaning to individual existence." They become fatalists caught in a meaningless circle of events leading nowhere. Under the influence of this cyclical worldview, the significance of individual attempts to better the world is lost in a fatalistic, all-powerful, universal cycle. Hindu societies, such as those in India, labor under this false perspective, and the people therefore have little motivation to change either the caste system or their economic poverty. Buddists, likewise, seek to minimize their perceived meaninglessness through minimizing life itself—even hiding from it.

The Marxist View of History

The Marxist view of history, as expressed by Karl Marx in his *Economics and Philosophic Manuscripts of 1844*, is simply: "The entire so-called history of the world is nothing but the creation of man through

Class Struggle
Resulting in the "Perfect Socialist State"

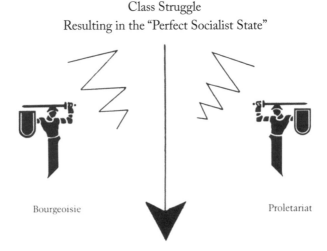

Bourgeoisie   Proletariat

human labor." His anti-Christian philosophy of history, and that of his many followers, has subtly permeated not only the totalitarian communist world but post-Soviet socialism and American culture. This historical materialism sees man as an economic unit caught in a class struggle between the bourgeoisie (the "haves") and the proletariat (the "have-nots").

Charles Beard, a follower of Marx and one of the most prolific materialist historians, molded the Hegelian dialectic and Marxist theory into scores of his works on American history. He deemphasized the Christian influence in America's founding, while disparaging the character of its Founders. The title of his first major work, *An Economic Interpretation of the Constitution*, illustrates how a Marxist perspective inclines a historian to view every event through the lens of Marx's economic prejudice.

Most of us, whether we know it or not, have been deeply influenced by this view of history. Popular films and television miniseries frequently portray history as a race conflict or class struggle between rich and poor. There can be no doubt that most of these entertainments, watched by hundreds of millions of Americans, reflect the influence of men such as Beard and their Marxist view of history. Their influence cannot be underestimated. *U.S. News & World Report* documented that most Americans believe that the fictional, often distorted historical dramas they watch are true.

The Marxist historian specializes in emphasizing the evils of free enterprise (e.g., robber barons). They deny or distort the fundamental base of our society: Biblical principles and their influence on and through individuals. All historical views that deny the sovereignty of the God of the Bible must of necessity distort the facts of history to fit their perspective. They require revisionism and will often tolerate many views—except one: the Providential view.

The "Who Cares?" Mentality

Presently, one of the most common historical views is the "who-cares?" dropout mentality. If history is, as the renowned historian Edward Gibbons said, the recounting of the crimes of the human species, why study it? Today, millions of Americans dislike history because they see it as irrelevant. "Today is what counts" and "We learn from history that we learn nothing from history" are typical clichés tossed around by bored history students who see their lives as chance evolutionary happenings. History, in this view, is meaningless, therefore of no interest, and the future is unpredictable, therefore without hope. With this attitude, the only sensible approach is to live for the moment. With the Roman gladiator, many Americans are saying, "Let us eat, drink, and be merry, for tomorrow we die."

The Existential View of History

History is meaningless (No interest)

The future is unpredictable (No hope)

Existential Moment
"eat, drink, and be merry for tomorrow we die."

Many Christians have subconsciously adopted this view of history. They undervalue their importance in a God-ordained plan for history and see themselves simply as individuals God has plucked out of an evil world who are now merely awaiting heaven. Their sense of connectedness to the past and their hope and planning for the future are lost in the din of the popular culture, where they are called to focus on self-improvement and satisfaction. This attitude eases the burden of guilt that lies heavily on the heads of American Christians because of our nation's moral crisis, but it does not alleviate their responsibility for it.

Ultimately, it is not the humanists, communists, or social deviants who are responsible for our present condition. Because these people are lost, we should not be surprised that they act like lost and bitter rebels. But it is the Christian community that has neglected its heritage and forgotten the history of America. We are the ones who should be expected to remember it and restore the knowledge of it to the American people as a whole. Until the Christian comes to grips with his historical duties, denouncing his existential perspective and reaffirming the Providential view of history, the renewal of our nation will be impossible.

The Predominant View of Our Ancestors

The Founders' passion for liberty was not primarily an inheritance from Rousseau, nor was it a reaction to the tyranny of kings who governed from afar. They were inspired chiefly by the worldview of the Reformation on law, history, education, and all other public and private affairs. When Calvin, Luther, and Knox proclaimed the sovereignty of God—even over the king—entire nations rose within a decade to challenge the political doctrines of tyrants who had oppressed the people of Europe for a millennium. This was the inheritance that the first settlers brought with them to the New World.

Ranke, the famous German historian, said, "John Calvin is the virtual founder of America." Bancroft, America's leading nineteenth-century historian, called Calvin simply, "the father of America." The world's foremost Reformation scholar, d'Aubigné, said:

> *Calvin was the founder of the greatest republics. The Pilgrims who left their country in the reign of James I, and, landing on the barren soil of New England, founded populous and mighty colonies, were his sons, his direct and legitimate sons: and…the American nation which we have seen growing so rapidly boasts as its father the humble Reformer born on the shore of Lake Leman.[3]*

Calvin shaped our republic because he unleashed a Biblical theology that laid open the profound sinfulness of all men and recognized that only by God's sovereign grace could men be redeemed. His teaching also emphasized that all men, including the king, were subject to the laws of God. But all of Calvin's systematic theology, whether the priesthood of all believers or the covenantal character of God's government, rested on the bedrock of God's sovereignty.

This emphasis on God's sovereignty endured in the generation of the Founders. Dr. Lorraine Boettner records that "about two-thirds of the Colonial population had been trained in the school of Calvin." Similarly, Bancroft notes that in 1776, the American populace was 98 percent Protestant and 66 percent Calvinist. The Providential view of God's sovereignty in and through history passed directly from the Reformers to the Founders.

Defining the Providential View

Noah Webster, the great educator and lexicographer who compiled and published the first American dictionary in 1828, defines *providence* as

> the care and superintendence which God exercises over his creatures.... Some persons admit a general providence, but deny a particular providence, not considering that a general providence consists of particulars. A belief in divine Providence is a source of great consolation to good men. By divine Providence is understood God himself.

In this definition, Webster, a devout Christian, expresses succinctly the Providential view of history. In writing that Providence "is a source of great consolation to good men," he alludes to the peace that comes from knowing that a just God presides over nations, and that His plan cannot be thwarted. The opposite is also true. If you are fighting the God of history and you learn of His Providence, it can be very unsettling.

One of the best definitions of the Providential view of history is given by the Rev. S. W. Foljambe. Writing in 1876, he said:

> It has been said that history is the biography of communities; in another and profounder sense it is the autobiography of Him "who worketh all things after the counsel of His will" (Ephesians 1:11) and who is graciously timing all events after the counsel of His Christ, and the kingdom of God on earth.[4]

In fact, this view of history is an important part of the Judeo-Christian tradition. D. W. Billington, in his book *Patterns in History*, says concerning the historical view of the apostles:

> The earliest Christians retained the attitudes to history found in the Old Testament. They continued to believe in divine

intervention, to conceive of the historical process as a straight line, and to see the panorama of world events as moving toward a goal.[5]

The Providential View of History

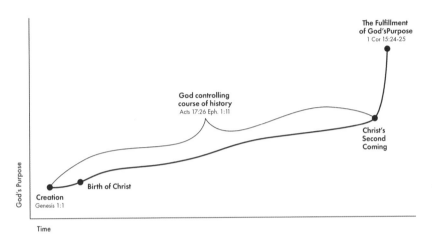

Speaking of Providence

Ample evidence of divine Providence surrounded our Founders. And they did not fail to give God the credit for both special Providence and their godly institutions.

William Bradford, in his *History of Plymouth Plantation*, tells of the Pilgrims' reliance on Providence in the midst of their many tragedies.

> *But these things did not dismay them (though they did sometimes trouble them) for their desires were set on the ways of God, and to enjoy His ordinances; but they rested on His Providence and knew whom they had believed.*[6]

George Washington made constant reference to God's Providence in his life and the life of the nation.

> *By the miraculous care of Providence, that protected me beyond all human expectations; I had four bullets through my coat, and two horses shot under me, and yet escaped unhurt.*[7]

> *It is the duty of all nations to acknowledge the Providence of Almighty God, to obey His will, to be grateful for His benefits, and humbly to implore His protection and favor.*[8]

Our Documents Confirm His Providence

The first charter for a successful English colony was issued on April 10, 1606. The Charter of Virginia stated:

> *We, greatly commending and graciously accepting of, the desires of the furtherance of so noble a work, which may by the Providence of Almighty God, hereafter tend to the glory of His divine majesty, in propagating of Christian religion to such people, as yet live in darkness and miserable ignorance of the true knowledge and worship of God, and may in time bring the infidels and savages living in those parts, to human civility and to a settled and quiet government.[9]*

Another founding document, the Fundamental Orders of Connecticut (1683), America's first constitution, acknowledges God's power and Providence in its preamble:

> *For as much as it has pleased the Almighty God by the wise disposition of His divine Providence so to order and dispose of things...*

The concluding statement of "The Declaration of the Causes and Necessity of Taking Up Arms" (Continental Congress, July 6, 1775) says:

> *With an humble confidence in the mercies of the Supreme and impartial God and ruler of the universe, we most devoutly implore His divine goodness to protect us happily through this great conflict, and to dispose our adversaries to reconciliation on reasonable terms, and thereby to relieve the empire from the calamities of civil war.[10]*

The Declaration of Independence, written July 4, 1776, concludes with a similar testimony by stating that their action was undertaken "with a firm reliance on the protection of divine Providence."

The above examples are just a sampling of the Providential view of history that held sway over much of American life well into the nineteenth century.

The History of Providence

The Founders of our nation were firm believers in the hand of Providence both in the general working of the world and in the particular events of their lives. They were familiar with competing concepts of history, but their Biblical worldview provided the foundation for their undertakings. Their belief in the Providence of God was borne out by their experience.

Providential Landing at Cape Cod

The landing of the Pilgrims at Cape Cod was an important Providential event. They were bound for Virginia, but the *Mayflower* was blown hundreds of miles off its course and ended up instead at Cape Cod. Because their patent did not include this territory, they consulted with the captain of the *Mayflower* and "resolved to stand for the southward…to find some place about Hudson's River for their habitation." But God did not allow them to do so. They soon encountered "dangerous shoals and roaring breakers" and were forced to return to Cape Cod. From there, they began their scouting expeditions to find a place to settle and finally discovered what is now Plymouth. Had they arrived a few years earlier, they would have been greeted by the fiercest tribe in the region, but in 1617, the Patuxet tribe that had occupied the area had been wiped out by a plague. It was perhaps the only place where they could have survived.[11]

A Special Man Sent from God

There was, however, one survivor of the Patuxet tribe, and the account of his survival further demonstrates the hand of God in history. This Native American, named Squanto, was kidnapped in 1605 by a captain named Weymouth and taken to England. There he learned English, and in 1614, he returned to New England on an expedition with Captain John Smith. Though Smith wanted to return him to his people, this was not God's timing. Shortly after Smith left for England, Squanto was again kidnapped.[12]

Captain Thomas Hunt lured Squanto and twenty-four other Natives on board his ship and, according to Bradford, intended to sell them into slavery in Spain. "But he [Squanto] got away for England and was entertained by a merchant in London, and employed to Newfoundland and other parts, and lastly brought hither into these parts by [Captain] Dermer."[13]

Dermer was on a voyage of discovery on the New England coast in 1618 and probably intended to use him as an interpreter with the Natives, but Squanto apparently jumped ship and headed for Plymouth, only to find that all of his tribe had been wiped out by the plague. After searching in vain for survivors, he attached himself to the neighboring tribe of the Wampanoag.

Fluent in English, he was led of God to offer his friendship and help to the Pilgrims when he learned of their presence at Plymouth. He joined with them thereafter and was converted to Christianity. Bradford says that he "was a special instrument sent of God for their good beyond their expectation."[14]

Without Squanto's help, they might not have survived, for he showed them how to plant corn, fertilizing it with fish. He also acted as their guide and, most important, was their interpreter in their dealings with the Wampanoag chief, Massasoit, in the crucial early days when it was vitally important to the Pilgrims to establish friendly relations with their Indigenous neighbors. With Squanto's aid as interpreter, a peace treaty that lasted fifty years was agreed upon, which treated both Natives and Pilgrims justly under the law. Through the hand of God, the Pilgrims did not share the fate of other English colonies in the New World that were wiped out by hostile Natives.

"New England Stood Still and Saw the Salvation of God"

In a later period of America's history, during the colonizing attempts of France, we encounter another striking instance of God's Providence. Wherever the French went, they only allowed faith practice in the Roman Catholic religion, and the New Englanders greatly feared them. The Stuart monarchs in England were sympathetic to France's Catholic monarch, but when firmly Protestant King William of Orange ascended the English throne, the French began to attack the English colonists in America with great savagery. The New

England forces, with the aid of a British squadron, captured Louisbourg in Nova Scotia. Here, God used the weather to the advantage of the New Englanders. "The English appear to have enlisted Heaven in their interest," wrote one of the town's residents later. "So long as the expedition lasted, they had the most beautiful weather in the world." No storms, no unfavorable winds, and no fog—which was most surprising for the area. After the capture of Louisbourg, the French sent half of their navy under the command of the Duc d'Anville "to lay waste the whole seacoast from Nova Scotia to Georgia."[15]

The Rev. Thomas Prince, pastor of the South Church in Boston, later preached a sermon of thanksgiving for God's protecting hand when New England was "a long while wholly ignorant of their designs against us."[16] Even when rumors reached them, they were not greatly worried because they understood that the British fleet would prevent the French from leaving the shores of France. But, unknown to the colonists, the French eluded Admiral Martin's squadron and slipped out to sea. But, as Rev. Prince observed:

> *While we knew nothing of Danger, God beheld it, and was working Salvation for us. And when we had none to help in America, He even prevented our Friends in Europe from coming to succor [help] us; that we might see our Salvation was His Work alone, and that the Glory belongs entirely to Him.*[17]

Having eluded the British, the proud French fleet "of about 70 sail" put to sea on June 20, 1746. As the vessels crossed the Atlantic, heading for Halifax, they were delayed at first in a prolonged calm and then encountered storms in which several ships were disabled by lightning. Pestilence broke out; then the entire fleet was scattered to the four winds by tremendous storms. By this means, "they were... so dispersed in the midst of the Ocean that by Aug. 26, they had left but twelve Ships of the Line and forty-one others."[18] On September 2, as they were nearing the dangerous shoals off the Isle of Sables, they encountered another violent storm and lost several more vessels.

When the Duc d'Anville's ship finally reached Halifax (or Chebucto, as it was then called), a lonely, isolated area, he fully expected to rendezvous with other French ships sent from the West Indies to meet him. The West Indies squadron had indeed been there but, discouraged by the long delay of d'Anville's fleet, had given up and left.

What had the New England colonists been doing all this time? Another New England pastor, Rev. Jonathan French, writes that as soon as the French vessels were sighted off the coast, the people were

> *filled with consternation. The streets filled with men, marching for the defence of the sea ports, and the distresses of women and children, trembling for the event, made...deep impressions upon the minds of those who remember these scenes. But never did the religion, for which the country was settled, appear more important, nor prayer more prevalent, than on this occasion. A prayer-hearing God stretched forth the arm of His power, and destroyed that mighty Armament, in a manner almost as extraordinary as the drowning of Pharaoh and his host in the Red Sea.*[19]

What happened was this: Shortly after his arrival at Halifax, the Duc d'Anville was so appalled at the loss of the major part of his fleet "and finding his few Ships so shattered, so many Men dead, so many sickly, and no more of his Fleet come in; he sunk into discouragement, and Sept. 15 died; but in such a Condition...it was generally thought he poisoned himself, and was buried without Ceremony."[20] More ships finally limped into port, but many of the men on board were ill, and their food supplies were fast running out. The commander who took d'Anville's place committed suicide only days after their arrival by falling on his own sword. The third in command ordered the men ashore to recruit French and Natives so that an attack on Annapolis could proceed. But before they could leave Halifax, between two and three thousand men died of a pestilence. Finally, the fleet's new commander, La Jonquiere, set sail on October 13, 1746, intending to attack Annapolis. He was probably unaware of the fact that on October 6, the New England colonies had set October 16 as a day of fasting and prayer for their deliverance. Rev. French describes the events that followed:

> *On this great emergency, and day of darkness and doubtful expectation, the 16th of October was observed as a day of FASTING AND PRAYER throughout the Province. And, wonderful to relate, that very night God sent upon them a more dreadful storm than*

*either of the former, and completed their destruction. Some over-
set, some foundered, and a remnant only of this miserable fleet
returned to France to carry the news. Thus NEW ENGLAND
STOOD STILL AND SAW THE SALVATION OF GOD.*[21]

The Hand of God
Rescues George Washington's Army

God's Providence played a great part in rescuing General Washington's troops when they were penned up in Brooklyn Heights by the
English General Howe in the early days of the revolution. Despite
the heavy losses Howe had inflicted on Washington's army, he had not
succeeded in capturing or destroying it. Now he prepared to lay siege
to the American forces on Long Island: some eight thousand men on
Brooklyn Heights. Washington realized he must retreat. But how?
The English forces surrounded him in a great semicircle, and behind
him British ships could close him off at any time. Then began Washington's desperate, bold strategy. He collected every vessel he could
find from rowboats to sloops, manned by fishermen from Gloucester
and Marblehead, and he set about to evacuate his troops by night. A
desperate measure, surely, and one doomed to failure. For wouldn't
the British see them in the moonlight or hear the splashing of their
oars and the many sounds of eight thousand men being transported,
however quiet they tried to be? But, as historian John Fiske writes:
"The Americans had been remarkably favored by the sudden rise of
a fog which covered the East River."[22]

In the morning, the British discovered to their astonishment that
their enemies had vanished—even taking with them their provisions,
horses, and cannons. Fiske observes that "so rare a chance of ending
the war at a blow was never again to be offered to the British com-
manders." But at the crucial, desperate moment, when Washington
had done all he could do, the hand of God intervened, providing the
critically needed elements so that neither by sight nor by sound were
the army's whereabouts known to the enemy.

Were all these events happy accidents or mere good luck? When
these and hundreds more striking instances of the Providential hand

of God in our history are put side by side, a pattern emerges that shows God's repeated protection of the new nation whose settlers had founded it for His glory.

A Firm Reliance on Divine Providence

The Founding Fathers were keenly aware of God's Providence and took care to see that the Declaration of Independence ended with the phrase, "And for the support of this Declaration, with a firm reliance on the protection of divine Providence, we mutually pledge to each other our lives, our fortunes, and our sacred honor."

During the Constitutional Convention, not only did Benjamin Franklin appeal for daily prayers, that they might be worthy of the support of divine Providence. George Washington, too, objected to arguments favoring halfway stopgaps intended to patch up the poorly working Confederation rather than follow through with a real plan of union. He rose from his presidential chair to his full, imposing height, and, his voice trembling with emotion, he declared: "If to please the people, we offer what we ourselves disapprove, how can we afterward defend our work? Let us raise a standard to which the wise and the honest can repair; the event is in the hand of God!"

His words were a bracing reminder of the need for stern resolve if they were to be worthy of God's Providential support. "From that moment," says historian John Fiske, "the mood in which they worked caught something from the glorious spirit of Washington."[23]

Today, as we once again recount the mighty deeds of God on our behalf and give Him the glory for these deeds, we too can expect a wave of hope to sweep our nation. The God of Abraham, Isaac, and Jacob—the God who preserved our forefathers as they covenanted to establish a nation for His honor—can sustain us in difficult times and enable us to follow His Providential plan for this nation into the future.

A Magnificent Optimism

On December 30, 1900, this poem was published in the *New York Journal*, America's most widely read newspaper at the time:

Faith is not dead, tho' priest and creed may pass,
For thought has leavened the whole unthinking mass.
And man looks now to find the God within.
We shall talk more of love, and less of sin.

In the century that followed, Americans certainly did talk more of love, yet sin continued to abound. The dream of goodness without a holy God has failed. But there is a potential blessing in humanism's collapse. The American people are increasingly looking for real solutions. In the past, we as a people have turned to God, as in the Great Awakening. God can turn the hearts of our people again.

Early Christians manifested "a magnificent optimism," according to historian Robin Lane Fox, even in the face of Roman hegemony and persecution. Their optimism was well rewarded, as the small sect that started with twelve disciples spread and permeated the Roman Empire in two centuries.

We too should be optimistic in our day. Our hope is built not upon the strength of our own resources, but upon the promises of God. As parents, we are promised that if we "train up a child in the way he should go;... he will not depart from it."[24] The psalmist declares, "How blessed is the man who fears the LORD, who greatly delights in His commandments. His descendants will be mighty on earth; the generation of the upright will be blessed."[25]

Just as He has given His people hope through His Scriptural promises, God has acted through history to spiritually renew entire generations in times of impending crisis and despair. There have been four great awakenings in American history. In each one, young people and their visionary faith played a significant role. The first Great Awakening in America had its roots in the Holy Club at Oxford, made up of Christian students like John Wesley and George Whitefield. The second Great Awakening gained great impetus from the revival at Yale under Timothy Dwight, the grandson of Jonathan Edwards. In 1795, fully one half of the student body was converted. In this troubled generation, America is ready for yet another student-led revival.

The Western world has been retreating from the God of the Bible for over two hundred years. We have sown the wind and are reaping the whirlwind. The thinkers who led the rebellion are gone. Charles Darwin, the prophet of evolution, died in 1882. Karl Marx, the theorist whose ideas inspired the communist revolutions and the greatest slaughters of the twentieth century, died in 1883. Julius Well Hauser, the founder of German higher criticism and modern liberal orthodoxy, died in 1918. Sigmund Freud, the father of godless psychology, died in 1939. John Maynard Keynes, the economist of the welfare state, died in 1946. John Dewey, the father of progressive secular education, died in 1952.

The ideas of these men have lingered long after their deaths and have tainted the thinking of whole generations. But God has providentially placed us in a time when we can not only expose the failures of their humanist dreams, but offer a dynamic, intellectually valid, historically proven, and Scripturally sound Christian faith. The vacuum left by the failure of the godless values of humanism must be filled. There exists a tension in modern culture as it awaits a new consensus. If Christian values are to prevail, then they will be championed by the children of godly parents who have been prepared for the challenge of such a time in history.

Life at the beginning of our third-millennium-A.D. era has much in common with life at the beginning of the first millennium. As in the Roman era, many today are not sure whether to prepare for peace or violence, prosperity or poverty, hope or despair. As then, numerous philosophies and religions today engage the attention of the masses yet fail to offer any real solutions to the problems of society. Christianity today, as it was then, is outside the major power centers in Western culture.

Like our first-century counterparts, we can look forward with great anticipation to what God is going to do in this seventh millennium of recorded history. Just as early Christianity grew through parental leadership and education, we can train our children to rise up and have a transforming impact in this century. There is no more important task than the daily discipleship of the world's future. And, as in the first century, we have every reason to exhibit a magnificent optimism.

Chapter 2 Study Questions

1. Can you paraphrase the Providential view of history in terms that explain its personal application and influence upon you as an individual?

2. This chapter states that neutrality is impossible. Is this statement, applied to historical study, also true of all areas of life? Why are Biblical presuppositions necessary to study man, English, economics, etc.?

3. Compare Noah Webster's definition of *providence* in his 1828 *Dictionary* with definitions given by later editions after his death. What is the impact of the definition of words? See, for example, comparative definitions of *sovereignty* and *love*.

4. What lifestyles are encouraged by the various historical world views? Which worldview do you hold to, and which is most prevalent in your circles?

5. Why can the Christian better comprehend such Providential events as those mentioned in this chapter? And, why are these events left out of all major histories that students read today?

For FREE bonus material & in-depth study on a variety of topics beyond what you find here in *The American Covenant,* visit WorldHistoryInstitute.com/free-downloads.

Chapter 2 Notes

1. *Harper's Magazine* (May 1980).

2. Paul Kurtz, *Humanist Manifestos I and II* (Amherst, NY: Prometheus Books, 1973), also available online at americanhumanist.org.

3. John Eidsmoe, *Christianity and the Constitution* (Grand Rapids: Baker Books, 1987), 18.

4. Verna M. Hall, *The Christian History of the American Revolution: Consider and Ponder* (San Francisco: Foundation for American Christian Education, 1976), 47.

5. D. W. Billington, *Patterns in History* (Downers Grove, IL: InterVarsity Press, 1979), 48.

6. Verna M. Hall, *The Christian History of the Constitution of the United States of America: Christian Self-Government* (San Francisco: Foundation for American Christian Education, 1975), 186.

7. George Washington (July 18, 1755), *Writings of George Washington*, Lawrence B. Evans, ed. (New York: G. P. Putnam's Sons, 1908), 1:152.

8. Ibid., (Thanksgiving Proclamation, October 3, 1789), 30:427.

9. "The First Charter of Virginia," April 10, 1606, *The Avalon Project*, avalon.law.yale.edu.

10. "Declaration of the Causes and Necessity of Taking Up Arms," *The Avalon Project*, avalon.law.yale.edu.

11. William Bradford, *Of Plymouth Plantation*, Samuel Eliot Morison, ed. (New York: The Modern Library, 1967), chapter XI.

12. Bradford Smith, *Bradford of Plymouth* (Philadelphia and New York: J. B. Lippincott Co., 1951), 189.

13. Bradford, *Of Plymouth Plantation*, 81.

14. Ibid.

15. George M. Wrong, *The Conquest of New France* (New Haven: University Press, 1918), 82–91.

16. *Mr. Prince's Thanksgiving Sermon on the Salvation of God in 1746* (Boston: D. Henchman, 1746), 21.

17. Ibid., 27.

18. Ibid., 28.

19. Rev. Jonathan French, *Thanksgiving Sermon*, November 29, 1798,

in Hall, *American Revolution*, 51.

20. *Mr. Prince's Thanksgiving Sermon*, 29.

21. Hall, *American Revolution*, 51; Exodus 14:13.

22. John Fiske, *The American Revolution*, 2 vols. (Boston and New York: Houghton, Mifflin & Co., 1898), 1:212.

23. John Fiske, *The Critical Period of American History: 1783–1789* (Boston and New York: Houghton, Mifflin & Co., 1898), 231–32.

24. Proverbs 22:6.

25. Psalm 112:1–2 NASB.

Chapter 3

America Is Not
the End of the World

Go therefore and make disciples of all nations [literally, "make the nations My disciples"].

Matthew 28:19

"LANDING OF THE PILGRIMS" BY CHARLES LUCY

Lastly, (and which was not least), a great hope & inward zeal they had of laying some good foundation, or at least to make some way thereunto, for the propagating & advancing the Gospel of the kingdom of Christ in those remote parts of the world; yea, though they should be but even as stepping-stones unto others for the performing of so great a work.

— William Bradford,

History of Plymouth Plantation

Chapter 3

America Is Not the End of the World

*I*s there a master plan for individuals and nations to be free? Is the loving Creator working in and through His children, created in His image, to reconcile the world to Himself? Or are we, as many materialist atheists would postulate, simply evolved animals born to die in a random universe? In each of the *six billion copies* of the Bible that have reached around the world, we find clear guidance into God's loving, unstoppable plan. Before we continue to destroy the foundations of America as a nation in covenant with God, it is important to step back and uncover God's revealed purpose in history to "set the captives free."[1] We also need to know our roles as individuals, families, and churches in His plan.

God's Purpose in History

What is God's purpose in history? Those who do not share the Providential approach to history would say that there is no definitive godly purpose to history. They see autonomous man or some fatalistic impersonal force making history. But the Biblical, Providential view of God's overall plan for His world and all His creation, which is being accomplished in history, underlies such passages as First Peter 4:11:

> *Whoever speaks, [let him speak] as one who speaks oracles of God; whoever serves, as one who serves by the strength that God supplies—in order that in everything God may be glorified through Jesus Christ. To Him belong glory and dominion forever and ever. Amen.*

Our task as stewards fulfilling God's will in history is to do all things to the glory of God.[2] The *Westminster Shorter Catechism* summarizes our purpose in light of God's plan, which is "to glorify God and enjoy Him forever."[3]

His Will: Our Commission

The Great Commission is given by Christ to His disciples as He speaks to them after His resurrection. He says in Matthew 28:18–20:

> *All authority in heaven and on earth has been given to Me. Go therefore and make disciples of all nations [literally, "make the nations My disciples"], baptizing them in the name of the Father and of the Son and of the Holy Spirit, teaching them to observe all that I have commanded you. And behold, I am with you always, to the end of the age.*

Matthew Henry, the premier Bible commentator of the founding era, said concerning the Great Commission:

> *What is the principal intention of this commission;... to disciple all nations. Admit them disciples; do your utmost to make the nations Christian nations.... The work which the apostles had to do was to set up the Christian religion in all places, and it was honorable work; the achievements of the mighty heroes [tyrants] of the world were nothing to it. They conquered the nations for themselves and made them MISERABLE; the apostles conquered them for Christ and made them HAPPY.*[4]

Pilgrim Governor Bradford shared this ambition, saying that the Pilgrims saw themselves as "stepping stones" for God's purpose. The Great Commission has provided the primary impetus for the building of Christian civilization around the world.

It is important to remember that the spread of Christianity is predicated upon one major driving force: the desire that God may be glorified through the preaching of the Gospel[5] and the reconciliation and replenishing of His world.[6] Of course, there have also been carnal motives for cultural development that have influenced Western culture (for example: greed, lust, survival, curiosity) but none as powerful, consistent, or driving as God's commission.

Passing the Torch of Christian Liberty

The expansion of Christian liberty is the observable westward phenomenon of the spreading of the Gospel of Christ as it took root and spread from the Mediterranean to Europe and on to the Americas. The story begins with the primitive Church spreading the Gospel of Christ to the entire Roman Empire before A.D. 70.[7] It should be noted that although the Gospel was preached to the four corners of the earth, it only became the dominant cultural influence as it moved westward from the Holy Land.

When all of history is seen as the unveiling of God's purpose within time and space, America's Christian history and the liberty that it produced can be viewed in a much more strategic light. Seen in the context of God's greater plan for the whole world, America can be placed in its proper perspective as an instrument for God's use, but not the pinnacle of history. America is not the final expression of the kingdom of God, but it is the frontier of Christianity's expansion and the first nation established fully on Christian ideals.

No "Manifest Destiny"

It is not our intention to portray Americans as God's chosen nation, as some modern religious cults have suggested. Nor are we trying to suggest that America has a "manifest destiny," or that she is destined to rule because of some inherent greatness. The idea of a manifest destiny grew up in the nineteenth century as a secularization of the original covenants of the Pilgrims and other colonists. God's purpose for America can be clearly seen in history through the covenants of our people and divine intervention in events.

That purpose is molded by the hand of the Creator, and it is to His glory that we as a nation have been used to spread His Gospel. Our forefathers understood that our commission was to spread the message of Christ to the world and build a Biblically based civilization.

They also understood that if they denied their commission, God would surely judge them and their nation.

God Prepares the Continents

The Lord spoke to Job and said: "Where were you when I laid the foundation of the earth? Tell Me, if you have understanding. Who determined its measurements—surely you know!"[8] Our God not only laid out the dimensions of the world, setting the boundaries of the sea, but He determined the appointed times and places of every nation and people. "And He made from one man every nation of mankind to live on all the face of the earth, having determined allotted periods and the boundaries of their dwelling place."[9]

Christian historians and scientists throughout much of American history clearly saw the hand of God in the creation and preservation not only of His world in general, but specifically of the North American continent. After analyzing the climates, natural resources, division of the oceans, and configuration of the rivers and mountains in light of God's Gospel purpose, Princeton geologist Arnold Guyot concludes concerning America:

> America, different in position, structure, and climatic conditions from both the other northern continents, seems destined to play a part in the history of mankind unlike that of Europe and Asia, though not less noble than either. America, therefore, with her cultured and progressive people and her social organization, founded upon the principle of the equality and brotherhood of all mankind, seems destined to furnish the most complete expression of the Christian civilization.[10]

Great historians also saw the hand of God at work in the forming of this continent in such a way that it would be preserved for a unique, Biblically minded, and Christian people. Emma Willard, historian, educator, and early pioneer for women's right to higher education, writes in her *History of the United States*: "In observing the United States, there is much to convince us that an Almighty, Overruling Providence, designed from the first to place here a great, united people."[11]

Forgetting this awareness of Providential provision, America has also lost sight of the purpose for which it was founded. A nation, like an individual, needs a purpose to succeed. Alien philosophies, such as cultural Marxism and secular materialism, are vying for our children's minds. We will point them to God's liberating purpose, or as Proverbs tells us, "Where there is no vision [Biblical revelation], the people perish."[12]

Powerful World-Changing Force

We have seen that America, though exceptional, is only a part of God's broader plan in history. So also are the people through whom God has carried out His historical initiative. The center stage of world history, when seen from a Christian perspective, is not dominated by class struggles, race wars, or the whims of potentates, but is flooded with light and meaning from the lives of simple believers in the Most High God. These self-governing Christians from all nations, ethnicities, and walks of life, have been and continue to be the most powerful world-changing force known to man. Let us see how these self-governing Christians were prepared to expand God's kingdom as he or she lived out the Great Commission in covenant with the Almighty.

The New Testament Church

Most histories of antiquity give but a few lines to the impact that Christianity has had in the world. The failure to recognize the historic centrality of the New Testament churches bears witness to the humanistic outlook of many historians. In their search for materialistic explanations of events, they ignore these seemingly insignificant people.

God set His people free from the bondage of sin and guilt, which had kept them as slaves.[13] This internal liberty, received through faith in Christ's atoning death and victorious ascension, made men free, whether in a Philippian jail[14] or in a stone quarry awaiting execution.[15] Internal liberty, however, finally manifested itself on a national scale. It was the Word of God unleashed in the hands of the individual that would, in time, liberate every area of life, both internal and external. Jesus Christ announced His plan to liberate men internally and externally in the first sermon of His ministry when He said:

> *The Spirit of the Lord is upon Me, because He has anointed Me to proclaim good news to the poor. He has sent Me to proclaim* LIBERTY *to the captives and recovering of sight to the blind, to set at* LIBERTY *those who are oppressed.*[16]

Churches: "Little Republics"

Through the teachings of Scripture and renewed commitments to God's precepts, the primitive churches were able to break with the pagan view of man that had dominated the world. Those churches demonstrated the Christian view of man, becoming themselves little Christian republics. In his book *The Genesis of the New England Churches*, Leonard Bacon says, "There are indications that in every place, the society of believers in Christ was a little republic."[17]

Women, slaves, gentiles, and children were all seen as important in the decisions of the Church; even the choice of leadership was the responsibility of the people, not a top-down religious class or hierarchy.

These early believers "turned the world upside down."[18] They did not have the completed Bible for more than two centuries, and even if they did, few of them could read. They were persecuted for almost three hundred years, and many died for their faith. They were like the mustard seed of which Jesus spoke: the smallest seed in the field, which would one day grow up into a tree where the birds of the air would lodge. The Kingdom of God was growing, and nothing could stop it.

By God's Providential hand, the New Testament, written by the apostles in the first century, became officially canonized in the third and fourth centuries. Having a completed Bible, great Church philosophers such as Augustine could articulate a Christian worldview encouraging real hope and reformation as opposed to the failed pagan philosophies. This prepared Christians to engage their culture on a sound moral and intellectual footing.

The Middle Ages saw a continued spread of the Chain of Christianity. Biblical thought and action overthrew paganism in Europe and England. Christian civilization became predominant. Even though the Word of God was not yet in the hands of the everyday person, monasteries and educated clergy preserved it. Soon, godly students of Scripture would realize that God intended His Word for all of His people. The stage was set for the Reformation.

The Morning Star of the Reformation

The Reformation began to emerge 150 years before Martin Luther hammered his famous theses to the church door at Wittenberg. It began in England with a clergyman named John Wycliffe, who is rightly called "the Morning Star of the Reformation." Wycliffe was educated at Oxford University, where he became a professor of divinity. He first gained prominence by his efforts to reform the Church in England, which had become corrupt and riddled with superstition. He was persecuted for his attempts but escaped execution through his friendship with a powerful nobleman.

Expelled from Oxford, he retired to a country pastorate. He began to see that his efforts at external reform of the Church were doomed to failure, for only as the people had the Word of God could they begin to reform their own lives—then the next step would be to reform the Church and then their society. At the time, only the educated clergy and nobility could read the Bible. Aside from general illiteracy, it was available only in Latin. Without waiting to gather a committee of scholars to tackle the immense task, Wycliffe began alone to translate the Bible into English, finishing his translation in 1381.

Taking the Bible to the People

As Wycliffe translated the Scriptures, he pondered the pressing problem of how to get God's Word to the people despite the opposition of court and clergy. God led him to teach a group of "poor preachers," who took his tracts and portions of the Bible as he translated them and distributed them to people throughout England. The people flocked to meetings on village greens, in chapels, and in halls, where the preachers read aloud to them from Scripture. They brought the

Bible to everyday people in their own language. However, a serious hurdle still confronted the preachers: few of the common people could read.

Literacy Program of the Poor Preachers

Undeterred, the preachers set about to teach the people to read, instructing men, women, and children so that they could understand the Scriptures for themselves. One observer who disapproved of God's Word being put into the hands of the everyday people wrote indignantly that Wycliffe's Bible had "become more accessible and familiar to laymen and to women able to read than it had…been to the most intelligent and learned of the clergy."

Detractors called his poor preachers and their followers "Lollards," a scornful name meaning "babblers," but their movement penetrated deeply into English life. Soon, followers of Wycliffe were everywhere and among all classes of people, from poor farmers and artisans to noblemen. One panic-stricken opponent claimed: "Every second man one meets is a Lollard!"[19]

An Entire Nation Awakened

Through the distribution and study of Wycliffe's Bible, an entire nation was awakened out of religious apathy and given a new sense of purpose.

The Pope, hoping to stem the tide of Reformation in England, summoned Wycliffe to Rome to undergo trial before the Papal Court. Wycliffe was too old and ill to go, however, and he died on December 31, 1384, while ministering to his parish church. Nevertheless, the Lollards continued long after his death as an effective underground movement, emerging into full light again in the time of the Pilgrims and other early-Christian settlers.

The hatred of Wycliffe's enemies followed him beyond the grave. In 1425, forty-one years after his death, the Church of Rome ordered his bones exhumed and burned, together with numerous books he had written. His ashes were cast into the River Swift, which flows near Lutterworth and, in the words of Thomas Fuller's eloquent eulogy:

The little river conveyed Wycliffe's remains into the Avon, the Avon into the Severn, Severn into the narrow seas, they to the main ocean. And thus the ashes of Wycliffe are the emblem of his doctrine, which now is dispersed all the world over.[20]

In the next two hundred years, many of God's servants would give their lives for the furtherance of His purpose, not seeing the full fruition of Christian liberty, but heralding its coming.

A Divine Time Bomb Brings Victory

Almost 150 years later, William Tyndale, a scholar educated at both Oxford and Cambridge, desired to translate the Scriptures into the English of his time, which had changed greatly since Wycliffe's day. Although he, like Wycliffe, faced stern opposition, he persisted.

In his *History of the Reformation in Europe in the Time of Calvin*, J. H. Merle d'Aubigné explains why:

He felt pressed to accomplish a vow made many years before. "If God preserves my life," he had said, "I will cause a boy that drives a plow to know more of the Scriptures than the pope."[21]

As God preserved his life, Tyndale remained faithful to his vow. In 1525, Tyndale's translation of the New Testament from the original Greek—rather than the Latin version used by Wycliffe—was published in Germany. Then he began work on the Old Testament.

After many years of toil, the last of which were spent as a prisoner in the Belgian city of Vilvorde, William Tyndale's translation of the Word of God into the English language was nearly completed. Before it could be published or distributed, Tyndale was burned at the stake as a religious heretic at the command of King Henry VIII on October 6, 1536. As the fire raged, Tyndale preached a sermon calling to his king to believe in Christ. "Lord, open the King of England's eyes!" were his last words.

Within twelve months of Tyndale's death, this same King Henry, having broken with the Roman Church, was advised that he needed his own Bible in every parish in the land to prove his independence from the Pope.

Tyndale's version was submitted to the king. Then, as the Reformation historian d'Aubigné relates, something remarkable happened:

> *Henry ran over the book: Tyndale's name was not in it, and the dedication to his Majesty was very well written. The King regarding...Holy Scripture as the most powerful engine to destroy the papal system...came to an unexpected resolution: he authorized the sale and the reading of the Bible throughout the kingdom.*

Henry little dreamed that he had just laid a divine time bomb under his own tyrannical throne by giving the Word of God to the people. Tyndale took the victory. Once again, God had taken the wrath of man to praise Him.[22]

Liberty Spreads as the Bible Is Unleashed

At the same time, on the European continent, the great reformers—Luther, Calvin, Zwingli, and others—began to systematically explain God's purpose for man and the way of salvation through faith alone. They reasoned from the Scriptures that the Lord does not divide people into hierarchies. "For God shows no partiality."[23] All people, whether king or pauper, rich or poor, regardless of race or status, can come to Him for salvation with equal access to His blessing.

The Scriptures, with its clear worldview, empowered English believers to resist the tyranny of the Tudor and Stuart dynasties and to establish accountable, representative government. But the persecution of true believers continued in England and Scotland.

In God's time, a small band of committed, exiled believers sailed to North America in 1620. The world would never be the same. Thousands of years of godly wisdom had paved the way for them. The discoveries of Columbus and inventions such as the sea compass made their travels possible. The invention of the printing press by Johannes Gutenberg and the eventual printing of the Geneva and King James Bibles made it possible for each family to have its own copy of the Bible. All of these events made possible the Biblical self-government that would characterize all of Colonial America.

These English farmers and artisans who set foot on Plymouth on December 12, 1620, came with few possessions. But each family had the Bible that provided the foundation for all their institutions. They had developed in their character all the elements necessary to lay the foundation of the world's first Christian constitutional republic. Liberty was on the march.

The Pilgrim governor, William Bradford, wrote the only authentic history of the entire Pilgrim saga. Bradford explains their passion for reaching the "remote parts of the world" with the liberating Gospel. When he tells their reasons for risking all to come to America, he says,

> *Lastly (and which was not least) a great hope and inward zeal they had of laying some good foundation, or at least to make some way there unto, for the propagating and advancing the Gospel of the kingdom of Christ in those remote parts of the world; yea, though they should be but even as stepping stones unto others for the performing of so great a work.*[24]

Of the small group of Pilgrims, one-half of them died of disease and cold the first winter of 1621. Those still living could have chosen to return to England on the *Mayflower* as it left in the spring. But every one of them chose to stay. They were willing to lay their lives down in the wilderness as stepping stones so that their heirs could enjoy unprecedented freedom and prosperity. We are those heirs!

Fulfillment of the Pilgrim Vision

One of the misconceptions in America today is that the Christianity of our forebears is fading. Yet, the opposite is true. In the twentieth century, the Christian faith grew exponentially worldwide. Authors such as Peter Jenkins, David Aikman, and Dinesh D'Souza have documented the evidence of this growth. For example, in 1900, there were approximately ten million Christians in Africa. By 2000, there were 360 million African believers—about one-half the total population on the continent. By 2018, there were more than 630 million Christians in Africa.

Other continents have experienced similar sweeping transformations. Only a few million Bible-believing Christians lived in Asia in the 1940s. That number is also growing dramatically, reaching 388 million by 2018. South America is seeing similar growth, with over 600 million believing Christians by 2018.

Christianity had spread largely in Europe until the seventeenth century. However, beginning with the Pilgrim's original Gospel vision, America established the world's first privately funded mission movement in the nineteenth century. This missionary movement spread the liberating truths of the faith worldwide. More missionaries have gone out from America than from all other countries of the world combined.

Today, approximately one-third of the world's population declare themselves to be Christians. "Ironically, while Europe has moved away from Christianity, the Christian religion has been expanding its influence in Central and South America, in Africa, and in Asia. For the first time in history, Christianity has become a universal religion. It is, in fact, the only religion with a global reach."[25]

Why has there been such an increase in Christianity in recent centuries? The central reason is the unleashing of the Bible throughout the world. Before the printing press, the Bible was chained to pulpits and available only in Latin and was read under penalty of death. The inventor of the movable-type printing press, Johannes Gutenberg, chose the Bible as the first book to be printed. He believed that this book would transform the world.

> *Yes, it is a press, certainly, but a press from which shall flow in inexhaustible streams the most abundant and most marvelous liquor that has ever flowed to relieve the thirst of men. Through it, God will spread His Word; a spring of pure truth shall flow from it; like a new star it shall scatter the darkness of ignorance and cause a light hithertofore unknown to shine among men.*[26]

The Prince of Preachers, C. H. Spurgeon (1834–92), agreed that the Bible, unleashed and taught, would increasingly free the nations:

> *There is not land beneath the sun where there is an open Bible and a preached Gospel, where a tyrant long can hold his place.... The religion of Jesus makes men think, and to make men think is always dangerous to a despot's power.*[27]

Chapter 3 Study Questions

1. What is God's purpose in history?

2. What is your responsibility in helping to fulfill that purpose?

3. Is the Great Commission applicable to nations as well as individuals?

4. Is America the "last act" in the geographic development of Christianity?

5. What progressive purposes of God can you discover in His development of the different continents?

6. Were early-American Christians aware of the hand of God in the forming of our continent?

7. During the Reformation, what was the major tool God gave to the individual to help him transform his life and his society?

8. What was the governmental form of the early Christian Church?

9. How many inventions and Providential events can you think of that have moved the Chain of Christianity to its present position?

10. What effect did the translation of the Bible by Wycliffe and Tyndale have on the individual?

11. What current events indicate a movement toward completing the Chain of Christianity?

For FREE bonus material & in-depth study on a variety of topics beyond what you find here in *The American Covenant*, visit WorldHistoryInstitute.com/free-downloads.

Chapter 3 Notes

1. Isaiah 61:1; Luke 4:18.
2. First Corinthians 10:31.
3. *Westminster Shorter Catechism*, Q. & A. 1, opc.org/sc.html.
4. Matthew Henry, *Commentary on the Whole Bible*, on Matthew 28:16–20, emphasis added.
5. Matthew 28:18–20.
6. Genesis 1:26–28.
7. Romans 1:8; Colossians 1:6, 23.
8. Job 38:4–5.
9. Acts 17:26.
10. Verna M. Hall, *The Christian History of the Constitution of the United States of America: Christian Self-Government* (San Francisco: Foundation for American Christian Education, 1975), 4.
11. Rosalie J. Slater, *Teaching and Learning America's Christian History* (San Francisco: Foundation for American Christian Education, 1975), 153.
12. Proverbs 29:18 KJV.
13. John 8:32–36.
14. Acts 16:25.
15. Acts 7:54.
16. Luke 4:18, emphasis added.
17. Leonard Bacon, *The Genesis of the New England Churches* (New York: Harper & Brothers, 1874), 23.
18. Acts 17:6.
19. J. R. Green, *Short History of the English People* (New York and London: Harper & Bros., 1898), 242.
20. Slater, *Teaching and Learning*, 168.
21. Ibid., 334.
22. Psalm 76:10.
23. Romans 2:11.
24. William Bradford, *Of Plymouth Plantation 1620–1647*, Samuel Eliot Morison, ed. (New York: Alfred A. Knopf, 2002), 25, emphasis added.
25. Dinesh D'Souza, *What's So Great About Christianity* (Carol Stream,

IL: Tyndale House Publishers, 2007), 9.

26. William Federer, *America's God and Country: Encyclopedia of Quotations* (St. Louis, MO: Amerisearch, Inc., 2000), 270.

27. Charles H. Spurgeon, "Joy Born in Bethlehem," in M. Water, ed., *Multi New Testament Commentary* (London: John Hunt, 1871), 195.

Chapter 4

The Individual Set Free

If you abide in My Word, you are truly My disciples, and you will know the truth, and the truth will set you free."

John 8:31–32

THE PILGRIMS AT PRAYER

They shook off this yoke of antichristian bondage, and as the Lord's free people, joined themselves by a covenant of the Lord into a church estate in the fellowship of the Gospel, to walk in all His ways, made known or to be made known unto them, according to their best endeavours, whatsoever it should cost them, the Lord assisting them.

— William Bradford
Of Plymouth Plantation

Chapter 4

The Individual
Set Free

*W*hat can one individual or family accomplish when they are in covenant with God? The following story provides one amazing answer to that question.

Jonathan Edwards and Sarah Pierrepont married in 1727. Edwards was the son of a minister and the only boy of eleven children. The couple had eleven children of their own, which continued a generational blessing that has populated America with godly offspring for centuries.

Jonathan believed in rising before the sun for prayer. He would then read a chapter of the Bible to his children before the day began. Though perhaps the greatest intellect produced in Colonial America, each day he took time out from his writing, pastoring, and mission work among the Natives to give one hour of undivided attention to his children.

During this time, he would go over their lessons or answer any questions they might have. Jonathan and Sarah Edwards shared the priority of training their progeny for service to God and man.

One hundred seventy-three years after their marriage, a study was made of some 1,400 of their descendants, revealing some amazing facts.

By 1900, this single marriage had produced thirteen college presidents, sixty-five professors, one hundred lawyers, the dean of an outstanding law school, thirty judges, fifty-six physicians, the dean of a medical school, eighty holders of public office, three United States senators, three mayors of large American cities, three state governors, one comptroller of the United States Treasury, and one vice president of the United States.

Members of the family had written 135 books and edited eighteen journals and periodicals. They had entered the ministry in droves, with nearly one hundred of them becoming missionaries overseas.

What can one person accomplish? What is the value of a single human life? The story of the Edwards family illustrates the power of covenant with God. The God who covenanted with Abraham, Isaac, and Jacob enters into covenant with *individuals* and empowers them to change the world in His name. God gives purpose to every individual life. We all have a role to play in this world-changing task.

For many generations, most Americans have been sheltered from facing the life-or-death decisions faced by our Founders: "Give me liberty or give me death." Our Founders understood that they were risking everything for liberty. As the Declaration of Independence says, "With a firm reliance on the protection of divine Providence, we mutually pledge to each other our lives, our fortunes, and our sacred honor." Many lost their lives, most lost their fortunes, but none lost his honor.

Most of us in our lifetime have taken for granted such things as our individual liberty: the right to make what we wish of our lives; to choose a profession; to live and work where we wish; to pursue happiness in our own way and enjoy the fruits of our labors; and, above all, the right to worship God according to the dictates of our conscience.

But we have forgotten that liberty was not always alive and well in the world. In fact, liberty is a relatively new experience for mankind. Less than 5 percent of people who have ever lived throughout history have known anything of what we would call freedom. Lasting civil and religious liberty for the individual only began with Christianity—the only exception being the ancient self-governing republic of the Hebrews. Through the suffering and sacrifices of innumerable believers over the centuries, America was finally able to realize lasting constitutional liberty.

If you believe that each person has an unalienable right to life, liberty, and the fruit of his or her own labors, you share in the Biblical idea of man, which holds the individual as precious to God. This concept of the uniqueness of the individual was completely foreign to the unbelieving ages of the world, when the individual was submerged in his tribe or nation, as anonymous as a grain of sand. Even the Israelites almost forgot the God-created individual of Genesis 1.

What Is the Dominion Mandate?

In Genesis, Moses wrote the story of creation. In the first four words of this book, God shatters the religious foundation of polytheism. "In the beginning, God…" At the very start, the Lord declares His sovereignty, preexistence, and oneness. There are no other gods or opposing forces of nature. He then proceeds to give His marching orders to His creature, man and woman:

> *Then God said, "Let Us make man in Our image, after Our likeness. And let them have dominion over the fish of the sea and over the birds of the heavens and over the livestock and over all the earth and over every creeping thing that creeps on the earth." So God created man in His own image, in the image of God He created him;* MALE *and* FEMALE *He created them. And God blessed them. And God said to them, "Be fruitful and multiply and fill the earth and subdue it, and have dominion over the fish of the sea and over the birds of the heavens and over every living thing that moves on the earth."[1]*

Here, in the first words spoken directly to His highest creation, created in His own image, God gives a world-encompassing commission to care for His creation. Since this commission is still in force, it does not permit us to escape our responsibility for the world's condition.

What About the Fall?

Was this great dominion mandate (sometimes called the "cultural mandate") canceled after the Fall? The Bible gives no evidence of such an assumption. In no way does God change His orders to His creation, except that man is condemned to earn his bread by the sweat of his brow and woman to bring forth her children in sorrow. But God does not give up the sovereignty of this world to Satan as some Biblical commentators have suggested. Quite the contrary, Satan is cursed, and his assured defeat is promised through the death and resurrection of Christ.[2]

Also, after the Fall, Cain and Abel offer the first fruits of their labor to God, which bears a clear relation to God's dominion mandate. By so doing, they declare God's ownership of the earth and their desire to be God's good stewards. And in Genesis 4:20ff., we also see individuals being named along with their vocations or commissions (such as cattlemen, musicians, and brass and ironworkers), illustrating the spreading of the mandate's application to every individual.

Again, after the Noahic Flood, God substantially repeats the dominion mandate in His first words of blessing spoken to Noah when he leaves the ark.[3] The Lord repeats His mandated plan for each individual.

Yet, just as men lost sight of their unique God-created individuality after the Fall, so they also lost sight of God's dominion mandate. Men twisted the *dominion* God had given them over the earth into *domination* over their fellow men. Instead of obeying God's command to cultivate the earth, men proceeded to destroy the creation entrusted into their care with endless wars over land, gold, and goods. Men forgot the one God and bowed down to other gods of their own creation.

God's Covenant with Abraham

The Hebrews alone continued to worship the one God, and through God's covenant with an individual, Abraham, He blessed their nation. For God tells Abraham that He will make a great nation from his seed and tells him: "In you shall all the nations be blessed."[4] It was God's intention that Abraham and his descendants would bring the unbelieving world back to God, restoring a right relationship between the individual and his Lord.

To prepare His people for their task, God gives them His merciful Law, His prophets, and His very presence. But rather than following God's plan of self-government under His Law, they demand to be ruled by a king, desiring to be like all the pagan nations around them.[5] Instead of transforming the pagan world, they conform to its view of man. Heedless of the warnings of their prophets, Israel is taken captive by a pagan people. But during the darkest days of the Babylonian captivity, the prophet Jeremiah predicts that one day, the Lord will write His Law on the hearts of His people.[6]

The Pagan Idea of Man

Despite the glorious promise of a New Covenant to come, Israel comes ultimately under the yoke of the greatest pagan power of antiquity: Rome. As American historian Richard Frothingham says of the pagan view of man that surrounded Israel:

> *The individual was regarded as of value only as he formed a part of the political fabric, and was able to contribute to its uses, as though it were the end of his being to aggrandize the State. This was the pagan idea of man. The wisest philosophers of antiquity could not rise above it.[7]*

The Greek philosopher Plato considered the State of primary importance, and the individual was only a cog in the machine of the State. The ideal State in Plato's *Republic* was essentially a commune that abolished family life in favor of an entire focus on serving the State. The "communism" he advocated was certainly repressive toward individuals' inalienable rights, as communism is today. Lenin said, "The goal of socialism is communism."

The State Becomes as God

Even Aristotle, a student of Plato whose wisdom is often quoted by early Church fathers, could not rise above this pagan idea that the State was of primary importance. (See Aristotle's *Politics*, book 1, chapter 2) As Frothingham says:

> *The State regarded as of paramount importance, not the man, but the citizen whose physical and intellectual forces it absorbed. If this tended to foster lofty civic virtues and splendid individual culture in the classes whom the State selected as the recipients of its favors, it bore hard on those whom the State virtually ignored—on laboring men, mechanics, the poor, captives in war, slaves, and woman.[8]*

Despite the low view of the individual in both Greece and Rome, God had purposes for these pagan states. As the great traders and colonizers of the ancient world, the Greeks took their beautiful and rich language wherever they went, so that Greek was spoken everywhere. Here was the language that would articulate the Gospel to millions in succeeding centuries.

The Greeks were philosophers and artists, but the Romans were practical men—builders of great roads, public buildings, and temples to house their numerous gods. These Roman creations show the monolithic nature of Roman culture and the impersonal public nature of Roman life in which the State—majestic and all powerful—overshadowed the individual, crushing him with its weight.

The Romans loved order and had great administrative ability. To a great extent, Rome succeeded in incorporating its conquered peoples into a national life, giving them the protection of its laws—something the old Oriental despotisms of Assyria and Persia had never done.

"Christ Entered a Dying World"

When Christ appeared, these two civilizations had prepared the way for His coming. God used these two national individualities—Greece and Rome—in a remarkable way. Through these two great pagan nations, God providentially connected the entire known world in one empire with a central administration providing general order, an unprecedented opportunity for communication with diverse peoples, and vast improvements in the ease and safety of travel.

Roman emperors may have persecuted Christians as a matter of policy, but the effect of their policies was to assist rather than inhibit the spread of Christianity.

There was then great need for the Messiah to rescue mankind. Millions of nameless individuals were caught in the web of Roman despotism. There was nowhere to flee from Rome's tyranny, which embraced the entire civilized world.

The state of this world was grim: Greek civilization was now dead; what had been best in Rome had died with the Republic. All semblance of the impartial rule of Roman law was over as the Emperor

Caesar Augustus gathered the reins of power into his own hands. He had ruled the Empire for thirty years when his decree "that all the world should be taxed" brought Mary and Joseph to Bethlehem. Israel was in slavery to the Romans, and their religion was in decay. There had been no prophets in Israel for four hundred years.

Into this great darkness, God sent His Son. Swiss historian Philip Schaff says of this wondrous event: "Christ entered a dying world as the author of a new and imperishable life."[9]

God revealed to individuals in the Old Testament their importance in His divine plan. In Psalm 8:4–6, the psalmist wonders at this importance:

> *What is man that You are mindful of him, and the son of man that You care for him? Yet You have made him a little lower than the heavenly beings and crowned him with glory and honor. You have given him dominion over the works of Your hands; You have put all things under his feet.*

Jesus restates God's original and unchanging purpose for mankind by expressing His love for each individual in the parable of the lost sheep:

> *What man of you, having a hundred sheep, if he has lost one of them, does not leave the ninety-nine in the open country, and go after the one that is lost, until he finds it? And when he has found it, he lays it on his shoulders, rejoicing. And when he comes home, he calls together his friends and his neighbors, saying to them, "Rejoice with me, for I have found my sheep that was lost." Just so, I tell you, there will be more joy in heaven over one sinner who repents than over ninety-nine righteous persons who need no repentance.*[10]

A New Spirit and a New Power in the World

New life in Christ gave the individual a new value unknown in the ancient world or its religions. It began the work of transforming individual lives in the midst of the most pervasive tyranny the world had known, where the pagan idea of man reigned supreme. As Frothingham says:

This low view of man was exerting its full influence when Rome was at the height of its power and glory. Christianity then appeared with its central doctrine, that man was created in the divine image, and destined for immortality; pronouncing that, in the eye of God, all men are equal. This asserted for the individual an independent value. It occasioned the great inference that man is superior to the State, which ought to be fashioned for his use. This was the advent of a new spirit and a new power in the world.[11]

God's plan of redemption was at last fulfilled in the person of His Son, Jesus Christ, who brought a higher law to individuals everywhere, a law addressed to the individual heart, illumining rather than abolishing the laws of Moses.

Internal Liberty and External Freedom

"The Gospel brings forth a higher standard of liberty than external law," writes Christian educator Rosalie J. Slater, for Christianity brings the

internal law of the Two Commandments of our Lord.... It was not until the Saviour of mankind appeared that men learned that external freedom was achieved by internal liberty—"the liberty wherewith Christ hath made us free."[12]

The Gospel of Jesus Christ is addressed to the individual man, woman, and child. Each is free to learn that, as Paul puts it, "I can do all things through Him [Christ] who strengthens me."[13] Christ brings liberty to the individual—both religious and civil liberty.

Right of Individual Conscience Unknown

The right of individual conscience was inconceivable to the pagan mind. Rome was happy to adopt the gods of its conquered peoples. It was very tolerant of all nations' religious beliefs because they were national religions.

The idea of an individual choosing his own religion, however, was unheard of. You were born into your religion; it was the religion of your fathers—of your nation. The Romans thought of Christianity simply as a Jewish heresy—and a very dangerous one, for not only had these Christians deserted the religion of their fathers, but they refused to bow down and worship the emperor. They were not "reliable" citizens of the State. So, the State persecuted them until Emperor Constantine adopted Christianity and made it the State religion in A.D. 312.

Even before Constantine's adoption, however, the Church had begun to lose its original self-governing nature. Now the individual Christian lost the last vestiges of control that he had over his church, which began to borrow the hierarchical structure of the pagan Roman State.

The Reformation Recovers the Gospel

In the previous chapter, we saw how the Reformation gave the Bible to the people, thus restoring to them the knowledge of the Gospel of Jesus Christ that had been kept in the hands of kings and priests. The sixteenth-century Reformation attempted to return to the Biblical doctrines and practices of primitive Christianity. It also demanded liberty of conscience for the individual Christian, asserting his right to read the Scriptures and, by the aid of the indwelling Holy Spirit, to interpret them for himself.

The Reformation asserted the Christian principle of individuality, a declaration of spiritual independence.

Christian Individuality and Humanistic Individualism

The individuality typified by the Pilgrims, however, was not the "do-your-own-thing" sort of humanistic individualism so prevalent today. Humanistic individualism implies a man-centered universe, with no moral absolutes to control man, and is an invitation to anarchy. Christian individuality implies a God-centered universe, with the individual controlled by God's laws, and is an invitation to enjoy Christ's law of liberty within the bounds of His unchanging order.

As we review our origins from the Christian perspective and recover our lost heritage of Christian principles, we shall be equipped as never before to go forward as world-transforming Christians, beginning with ourselves, then our families, churches, schools, communities, states, and our nation.

Today, many signs that mark a revival of respect for the individual's God-given rights are impacting world events. Grassroots, Biblically based social and political movements in America are awakening the dormant conscience of a nation careening toward socialism. Many Americans are becoming increasingly concerned about the rights of the unborn, the handicapped, the aged, the property owner, and the family.

Unfortunately, many Americans have largely forgotten the power of the individual in light of a Biblical view of man and government—a power that undermines tyranny and brings liberty to cultures that are in bondage.

We, as our Pilgrim Fathers did, need to see that neither the worldly power nor the social position of an individual determines his capacity for changing the world. An American individual, burdened with taxation and struggling to raise a family, often questions whether one lone voice can ever be heard—whether it is worth trying to change the status quo.

The Providential view of life and history restores hope and inspires people, like the Pilgrims were inspired, to risk much in order to become God's world changers.

Reformation without Tarrying for Any

Roused by their growing knowledge of the Bible, which Henry VIII made it legal to read, many English Christians learned that the Church in which they had grown up had strayed far from the original model in the New Testament. Many wished to reform the national Church.

But, in addition to these Puritans, as they soon were called, were the men and women known as Separatists, the most famous of whom later became the Pilgrims. The Separatists desired to disengage themselves from the authority of the national Church in order to practice Christian self-government and to teach their children to do the same.

A courageous young minister, Robert Browne, was thrown into prison repeatedly for preaching separation from the national Church and the individual's "reformation without tarrying for any." He was finally forced to flee to Holland. But his words took hold of many still in England struggling with the great question of whether to remain in the Church of England and try to reform it or to denounce the concept of the national Church as unscriptural.

In the little town of Scrooby in the north of England, the idea of "reformation without tarrying for any" began to take effect. Here, three individuals—future leaders of the Pilgrims—struggled with this question.

The Church was built on the blood of the martyrs, as we have learned from the lives of great reformers like Wycliffe and Tyndale. These Christians were willing to pay the ultimate price for obeying God rather than man and for exercising their God-given individuality. Their work set the stage for a fuller flowering of the individual. For this next great step, the most unlikely cast of characters was assembled—people without power, money, or position. Nevertheless, they were to plant the seed of Christian liberty in a new world.

William Brewster

This remarkable Christian lived three lives—as confidential secretary to William Davison, a prominent member of Queen Elizabeth's court; then, after Davison's fall from favor, as a Separatist leader in England and Holland; finally, as the great spiritual leader of the Pilgrims in the Plymouth Colony.

After he returned from court to the quiet village of Scrooby, in East Anglia, he took over his ailing father's post as Her Majesty's postmaster and the Archbishop of York's bailiff in charge of his estates in the area. He set out to reform the Church of England from within. He sought good preachers for local churches and paid them out of his own pocket. (Many churches went without preaching for years on end, since Queen Elizabeth plainly preferred the reading of government-approved homilies to sermons that reflected individual interpretation of Scripture.)

When the Church of England demanded more rigid conformity to its rituals and rejected the right of individuals to hear unauthorized preachers, Brewster finally decided to separate from the Church and to covenant with other Christians in his area to form a Scriptural congregation. As Pilgrim historian Bradford records in his *History of Plimoth Plantation*:

> *They shook off this yoke of antichristian bondage, and as the Lord's free people, joined themselves (by a covenant of the Lord) into a church estate, in the fellowship of the Gospel, to walk in all His ways, made known or to be made known unto them, according to their best endeavours, whatsoever it should cost them, the Lord assisting them.[14]*

After the church formed by mutual covenant, Bradford relates how Brewster "was a special stay and help unto them."[15]

> *They originally met at his house on the Lord's Day (which was a manor of the bishop's) and with great love he entertained them when they came, making provision for them to his great charge.... And when they were to remove out of the country he was one of the first in all adventures.[16]*

Brewster bore all the ensuing trials in England, Holland, and America with unfailing resolution and good cheer. Later, when the Pilgrim Church was without a minister in the New World, he preached twice every Sunday and brought many to Christ. Bradford says that throughout his life, Brewster was a highly effective evangelist. "He did more in this behalf in a year," the Pilgrim historian remarks, "than many...do in all their lives."[17]

John Robinson

John Robinson was an eminent professor and dean at Cambridge University in the 1590s. As a brilliant student of the Scriptures, he became appalled at the corruptions and false teaching of the established Church controlled by Queen Elizabeth.

But Robinson made the career-ending decision to teach the truth about the unbiblical practices of the Queen's Church. As a result, he lost his high position and was prohibited by the government and the university from ever preaching in public again.

He and his wife and family returned to the Scrooby area to stay with relatives. He struggled in his heart about whether to leave the established tyrannical Church of England. He knew his career would be over, and he would live as an outcast from English society.

But at last, he did break those bonds and joined the Separatist congregation that met at Scrooby Manor. He was to become one of the most intelligent, committed, and loving leaders of the Church in history.

Perhaps Pastor John Robinson's greatest legacy is his writing and teaching on the Biblical foundations of freedom. While in exile in Leyden, Holland, Robinson became a respected professor at the University of Leyden—the greatest university in the world at the time. There he worked shoulder to shoulder with Professor Peter Cunaeus and other foremost scholars in the world on the subject of the Hebrew republic, a field widely studied at that time.

There is no doubt that Pastor Robinson conveyed the timeless model of the ancient Hebrew republic to his leaders, who would soon lay the foundation for America's constitutional republic. Pastor John Robinson is the forgotten Founding Father of America.

For twenty years, he taught these principles in depth to his persecuted and beloved Pilgrim Church. More than any other man, John Robinson prepared a people to take dominion over a wilderness to the glory of God. Through his godly wisdom, he taught the Pilgrims individual Christian self-government, and through the example of his Christian compassion, he taught them the value of Christian unity. Bradford writes:

> *His love was great towards them, and his care was all ways bent for their best good, both for soul and body; for besides his singular abilities in divine things (wherein he excelled), he was also very able to give directions in civil affairs, and to foresee dangers & inconveniences; by which means he was very helpful to their outward estates, and so was every way as a common father unto them.*[18]

William Bradford

Young William Bradford was destined to be the leader of the Pilgrims in America. He began his life in the village of Austerfield, England. His parents died when he was only a small child. He was raised by his uncles, who trained him to be a yeoman farmer on his own land. It was the Elizabethan Age—a carnal age. Teens were encouraged to venture into Sherwood Forest to celebrate the summer solstice and party all night long.

But Bradford endured a long childhood illness. While recovering, he began to read the Scriptures with great interest. As a young teen, a friend invited Bradford to a church in nearby Babworth to hear the Rev. Richard Clyfton preach. Young Bradford was so impressed with Clyfton's Scriptural preaching that he continued attending the Babworth church until Clyfton withdrew to become minister of the small Separatist congregation at Scrooby. Despite enormous pressure upon him to remain in the Church of England, young Bradford decided

> to withdraw from the communion of the parish-assemblies, and engage with some society of the faithful that should keep close unto the written Word of God, as the rule of their worship.... Although the provoked rage of his friends tried all the ways imaginable to reclaim him from it, unto all...his answer was... "Nevertheless, to keep a good conscience, and walk in such a way as God has prescribed in His Word, is a thing which I must prefer before you all, and above life itself."[19]

When Bradford started attending the small Separatist church that met at Scrooby Manor, he found a father in William Brewster, who shared his Cambridge education with the talented youth. Bradford was to become not only an outstanding Pilgrim leader in the New World, serving as the governor of the Plymouth Colony for thirty-three years, but also the author of the *History of Plymouth Plantation*. In this account of the Pilgrims, Bradford produced the first great literary work written on these shores.

At the end of a long and productive life, Bradford wrote a summary of the impact of his beloved Pilgrims. He said,

Thus out of small beginnings greater things have been produced by His hand that made all things of nothing, and gives being to all things that are; and as one small candle may light a thousand, so the light here kindled hath shone unto many, yea in some sort to our whole nation; let the glorious name of Jehovah have all the praise![20]

These three individuals—a village postmaster/bailiff, an obscure clergyman, and a young farmer—little dreamed of the marvelous ways in which God would use them in the succeeding years. But they had heeded Paul's admonition: "Do not be conformed to this world, but be transformed by the renewal of your mind, that by testing you may discern what is the will of God, what is good and acceptable and perfect."[21] Renewed and transformed by God, their joy was great, as was their love for each other. But soon these transformed Christians were persecuted severely for refusing to conform to the Church of England.

The Perfect Storm of Providence

These three men, along with their faithful, persecuted friends and families, were brought together in a perfect storm of Providence.

If John Robinson had not left his powerful position at Cambridge; if William Brewster had not escaped the court of Queen Elizabeth and come back to Scrooby; and if William Bradford had not chosen God over the orgies of Sherwood Forest, there may have never been a United States of America. These and all of the providential miracles that are told in these chapters should cause our hearts to be filled with love for the Lord, the Author of liberty.

The Seed of Our Institutions

As we return to the Pilgrim story, we find the above leaders founding an underground Church in the midlands of England. King James I inherited the throne of England in 1603. He vowed to imprison or kill every citizen in England who disagreed with his tyrannical "religion."

The Pilgrims, seeing their friends imprisoned or killed, chose to flee to Holland. After two failed attempts to escape, most of them made their way to Leyden, Holland, the only sanctuary of freedom in the world at that time.

In Holland, they found toleration, although not full religious liberty. Here their pastor, John Robinson, instructed them in the Scriptures, and here they forged strong bonds of Christian fellowship and learned to be a self-governing people. But after twelve years in Holland, they were guided by God to leave that land for the wilderness of America.

In the next chapter, we shall see the foundation they laid for Christian civil government in the New World. Among the Pilgrims, we find many other important foundations. We can trace the lineage of many of our nation's most hallowed institutions back to these dedicated Christians. The Biblical principles that guided and sustained them through danger and difficulty are enshrined in the covenant that founded our nation. For these reasons, we shall be referring often to this small band of dedicated Christians who illustrate so vividly what the individual can do when Christ has set him free.

For FREE bonus material & in-depth study on a variety of topics beyond what you find here in *The American Covenant,* visit WorldHistoryInstitute.com/free-downloads.

Chapter 4 Study Questions

1. Why is the individual important?

2. What is entailed in the dominion mandate? What does it include, and what does it *not* include?

3. What was the pagan idea of man and government?

4. Why did the pagan civilizations of Greece and Rome make the State paramount in their system and man secondary?

5. Why does the "inward law" brought by Jesus Christ help us to fulfill the "outward law" of Moses?

6. What was the Reformation in its essence?

7. Do we need reformation today? In what ways?

8. What happens when individualism is divorced from Christianity? What effects does it produce?

9. What happens to the relations between individuals in a man-centered, rather than God-centered, world?

10. Do we Christians today think of ourselves primarily as individuals, or do we think of ourselves primarily as members of groups—religious, economic, and social?

11. Are Christians persecuted today? By whom? Why?

12. Where does one find God's principle of individuality?

Chapter 4 Notes

1. Genesis 1:26–28, emphasis added.

2. Genesis 3:14–15.

3. Genesis 9:1–4.

4. Galatians 3:8, referencing Genesis 12:3.

5. First Samuel 8.

6. Jeremiah 31:33.

7. Verna M. Hall, *The Christian History of the Constitution of the United States of America: Christian Self-Government* (San Francisco: Foundation for American Christian Education, 1975), 1–2.

8. Ibid.

9. Philip Schaff, *History of the Christian Church*, 8 vols. (Grand Rapids, MI: Eerdmans, 1978), I:59.

10. Luke 15:4–7.

11. Hall, *The Christian History of the Constitution*, 2.

12. Rosalie J. Slater, *Teaching and Learning America's Christian History* (San Francisco: Foundation for American Christian Education, 1975), 159.

13. Philippians 4:13.

14. Hall, *The Christian History of the Constitution*, 185.

15. William Bradford, *Of Plymouth Plantation: 1620–1647*, Samuel Eliot Morison, ed., (New York: Random House, 1967), 326.

16. Ibid.

17. Ibid., 327.

18. Hall, *The Christian History of the Constitution*, 190.

19. Cotton Mather, *Life of William Bradford*, in *The Story of the Pilgrim Fathers* (London: Ward & Downey, 1897; Boston, New York: Houghton, Mifflin & Co., 1897; New York: Klaus Reprint Co., 1969), 40.

20. Bradford, *Of Plymouth Plantation*, 236.

21. Romans 12:2.

Chapter 5

God's World Changers

For freedom Christ has set us free; stand firm therefore, and do not submit again to a yoke of slavery.

Galatians 5:1

GOV. WINTHROP ARRIVES AT SALEM ON THE *ARBELLA* (1630)

Thus stands the cause between God and us, we are entered into Covenant with Him for this work…. Now if the Lord shall please to bear us, and bring us in peace to the place we desire, then hath He verified this Covenant and sealed our Commission.

— John Winthrop,
"Christian Charitie: A Modell Thereof"

Chapter 5

God's World Changers

*M*any Americans today question the assertion that the self-governing Christian is a world changer. Perhaps the average churchgoer they know does not appear to be transforming society.

Yet, Scripture sees the Christian as more than a man who does good and avoids evil. He has within him, because of his faith in Christ, all the power to subdue God's earth to His glory.

Throughout this book, we speak of this vital individual as the self-governing Christian. Before we give an historical survey of the impact of God's world changers, let us begin by defining self-government.

Today in America, our tendency is to think of the word *government* in purely external terms: as *they*—the people in city hall, statehouse, or the national government. To us they are the government. So, at first, the term *self-government* seems strange. If used in a humanistic sense—suggesting that every man is free to govern himself however he wishes without reference to God's moral law—then self-government becomes anarchy. The meaning of the term *self-government* as our Founders understood it can only be grasped when we are willing to be governed by the Scriptures.

Christ's Internal Government

Christ's government is internal, resulting in the Christian becoming self-governing, but always in accord with God's laws. Self-government that ignores God's laws or defies them is not true self-government and leads not to liberty, but to the bondage Jesus refers to in John

8:34–36: "Everyone who practices sin is a slave to sin." Only when the Son sets you free are you free indeed.[1]

Pilgrim Self-Government

The Pilgrims clearly understood the basis of their self-government. A passage on self-government from Scripture that they must have heeded well is: "For if someone does not know how to manage his own household, how will he care for God's church?"[2]

As soon as the Pilgrims settled in their Dutch haven in the city of Leyden, the question of caring for the Church of God was much on their mind. Here, in hospitable Holland, the Pilgrims entered into the important second stage of their development as self-governing Christians, a stage which had just begun in England. It was now their task to establish firmly their new self-governing church. For guidance, they turned to the New Testament model.

Spontaneous Associations

They discovered that the New Testament churches were spontaneous associations of believers: "Individuals and families, drawn toward each other by their common trust in Jesus the Christ…became a community united, not by external bonds, but by the vital force of distinctive ideas and principles."[3]

They also learned that the organization of the church at Jerusalem was essentially democratic. In Leonard Bacon's words, "In every place the society of believers in Christ was a little republic." So, in common with all Separatist churches that had similarly studied the New Testament, the Pilgrims set up a congregational form of government whereby they governed themselves through elected officers.

Their sworn enemy was the corrupt Church of England and its centralized episcopacy, which was, in turn, controlled by the Crown. Looking back through history, they learned how this had come about.

The Church Corrupted

The self-governing Christians of the New Testament churches had only delegated their powers to their church officers to conduct the business of the Church. But, under pressure of persecution in the days before Constantine adopted Christianity, they gradually granted more and more "emergency powers" to their leaders. By A.D. 300, the Church had adopted a centralized episcopal form of government, although their bishops were still democratically elected by the congregations.

The self-government of God's people at this time can teach many lessons for us today. The importance of knowing our history is highlighted by the fact that the early Christians let their powers of self-government slip away from them because, unlike us today, they had no experience to guide them. Leonard Bacon asks, "Why should they be jealous for their liberty? How should they be expected to detect and resist the beginning of lordship over God's heritage?"[4]

But when Constantine adopted Christianity as the state religion in A.D. 312, the self-governing Christian soon lost the last vestiges of control over his church. It was no longer the spontaneous, self-governing association of believers, but a hierarchical structure with power at the top dictating its will to the people below.

The One, the Few, and the Many

The Pilgrims had suffered severely enough from a State-controlled episcopacy to know it was not in accord with Christ's Law of Liberty. Their pastor, John Robinson, wrote down his thoughts on the three basic forms of government known to the world. He concluded that all three forms had their place in the Church of Christ. They were

> *monarchical, where supreme authority is in the hands of one; aristocratical, when it is in the hands of some few...; and democratical, in the whole body, or multitude.... In respect of Him the head, it is a monarchy, in respect of the eldership, an aristocracy, in respect of the body, a popular state.*
>
> *The Lord Jesus is the King of His Church alone, upon whose shoulders the government is, and unto whom all power is given in heaven and earth.... But [Christ has committed this power to] His Church,[5]*

anointing all men as kings and priests unto God.

In Christ's Church, Robinson maintained, each member functioned as a king by guiding and governing himself "in the ways of godliness" and as a priest by offering up "prayers, praises, and thanksgiving"—but all in accord with "those special determinations which the Lord Jesus, the King of kings hath prescribed." Even the least member of the Body of Christ "hath received his drop…of this anointing, so is not the same to be despised." Robinson then dealt with the question of how a congregation of kings and priests could all govern without ensuing chaos!

> *Someone or few must needs be appointed over the assembly [for]… discussing and determining of all matters, so in this royal assembly, the Church of Christ, though all be kings, yet some most faithful and most able, are to be set over the rest…[and] charged…to minister according to the Testament of Christ.*[6]

But, Robinson warned, this government by elected representatives did not involve any lordship over God's people, for these representatives were but to serve their brothers and sisters in Christ, "affording the Lord and them their best service."[7] This is confirmed by the Scriptures in First Peter 5:3, where the elders are exhorted not to be lords over God's heritage but to be examples to the flock.

This was the structure of the Pilgrim Church under Pastor Robinson's inspired leadership: Christ the King giving to each member self-government; then the Christians, forming the Body of Christ, electing representatives from among themselves to carry on the work of the Church.

By the time the truce between Holland and Spain was drawing to a close and war clouds were gathering, the Pilgrims were well grounded in Christian government of themselves and their church and were ready to take on the challenge of the next step in God's plan for them.

Protracted negotiations with the Virginia Company of London for a patent to plant a colony in America were discouraging to many of the Pilgrims and, in the end, it was only a small number of Robinson's congregation who were willing to be among the first to go. Robinson decided, reluctantly, that he must stay behind with the greater number. Meanwhile, Elder William Brewster would accompany the Pilgrims to America and minister to their spiritual needs.

The Floating Republic

Fewer than half of the 102 passengers on the *Mayflower* were Pilgrims. The merchant adventurers who helped finance the venture had recruited the rest. Some of these strangers were to become excellent citizens of the new colony, but others were dishonest troublemakers who caused many difficulties.

Wisely foreseeing how greatly their capacities for self-government would be tested, Pastor Robinson wrote the Pilgrims a farewell letter containing much useful counsel on self-government. He urged them first of all to renew their repentance with God daily, and after this, "peace with God" and their own consciences, "carefully to provide for peace with all men," and neither to give offence "nor easily to take offence being given by others." He knew that because many of the travelers were strangers to the Pilgrims, the Pilgrims would "stand in need of more watchfulness this way, lest when such things fall out in men and women as you suspected not, you be inordinately affected with them."[8]

The Pilgrim Body Politic

Then, moving from Christian self-government to the sphere of Christian civil government, Robinson wrote:

> *Lastly, whereas you are to become a body politic, using amongst yourselves civil government,… let your wisdom and godliness appear not only in choosing such persons as do entirely love and will diligently promote the common good, but also in yielding unto them all due honor and obedience in their lawful administrations; not beholding in them the ordinariness of their persons, but God's ordinance for your good.[9]*

In the prayer concluding his letter, he asked the Lord to guide them "inwardly by His Spirit, so outwardly by the hand of His power." God did, indeed, guide them through the perilous voyage. His Providential hand saved their lives in miraculous ways from the fury of the storms that battered the *Mayflower*, and He brought them safely to His destination for them.

Then He gave them the wisdom to see what must be done to quell the mutinous murmurs of some of the strangers on board who, as Bradford relates, said that when they got ashore, "they would use their own liberties; for none had power to command them, the patent they had being for Virginia and not for New England."[10]

America's Founding Covenant: The Mayflower Compact

Because of these "discontented and mutinous speeches," the Pilgrim leaders, Deacon Carver, Elder Brewster, and the young William Bradford, realized that their civil government would have to be placed on a firm Christian base before leaving the ship, or a state of anarchy would ensue. The Pilgrims accomplished this in their vitally important document, the Mayflower Compact.

> *In the name of God, Amen. We whose names are underwritten, the loyal subjects of our dread sovereign lord, King James, by the grace of God, of Great Britain, France, & Ireland king, defender of the faith, &c., having undertaken, for the glory of God, and advancement of the Christian faith, and honour of our king & country, a voyage to plant the first colony in the Northern parts of Virginia, do by these presents solemnly & mutually in the presence of God, and one of another, covenant & combine ourselves together into a civil body politic, for our better ordering & preservation & furtherance of the ends aforesaid; and by virtue hereof to enact, constitute, and frame such just & equal laws, ordinances, acts, constitutions & offices, from time to time, as shall be thought most meet & convenient for the general good of the colony, unto which we promise all due submission and obedience.[11]*

This was to be the first of many such covenants, agreements, and constitutions written by each colony. These various covenants form one of the pillars of American constitutional government.

In discussing the Mayflower Compact, Professor Andrew McLaughlin, a leading scholar in the field of American constitutional history, says that "it is impossible…to neglect the word 'covenant,' and not see in the compact the transmutation of a church covenant into the practical foundation of a self-governing community."[12]

Communal Farming Fails

In the difficult days that lay ahead, the Christian character and self-government the Pilgrims had learned, and the strong bonds of Christian fellowship forged at Scrooby and tested in Holland, stood them in good stead. After the first disastrous winter, in which more than half of them died, amazingly, none of the survivors returned to England when the *Mayflower* finally left for the Mother Country.

But the little colony nearly foundered because of the collective economic system the merchants in London had imposed on it, all the settlers working only for the joint partnership and being fed out of the common stores. The land, too, and the houses they built on it were to be the joint property of the merchants and colonists for seven years and then divided equally on the death of Deacon Carver, who had been the Pilgrim governor. Young William Bradford, then only thirty years old, was elected their new governor and soon proved the high quality of his leadership.

The agreement with the merchants had caused much resentment among Pilgrims and "strangers" alike and reduced productivity. Finally, Bradford saw that bold, decisive action was needed. As he wrote later in his history:

> *After much debate of things, the Governor (with the advice of the chiefest amongst them) gave way that they should set corn every man for his own particular, and in that regard trust to themselves.*[13]

Free Enterprise Succeeds

Bradford assigned a plot of land to each family to work. "This had very good success; for it made all hands very industrious," he wrote. From then on, there was never a famine at Plymouth. Bradford's comments on this event are significant.

> *The experience that was had in this common course and condition, tried sundry years, and that amongst godly and sober men, may well evince the vanity and conceit of Plato and other ancients,... that the taking away of property, and bringing in community into*

a commonwealth, would make them happy and flourishing; as if they were wiser than God, For this community...was found to breed much confusion and discontent, and retard much imploy-ment that would have been to their benefit and comfort.[14]

An abundant harvest resulted from Governor Bradford's decision to establish individual enterprise. This experience was in sharp contrast to what happened in the Virginia Colony. Both colonies were planted to the glory of God. The Virginia Colony's charter, like the Mayflower Compact, makes this abundantly clear.

We greatly commend and graciously accept their desires for the furtherance of so noble a work, which may, by the Providence of Almighty God, hereafter tend to the glory of His divine Majesty, in propagating of Christian religion to such people as yet live in darkness and miserable ignorance of the true knowledge and wor-ship of God.

Many of the early settlers at Jamestown, however, were soldiers of fortune intent on mere economic gain. In addition, they went to Virginia without their families and with no intentions of settling there permanently. The desire for external gain—to find and seize the gold and pearls the Natives were rumored to possess—was in sharp contrast to the Pilgrims' desire to found their colony for internal liberty of conscience.

Pioneers of Liberty

Although it never became a large colony and was later absorbed by its neighbor, the Massachusetts Bay Colony, Plymouth exercised a profound influence on Massachusetts and the other colonies that developed later in Connecticut and Rhode Island.

The colony of Salem had started out to plant a Puritan branch of the Church of England in the New World, but it was not long before the colonists began to have different views of Church government.

The leader of the Salem colonists, John Endicott, was deeply impressed by the Separatists at Plymouth. Governor Bradford had sent the Pilgrims' physician, Deacon Fuller, to help the Salem people when they suffered from a terrible epidemic in 1628. Fuller labored to heal their sick and then, before returning to Plymouth, he took time to correct some of Endicott's misconceptions about the Separatists.

Endicott sent a warm letter of thanks to Governor Bradford for all that Fuller had done to help them and mentioned how glad he was to have learned about their religious views. Soon after, in 1629, Endicott took the lead in effecting a remarkable change.

He and the other Puritans at Salem decided that—unlike the Church of England, which accepted everyone within its territory—their church would only include those who had made a profession of faith. To this end, one of their ministers drew up a statement for those joining the church "solemnly to enter into a covenant engagement one with another, in the presence of God, to walk together before Him according to His Word."[15]

Governor Bradford and William Brewster from Plymouth were invited to the special day set aside for the forming of the new church. Although the voyage across the bay was delayed by headwinds so that they arrived too late to afford the Salem congregation their "direction and assistance," they had the joy of learning that the new church had been formed, as theirs had been, by covenanting with the Lord, and that the people had freely elected their own church officers.

The church that had been brought over the ocean now saw another church, the first-born in America, holding the same faith in the same simplicity of self-government under Christ alone.[16]

The Great Exodus of Persecuted Believers

By 1630, the great Puritan exodus from England was underway. Renewed persecution by Charles I and Archbishop Laud gave a strong impetus to the desire many Puritans had long cherished of leaving England for a land where they could worship God in accord with the Scriptures.

Unlike the Pilgrims, the new colonists who arrived on the New England coast in 1630 were men of means. "Some of them came from stately homes and were possessed of wealth and social position," historian John Brown points out, "while others had occupied influential positions as ministers of the Church."[17]

During the remainder of Charles I's reign, England was drained of some of its best intellects and a great deal of money. In his 1731 book *History of the Puritans*, Daniel Neal observes:

> *Upon the whole it has been computed that the four settlements of New England, viz. Plymouth, the Massachussets Bay, Connecticut, and New Haven...drained England of four or five hundred thousand pounds in money (a very great sum in those days); and if the persecution of the Puritans had continued twelve years longer, it is thought that a fourth part of the riches of the kingdom would have passed out of it through this channel.*

These men who in 1629 were preparing to establish a new colony in New England were unwilling to do so if the Massachusetts Bay Company remained merely a commercial trading body headquartered in London and subject to interference from the king. But how could they hope to set up a colony that would not be controlled by the home government? As they prayed about this, divine Providence provided a way.

In March 1629, a royal charter was granted to the Company to create a new corporation. The charter specified that a governor, deputy governor, and eighteen assistants would be empowered to make all reasonable laws for the colony. But the question of where these officers would hold their meetings was simply not mentioned in the charter, and—providentially—the autocratic King Charles did not notice this glaring omission and signed the charter! This was done the same week he dissolved Parliament and vowed to rule England alone.

Thus, while annihilating representative government in England with one hand, with the other he unwittingly created a self-governing colony in America. In July 1629, the Massachusetts Bay Company simply voted to transfer the government of the plantation from England to the new colony. This allowed it to establish an independent, self-governing colony where, like their Pilgrim neighbors, they could worship the Lord according to the dictates of their conscience. Edward Eggleston notes:

From the point of view of our later age, the removal of the charter government to America is the event of chief importance in this migration.... The ultimate effect of this brilliant stroke was so to modify a commercial corporation that it became a colonial government as independent as possible of control from England. By the admission of a large number of colonists to be freemen—that is, to vote as stockholders in the affairs of the company, which was now the colony itself, and a little later by the development of a second chamber—the government became representative.

The Moses of a New Exodus

On March 23, 1630, some one thousand Puritans embarked for New England on four well-provisioned ships. Arranging such an expedition had been an enormous burden, but in John Winthrop, the Company found a man who was fully equal to the task. "He was a man of remarkable strength and beauty of character," writes John Fiske. "When his life shall have been adequately written,... he will be recognized as one of the very noblest figures in American history."[18]

From early youth he had that same power of winning confidence and commanding respect for which Washington was so remarkable; and when he was selected as the Moses of the great Puritan exodus, there was a wide-spread feeling that extraordinary results were likely to come of such an enterprise.[19]

The son of a prosperous country lawyer from Suffolk, Winthrop had followed his father's footsteps into a career in the law and gave up a lucrative position as attorney in the Court of Wards in order to emigrate to New England. He was to deplete his estate in Suffolk substantially in order to help sustain the Bay Colony in its early years.

A City upon a Hill

While at sea on board the flagship, the *Arbella*, this thoughtful, self-sacrificing Christian leader wrote an important paper known today as "A Model of Christian Charity," which he shared with his fellow Puritans. It is an eloquent statement of their motives and goals for the new colony. First of all, Winthrop wished them to remember who they were. "We are a company, professing ourselves fellow members of Christ,… knit together by this bond of love," he tells them.

And what was to be their purpose? He writes that the work they had in hand was to seek a place to live together "under a due form of government, both civil and ecclesiastical." But theirs was not to be a mere legal agreement. As in the Mayflower Compact, their relationship to God and to each other is described in covenantal terms:

> *Thus stands the cause between God and us, we are entered into Covenant with Him for this work…. Now if the Lord shall please to bear us, and bring us in peace to the place we desire, then hath He verified this Covenant and sealed our Commission.*[20]

With a clear vision of their place in history, Winthrop prayed that God

> *shall make us a praise and glory, that men shall say of succeeding plantations: the Lord make it like that of New England for we must consider* WE SHALL BE AS A CITY UPON A HILL, *the eyes of all people are upon us; so that if we shall deal falsely with our God in this work we have undertaken and so cause Him to withdraw His present help from us, we shall be made a story and a byword [laughingstock] through the world.*[21]

This stands as a reminder to twentieth-century American Christians of our duty. Are not the eyes of the world, as well as the eyes of God, focused upon America today, critically evaluating how well we are living out the principles of our founding covenants?

The Puritans Cling to a State Church

The great desire of the Puritan was to be self-governing in accord with God's laws. But the Puritans' zeal and strength of character must be tempered with Pilgrim compassion. This tempering process had already begun with Deacon Fuller's visit to Salem. Historian Edward Eggleson notes that

> *the Church discipline and the form of government in Massachusetts borrowed much from Plymouth, but the mildness and*

semi-toleration—the "toleration of tolerable opinions"—which Robinson had impressed on the Pilgrims was not so easily communicated to their new neighbors who had been trained in another school.

The Puritans wanted a self-governing colony, but one in which political power remained in the hands of their fellow Puritans. They still clung to a State Church.

How Much Self Government?

Many more vessels bringing new settlers from England followed the *Arbella* and her sister ships. Soon, Boston was established, and other settlements sprang up all over Massachusetts Bay. These towns followed Salem's lead in establishing their churches by covenant in emulation of their Pilgrim neighbors.

But the Puritans continued to disavow Separatism. They still considered themselves members of the Church of England, but now liberated from its corruptions. While united with regard to their Church government, soon conflict arose concerning the colony's civil government. Originally, the colonists intended that the freemen elect the governor, deputy governor, and the assistants. But as early as October 1630, an attempt was made to transfer power from the freemen to the governor, deputy governor, and assistants.

Some proposed that the governor be elected not by the freemen, but by the assistants. Sinful men love to collect power to themselves! When the government in Boston attempted to levy a special tax for frontier fortifications against a possible attack by the French, strong objections were raised by colonists in outlying settlements. They pointed out that according to English law, they could not be taxed except with their own consent. They insisted that the power to tax lay with the whole body of the people, that is, with the freemen of the colony.

The Boston elite backed down, permitting all freemen to elect the governor, deputy governor, and assistants. Historian John Brown notes:

*There was also an extension of self-government in the arrange-
ment that every town should send two representatives to advise
the governor and assistants on the question of taxation.*[22]

The latter was certainly a step toward liberty. But in 1631, a decision
partially counteracted it. They decided that "no man shall be admitted
to the freedom of this body politic, but such as are members of some
of the churches within the limits of the same."[23]

This provision that none but church members could vote or hold
office narrowed the franchise considerably and did not satisfy many
people. At the time, the church maintained a very high bar for membership. Why, they asked, should non-church members be disenfran-
chised and yet still be obliged to fulfill their civic duties? Why should
they have no say in regard to making or executing the laws that were
to govern them and in support of which they paid taxes?

Another Kind of Puritan

One of those to object was a remarkable Puritan pastor from Essex,
England, who arrived in the Bay Colony in 1633. The Rev. Thomas
Hooker was a learned man who (like so many other Puritans) had
been educated at Cambridge University and had become one of
England's most eloquent supporters of Scriptural Christianity.

Unfortunately, he was so eloquent that he attracted the attention
of William Laud, the Archbishop of Canterbury. Learning that Laud
was planning to arrest him, Rev. Hooker escaped to Holland in 1630.
There he lived for three years until he felt that the Lord called him
to New England.

Soon after his arrival in the Bay Colony, Hooker became pastor
of the church at Newtown (now Cambridge). He had not long been
in the colony when he became disturbed concerning the question of
restricted voting rights. He expressed these concerns in a letter to
John Winthrop, now Governor Winthrop, who replied to him that
"the best part is always the least, and of that best part the wiser part is
always the lesser."[24] Great as he was as a conscientious Bible-believing
Christian leader, Winthrop could not transcend the elitist outlook of
the Puritan aristocracy. But Rev. Hooker could not concur with his
views and replied:

> *In matters which concern the common good, a general council, chosen by all, to transact businesses which concern all, I conceive most suitable to rule and most safe for relief of the whole.*[25]

Nor could he agree with Winthrop that the assistants should be elected for good behavior, that is, for life, unless guilty of some serious misdeed. Later, Hooker wrote to Winthrop:

> *I must confess, I ever looked at it, as a way which leads directly to tyranny and so to confusion, and must plainly profess, if it was in my liberty, I should choose neither to live, nor leave my posterity, under such a government.*[26]

Another Great Migration

But Governor Winthrop and the Boston Puritans were adamant. So, in June 1636, Rev. Thomas Hooker and his congregation at Newtown—some one hundred people—left the Massachusetts Bay Colony to settle in the Connecticut Valley. The congregations of Dorchester and Watertown followed them.

By May 1637, eight hundred people had moved from the Boston area to populate Windsor, Wethersfield, and Hartford. In the end, the Bay Colony lost not just a few individuals, but virtually three whole towns in this dispute over self-government.

For a year, these Connecticut towns consented to be governed by a board of commissioners from Massachusetts, but then they assembled together and elected their own representatives in a general court held in Hartford in 1638.

For many years, historians did not know the critical role Thomas Hooker had played in producing the new government and its landmark constitution. But in the middle of the nineteenth century, a little volume in which someone had transcribed notes in cipher on sermons and lectures given by Rev. Thomas Hooker and others was found in Windsor. In this volume was discovered a digest of the remarkable, statesmanlike sermon Hooker gave before the general court on May 31, 1638.

Hooker took Deuteronomy 1:13 as his text: "Choose for your tribes wise, understanding…men, and I will appoint them as your heads."

He told the people that "the foundation of authority is laid…in the free consent of the people" and that "the choice of public magistrates belongs unto the people by God's own allowance." He continued to assert that they who have the power to appoint officers and magistrates have the right also "to set the bounds and limitations of the power and place unto which they call them."

The various points Rev. Hooker enumerated in his sermon formed the basis of the Fundamental Orders of Connecticut, which were adopted as the Constitution of Connecticut by the freemen of the three towns assembled in Hartford on January 14, 1639.

In the Fundamental Orders of Connecticut, we have a document far ahead of its time in recognizing the origin of all civil government as derived from God and "the agreement and covenant of the whole body of the governed." In this remarkable work, the American Covenant, begun by the Mayflower Compact, developed into a full-fledged body of laws. Historian John Fiske sums up its historical importance:

> *It was the first written constitution known to history that created a government, and it marked the beginnings of American democracy, of which Thomas Hooker deserves more than any other man to be called the father.*

Furthermore, according to Fiske, the government of the United States is "in lineal descent more nearly related to that of Connecticut than to any of the other thirteen colonies."

> *The most noteworthy feature of the Connecticut republic was that it was a federation of independent towns and that all attributes of sovereignty not expressly granted to the General Court remained, as of original right, in the towns.*

Here, in the Fundamental Orders, is a microcosm of the Federal Constitution to come.

A Distinct Departure

Significantly, the Fundamental Orders did not require church membership in order to vote or hold most offices. An exception was the governor, who must be a member of "some approved congregation." This was a distinct departure from the Puritan view of civil government as an elitist form of rule, which in practice meant rule of the State by a specific Christian denomination with its specific interpretation of Scripture.

Yet Hooker in no way attempted to secularize the State or separate it from Biblical Law. On the contrary, the document reflected the sincere Biblical consensus of the people. It acknowledged that wherever a people are gathered together, the Word of God requires them to set up "an orderly and decent government established according to God." Thus did they "enter into combination and confederation together to maintain and preserve the liberty and purity of the Gospel of our Lord Jesus Christ."

Providentially, this little federal republic grew until, in John Goodwin's words,

> *It became the strongest political structure on the continent, as was illustrated in the remarkable military energy and the unshaken financial credit of Connecticut during the Revolutionary War.*

It was Connecticut, too, that broke the deadlock at the Constitutional Convention of 1787 with its compromise by which it was decided that the states would be represented equally in the Senate but on the basis of population in the House of Representatives. If there is any doubt that a single person can accomplish great things for God, let the example of Thomas Hooker erase it.

Liberty of Conscience

The hand of God may also be seen in the founding of the colony called Providence, where they at last achieved full religious liberty. When young Separatist Roger Williams arrived in the Bay Colony in 1631 as a refugee from the tyranny of Charles I, he refused a post as a teacher in the church of Boston because it would not renounce all fellowship with the Church of England. An eloquent, inspiring preacher, warmhearted and earnest, Williams served as minister at Plymouth and then at Salem.

His uncompromising views, however, in regard to having dealings with the Church of England caused much controversy. When he advanced the argument that the King of England had no title to land held by the Natives and therefore no authority to issue the charter under which the Massachusetts Puritans were trying to enforce religious uniformity on everyone, he ran into trouble. His demand for liberty of conscience for the self-governing Christian resulted in his trial and banishment from the Bay Colony in 1635.

Driven into the wilderness, he purchased land from the Natives and founded Providence, which soon attracted many who had been persecuted for their religious convictions.

The settlers under Roger Williams at Providence entered into a written covenant of obedience

> *to all such orders and agreements as shall be made for public good of the body in an orderly way, by the major consent of the present inhabitants...incorporated together in a Towne fellowship.*[27]

Thus, the banishment of Roger Williams from Massachusetts resulted in the establishment of liberty of conscience in the colony of Providence. Once again, God used "the wrath of men to praise Him" and brought about another step in the development of Christian self-government.

In 1639, Baptists, who like the Separatists, believed in self-governing churches and were strongly opposed to any national Church, began to take refuge at Providence. Pastor Roger Williams was impressed with their doctrine that adult rather than infant baptism was Scripturally appropriate. He was baptized and helped to found at Providence the first Baptist church in America.

Although he did not remain a Baptist for long, feeling continually driven to seek "a purer form of Christianity," his impassioned stand for liberty of conscience enabled the Baptists and other dissenters to have the freedom to develop their own self-governing churches in accord with individual Christian conscience.

The Massachusetts Body of Liberties

Meanwhile, the colonists in Massachusetts Bay were becoming increasingly restless. They complained that too much power still remained in the hands of the magistrates and demanded a code of laws that would define and secure the rights of all.

It was the Rev. Nathaniel Ward of Ipswich who was responsible for another landmark in American history: the Massachusetts Body of Liberties. As the famous New England historian John Palfrey points out: "Ward was capable of the great business to which he was set.... He announced the principal that life, liberty, or property was not to be invaded except by virtue of express law."

> *The Body of Liberties...first lays down those fundamental principles relating to the sacredness of life, liberty, property, and reputation, which are the special subject-matter of a Bill of Rights. It then goes on to prescribe general rules of judicial proceedings to define the privileges and duties of freemen; to provide for justice to women, children, servants, and foreigners, and for gentle treatment of the brute creation.*

This concept of a detailed enumeration of individual rights was to reappear in the first Ten Amendments to our Federal Constitution.

William Penn, Founder of Pennsylvania

Another colony that made important contributions to the development of Christian self-government in America was Pennsylvania, established by the Quaker William Penn. Although it was a proprietary colony—i.e., the Crown vested Penn with the right to govern it—he had no desire to be an autocratic ruler. On the contrary, he told the settlers that they were "at the mercy of no governor" and assured them, "you shall be governed by laws of your own making, and live a free and, if you will, a sober and industrious people."

Penn believed that God had planted his colony and that He would "bless and make it the seed of a nation." Therefore, he was determined to "have a tender care to the government, that it will be well laid." Since he had been imprisoned in the Tower of London for heresy and again in Newgate Prison for defending the Quaker faith, he was deeply compassionate toward all victims of religious intolerance.

The Frame of Government that Penn spent much time and thought in writing, and which he signed on April 25, 1682, established religious liberty in Pennsylvania.

> *All persons living in this province, who confess and acknowledge the One Almighty and Eternal God to be the Creator, Upholder, and Ruler of the world, and that hold themselves obliged in conscience to live peaceably and justly in civil society, shall in no wise be molested or prejudiced for their religious persuasion or practice, in matters of faith and worship; nor shall they be compelled at any time to frequent or maintain any religious worship, place, or ministry whatsoever.*

This document vested the government in the governor and freemen through an elected provincial council and an assembly of all the freemen in the province. In this colony, established by a God-fearing man on Christian principles, we witness the continual drive of self-governing Christians, in Penn's words,

> *to make and establish such laws as shall best preserve true Christian and civil liberty, in opposition to all unchristian, licentious, and unjust practices, whereby God may have His due, Caesar his due, and the people their due.*

Standing Fast in Liberty

These outstanding Christian leaders—William Bradford, John Winthrop, Thomas Hooker, Roger Williams, Nathaniel Ward, and William Penn—show what great things God can accomplish through self-governing Christians. By the efforts of these individuals and many others of diverse denominations, self-government was established in America.

There is no limit to what we as self-governing Christians can accomplish today when we understand our history and stand firm in the liberty for which Christ has set us free.[28]

Following in their footsteps, it is our solemn responsibility to become active, self-governing Christians in our homes, our churches, our schools, and at all levels of our government. We need to participate in Christian civil government by supporting capable, godly individuals for elective office and lending our own talents to this field if the Lord so leads us.

It is time to reform our public schools, where the worldview of secular humanism holds sway, where our Christian history is ignored, and where prayer is prohibited and the Bible is merely a cultural artifact.

As you relearn the inspiring principles of our Christian history and teach them to your children in your homes and schools, you will be a "repairer of the breach, the restorer of streets to dwell in."[29] Thus we will ensure that our children will have—and be able to maintain—their precious heritage of liberty and self-government.

The sacrifice of thousands of self-governing individuals over hundreds of years won liberty for us. By the 1840s, the storm clouds of division in our nation were gathering. Robert C. Winthrop was a statesman, a sincere believer, and the direct descendant of his namesake John Winthrop, founder of Boston. On May 28, 1849, Robert Winthrop spoke to the Massachusetts Bible Society in Boston. He gave a profound warning for our nation, then facing civil war, to turn back to the Bible or face catastrophe. Not enough Americans heeded his warning then, and over 600,000 of them died in the horrific Civil War.

Our present cultural crisis is every bit as desperate as the one Winthrop warned of in 1849. If left to fester, it may pulverize our constitutional republic into oblivion. Before we allow it to slip from our grasp, we should pause and consider Winthrop's profound words. They call us to renew our personal covenant and corporate American covenant with God:

> *The voice of experience and the voice of our own reason speak but one language.... Both united in teaching us, that men may as well build their houses upon the sand and expect to see them stand, when the rains fall, and the winds blow, and the floods come, as to found free institutions upon any other basis than that of morality and virtue, of which the Word of God is the only authoritative rule, and the only adequate sanction.*

All societies of men must be governed in some way or other. The less they have of stringent State government, the more they must have of individual self-government. The less they rely on public law or physical force, the more they must rely on private moral restraint.

Men, in a word, must necessarily be controlled either by a power within them, or by a power without them; either by the Word of God, or by the strong arm of man, either by the Bible, or by the bayonet.[30]

Chapter 5 Study Questions

1. What kind of society do you have when external government is primary? And when internal Christian self-government is primary?

2. Why is a knowledge of the past important to preserve our liberty today?

3. What system of government did the Pilgrims discover in the New Testament?

4. Was this system democratic or republican?

5. Did the element of monarchy enter into the New Testament Church? In what way?

6. The bishops of the Episcopal Church of England had monarchical powers. Why was this not in accord with the New Testament Church?

7. Who was monarch in the New Testament churches and the Pilgrim Church?

8. What effect did the Pilgrims have on the Puritans?

9. What is a major pillar of American constitutionalism?

10. Why did the collective economic system in Plymouth fail?

11. Were the Christian ministers and laymen active in civil government in Colonial days or did they leave it to others?

12. As self-governing Christians, what is our duty in relation to civil government?

13. Why is it important for our children to learn the principles of Christian self-government as shown in our Christian history?

Chapter 5 Notes

1. John 8:36.
2. First Timothy 3:5.
3. Verna M. Hall, *The Christian History of the Constitution of the United States of America: Christian Self-Government* (San Francisco: Foundation for American Christian Education, 1975), 16.
4. Ibid., 19.
5. John Robinson, *The Works of John Robinson, Pastor of the Pilgrim Fathers*, Robert Ashton, ed., 3 vols (London: John Snow, 1851), 2:140–41; Revelation 1:6.
6. Robinson, *The Works of John Robinson*, 141.
7. Ibid.
8. Hall, *The Christian History of the Constitution*, 198–99.
9. Ibid., 200.
10. Ibid., 204.
11. Ibid., 204.
12. Andrew C. McLaughlin, *Foundations of American Constitutionalism* (New York: New York University, 1932; Fawcett World Library, 1961), 17.
13. Hall, *The Christian History of the Constitution*, 213.
14. Ibid., 213.
15. Leonard Bacon, *The Genesis of the New England Churches* (New York: Harper & Brothers, 1874), 475.
16. Ibid., 477.
17. John Brown, *The Pilgrim Fathers of New England and Their Puritan Successors* (Pasadena, TX: Pilgrim Publications, 1970), 255.
18. John Fiske, *The Beginnings of New England or The Puritan Theocracy in Its Relation to Civil and Religious Liberty* (Boston, New York: Houghton, Mifflin, 1900), 102.
19. Ibid.
20. H. Sheldon Smith, Robert T. Handy, Lefferts A. Loetscher, *American Christianity: An Historical Interpretation with Representative Documents, vol. 1: 1607–1820* (New York: Charles Scribner's Sons, 1960), 100–101.

21. Ibid., 102, emphasis added.

22. Brown, *The Pilgrim Fathers*, 291.

23. Fiske, *The Beginnings of New England*, 109.

24. Ibid., 124.

25. Ibid., 124.

26. Peter Marshall and David Manuel, *The Light and the Glory* (Old Tappan, NJ: Fleming H. Revell, 1977), 207.

27. McLaughlin, *Foundations*, 34.

28. Galatians 5:1.

29. Isaiah 58:12.

30. Verna M. Hall, *The Christian History of the American Revolution: Consider and Ponder* (San Francisco: Foundation for American Christian Education, 1976), 20.

Chapter 6

Who Owns You and Your Property?

Ye are not your own. For ye are bought with a price: therefore glorify God in your body, and in your spirit, which are God's.

First Corinthians 6:19–20 KJV

SIGNING OF THE DECLARATION OF INDEPENDENCE
(DETAIL) BY JOHN TRUMBULL

Just as the Mayflower Compact united the Pilgrims in their shared Biblical vision of the body politic, so now the Declaration united a whole people in a solemn covenant.

Chapter 6

Who Owns You and Your Property?

*T*here is perhaps no more important question to address at this critical hour of American history than "Who owns you and your property, God or Caesar?" If we do not settle this issue and settle it soon, what is left of our estates, our families, and our religious liberty will be confiscated by the humanist State.

Over the past hundred years, we, the American people, have been slowly boiled, so to speak, like an unwary frog, in a pan of candy-coated historical and theological distortions. Today, we devote five months of every year to work as servants of the statist bureaucracy. That is how long it takes us to work off the tax burden at all levels. The Roman Empire fell with a tax burden of just over 20 percent, while we in America are facing well over a 40 percent tax burden.

The Founders were much more distrustful of government and its tendency to accrue power than we are today. For example, George Washington warned: "Government is not reason, it is not eloquence—it is force! Like fire, it is a dangerous servant and a fearful master."[1] Thomas Jefferson was also skeptical of the ability of government to respect the rights of citizens:

> *It would be a dangerous delusion were a confidence in the men of our choice to silence our fears for the safety of our rights. That confidence is everywhere the parent of despotism.... Our constitution has accordingly fixed the limits to which, and no farther, our confidence may go.... In questions of power, then, let no more be said of confidence in man, but bind him down from mischief by the chains of the Constitution.*[2]

George Mason, the father of the Bill of Rights, agreed:

From the nature of man, we may be sure that those who have power in their hands will not give it up while they can retain it. On the contrary, we know that they will always, when they can, rather increase it.[3]

Many in our nation, when warned of these facts, shrug their shoulders and say such things as, "That is the cost we must pay for our societal benefits," or, "Render unto Caesar the things that are Caesar's." They fail to recognize that whoever determines how you use your property will become your lord. The real question facing us today, is: Who is sovereign?

The Question Is: Who Is God?

A nation's, as well as an individual's, view of property and liberty will be determined by whom it views as the ruler of this world. We have already seen in past chapters that the humanist—whether Greek, Roman, Russian, or American—sees man, and more practically, the corporate man—"the State"—as sovereign. This belief dominates modern scholarship, the curriculum of most public schools, and the halls of Congress.

But, how did this happen? In the past century, an alarming doctrine, which sees Satan as the sovereign of this world, has been accepted by many in Christian circles. Many Bible teachers today see Jesus as an absentee King concerned exclusively with building and maintaining His Church until He returns to earth. They see Jesus as having the authority and right to rule, but as having given over powers to subjugate the world temporarily to Satan.

The view of the secular humanist is even more extreme. God does not even enter his considerations. He thinks of God as irrelevant if he thinks of Him at all. The sole contender for the title of sovereign is autonomous man, who holds title to his property by his own authority and makes use of it according to rules of his own creation.

The worldview of the reformers radically opposed these two views. Reflecting the Biblical worldview of the Reformation, generations of colonists saw God as sole sovereign over men and their property. Jesus Christ they saw as the ruler of the earth[4] and Satan, a defeated foe.[5]

Our attitude toward the issue of sovereignty is of paramount importance, because it affects every area of life. Here is the contrast:

Worldview of the Reformation and Early America	Worldview of Many Twentieth-Century Christians
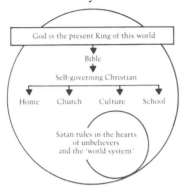	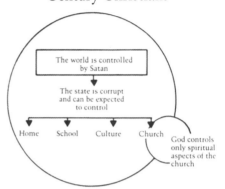

If you see God ruling the earth:	*If you see Satan ruling the earth:*
1. Your commission is to subdue the earth and build godly nations through evangelizing and discipleship.	1. Your commission is just to concentrate on saving souls from this evil world.
2. You see Christian culture as leavening all areas of life, replenishing the earth, and blessing all mankind.	2. You see Christian culture as a counterculture, an isolated, persecuted minority in an evil world.
3. All of God's world is His and every activity in life is a religious activity, to be seen as a spiritual work of God.	3. Church activity is primary and spiritual, while worldly pursuits are secular and to be dealt with only as a necessity.
4. Reformation is expected if a nation is obedient to God's Word.	4. Reformation is impossible, since things must get worse because Satan is in control.

Worldview of the Secular Humanist

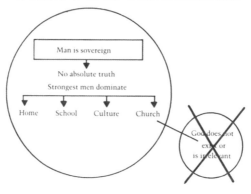

If you see man as ruling the earth:

1. Your commission is whatever you choose to do with your life, since man is autonomous.

2. You see Christian culture as old fashioned, irrelevant, and restrictive.

3. All human activity is guided by human reason and evolution. Man is just a higher animal in a mysterious universe.

4. Reformation is unnecessary and impossible, since there are no absolute principles to which man should reform.

The above contrasts illustrate the importance of ideas in determining consequences. To the degree that Christians have abdicated their leadership role and denied the sovereignty of Jesus Christ, humanism has filled the void.

Who Owned the Property of Our Founders?

In view of the foregoing, it is not surprising that the word *property* has a diminished value in today's dictionaries, which define it superficially and in strictly materialistic terms. One dictionary defines it simply as "that which a person owns; the possession or possessions of a particular owner. Goods, land, etc.; A piece of land or real estate." If this is our only sense of property, it is easy to be deluded by claims made by socialists and communists that *property rights* are separate from *human rights* and are far less important. Such an external view of property does not show its connection with the individual's life and liberty.

This partial, purely external view of property was not shared by the Founding Fathers, who fought the Revolutionary War in defense of their God-given liberty and property. Noah Webster's 1828 *Dictionary* sheds much more light on what the word *property* meant to our forefathers:

> *The exclusive right of possessing, enjoying, and disposing of a thing; ownership. In the beginning of the world, the Creator gave to man dominion over the earth, over the fish of the sea and the fowls of the air, and over every living thing. This is the foundation of man's property in the earth and all its productions…. The labor of inventing, making, or producing any thing constitutes one of the highest titles to property…. It is one of the greatest blessings of civil society that the property of citizens is well secured.*

If the Pilgrims had been asked: "Who owns you and your property?" they would have answered in a word: God. Then, they might have added: "We are free men who have been bought with a price." They recognized that they could not be any man's property because they were God's property. "For ye are bought with a price: therefore glorify God in your body, and in your spirit, which are God's."[6] And, as Paul also said, "For we are His workmanship, created in Christ Jesus for good works, which God prepared beforehand, that we should walk in them."[7]

Opposing Views of Property

Experiences of Jamestown and Plymouth, the first two colonies, illustrate two different views of property. In Plymouth, the Pilgrims strove to be self-supporting and, through Governor Bradford's wisdom in establishing private enterprise, they succeeded. They neither stole from the Natives nor demanded by the sword that the Natives barter their corn.

At Jamestown, the situation was different. As we have seen, many of the first settlers were hardened soldiers of fortune or men on the run from English law, coming to America in search of gold or other treasure. They were not interested in planting corn but preferred to barter with the Natives for their food—or seize it by force.

Forced Labor and Low Productivity

While the tough, intrepid Captain John Smith was with them, he was often obliged to force them to work at the point of the sword. The colonists' unruly behavior demanded strong external government. After Smith returned to England, records William Robertson, "everything tended fast to the wildest anarchy." Many colonists were

> *so profligate, or desperate, that their country [England] was happy to throw them out as nuisances in society. Such persons were little capable of...the strict economy, and persevering industry, which their situation required.*[8]

God's Providence Saves Jamestown

But, along with these unruly settlers, there was a strong, if small, nucleus of God-fearing, hard-working farmers and artisans—Virginia's future hope. When a terrible famine ensued, five hundred settlers were reduced to sixty gaunt survivors in a mere six months. Just as they were abandoning Jamestown in a desperate attempt to reach Newfoundland, the hand of God intervened, honoring the efforts of this faithful remnant. He had a plan for Virginia and would not have it abandoned. Robertson recounts that

> *Before [Sir Thomas] Gates and the melancholy companions of his voyage had reached the mouth of the James River, they were met by Lord Delaware with three ships that brought a large recruit of provisions.*[9]

Free Enterprise Brings Prosperity while Socialism Fails

But the Virginia Colony's progress was still painfully slow. New settlers arrived with the same desire for quick gain, and the problems in productivity recurred. Because there were still those who preferred to get their supplies through plunder rather than productivity, a later governor, Sir Thomas Dale, finally invoked martial law in order to force production of the food they so desperately needed.

But, as in the case of the Plymouth Colony, the early settlers of Virginia were also fed "from the common kettle." As it had at Plymouth, this acted as a discouragement to those who were trying to work conscientiously, for the most idle and irresponsible were rewarded equally with the hard working and conscientious. According to Robertson,

> *It was computed that the united industry of the colony did not accomplish as much work in a week as might have been performed in a day, if each individual had laboured on his own account.*[10]

The harsh, arbitrary rule that Dale meted out could not go on forever; it was self-defeating, because the moment it was relaxed, the problems recurred. Finally, he divided part of the land into small plots and gave one to each individual as his property.

> *From the moment that industry had the certain prospect of a recompense [reward], it advanced with rapid progress.*[11]

Poor Stewards of God's Property

By 1619, a new type of colonist had begun to come to Virginia with plans to settle and work, and young women came from England to become their wives.

Many of the colonists who went to Jamestown, like those who came before from Spain and France, were intent on quick gain. Their new "gold" was tobacco, a crop they knew would sell at a high price. With total lack of foresight and self-control, they planted tobacco everywhere—even in the streets of Jamestown—and neglected to raise adequate provisions of food.

The result was that, pressed by lack of food, they began again "to renew their demands upon the Indians, who seeing no end of those exactions, their antipathy to the English name revived with additional rancor, and they began to form schemes of vengeance."[12] These schemes later took effect in the Massacre of 1622, which almost wiped out the colony. But again, God saved it from complete extermination through a Christian Native's timely warning of the plot, which helped save many lives.

The Representative System

In 1619, another event of great importance took place. A representative body, similar to the English House of Commons, was established, through the efforts of a Christian statesman, Sir Edwin Sandys, who was then treasurer of the Virginia Company. The House of Burgesses, the first representative legislative body in America, was an important step in the direction of self-government for the colony. By God's Providence, this seed was to bear much fruit one hundred years later, when Virginia became the home of the nation's greatest statesmen.

Life, Liberty, and Property

In the struggle for liberty that culminated in the Declaration of Independence, the individual's right to his property played a central role. In Boston, the revolutionary battle cry was "Liberty and Property!" At the time of the Stamp Act in 1765, an organization called the Sons of Liberty was formed to resist the Act "by all lawful means." People marched through the streets of Boston to a gathering under an elm named the Liberty Tree, calling out, "Liberty, Property, and no Stamps!"[13]

Throughout the colonies, life, liberty, and property were spoken of as a single unit. This was because John Locke, an English philosopher, had been inspired to present them as interconnected and inseparable. The writings of "the great Mr. Locke" were widely read throughout the colonies. In his famous 1689 treatise, *Of Civil Government*, Locke speaks of men's "Lives, Liberties, and Estates, which I call by the general Name, Property." He asserts that the

> great and CHIEF END therefore, of Men's uniting into Commonwealths, and putting themselves under Government, IS THE PRESERVATION OF THEIR PROPERTY.[14]

"We Are His Workmanship"

Locke's treatise closely examines property from the Biblical perspective. Echoing the words of the apostle Paul, Locke wrote:

For Men being all the Workmanship of one Omnipotent, and infinitely wise Maker: all the Servants of one Sovereign Master, sent into the World by His Order and about His Business, they are His Property, whose Workmanship they are, made to last during His, not one another's Pleasure.[15]

Locke also refers to "those Grants God made of the World to Adam, and to Noah, and his Sons," which make it clear that God "has given the Earth to the Children of Men, given it to Mankind in common."[16] Locke is not advocating primitive communism or socialism. As he explains, "God, who hath given the World to Men in common, hath also given them reason to make use of it to the best Advantage of Life and Convenience."[17]

A Property in His Own Person

What follows was to strike a very responsive chord in the minds of America's Colonial leaders of the Revolutionary period.

Though the Earth and all inferior Creatures be common to all Men, yet every Man has a Property in his own Person: This no Body has any right to but himself. The Labour of his Body, and the Work of his hands, we may say, are properly his. Whatsoever then he removes out of the State that Nature hath provided, and left it in, he hath mixed his Labour with, and joined to it something that is his own, and thereby makes it his Property.[18]

Biblical Authority for Property

Because God did not intend the earth to remain "common and uncultivated," He gave it "to the use of the industrious and rational, and Labour was to be his title to it."[19] God did not give the earth "to the Fancy or Covetousness of the Quarrelsome and Contentious," Locke adds. In other words, Locke is acknowledging the Biblical cultural commission, or dominion mandate. He is saying that the commission to take dominion over the land is to be divided up in individual industrious, character-filled individuals.

The intent of God in His dominion mandate was not for a small elite in government to take dominion over the fruit of an individual's labor and property. In fact, five of the Ten Commandments focus specifically upon defending the family and private property.

Conscience the Most Sacred Property

James Madison, who was to become known as the "Father of the Constitution," from early youth devoted himself to the study of history, particularly political history. He was familiar with all that had been written on the subject from the time of Aristotle. Like our other Founding Fathers, he was thoroughly familiar with the writings of John Locke and considered them ideal for educating youth in sound political principles.

In an essay titled "Property," Madison gives a succinct and penetrating analysis of property from the Christian point of view:

> PROPERTY.... In the former sense, a man's land, or merchandise, or money, is called his property. In the latter sense, a man has a property in his opinions and the free communication of them. He has a property of peculiar value in his religious opinions, and in the profession and practice dictated by them.... He has an equal property in the free use of his faculties, and free choice of the objects on which to employ them. In a word, as a man is said to have a right to his property, he may be equally said to have a property in his rights.... GOVERNMENT IS INSTITUTED TO PROTECT PROPERTY OF EVERY SORT.... CONSCIENCE IS THE MOST SACRED OF ALL PROPERTY.[20]

Property: Internal and External

These views held by Locke and Madison show that they thought of property as being first of all internal:

- *Man has a property in his person*
- *Man has a property in the free use of his faculties*
- *Conscience is the most sacred of all property*

To these Christians, external property was something the individual produced from within by his abilities. And the quality of what he produced was also determined internally. "The good person out of his good treasure brings forth good, and the evil person out of his evil treasure brings forth evil."[21]

John Locke was a lifelong member of the Church of England, but he advocated religious toleration. His many essays on the validity of the Christian faith vouch for the fact that he was a devout believer in Jesus Christ. Many of America's Founders were Church of England men, and they turned mainly to Locke for clarification of their views on man's natural, God-given rights to life, liberty, and property. Such men as Madison, George Mason, and Patrick Henry were Christian leaders thoroughly familiar with John Locke's writings. Thomas Jefferson, during difficult times in his life, may have questioned the deity of Christ, but throughout his life, he acknowledged the moral system of Jesus as the greatest the world had ever known.

Political Principles of the New England Clergy

In New England, political leaders like Samuel and John Adams heavily quoted or paraphrased Locke's writings. The clergy began quoting him in sermons as early as 1738. These ministers carefully taught their congregations the principles of Christian liberty. In the period between 1774 and 1776:

Old and New Testament and classic writers…and often "the great Mr. Locke" were cited [by the clergy] in proof of the duty as well as the right to resist tyranny and any attack upon the rights of men.[22]

Referring to liberty as man's Christian birthright, Rev. Gad Hitchcock, of Massachusetts, said in a 1774 sermon:

Every man that is born into the world, as Mr. Locke, that prince of philosophers hath said, "is born to it" and every member of civil and religious society has an unalienable title to, and concern in it [the inalienable right to property in all forms].[23]

No Taxation without Representation

Ever since the days of the Stamp Act in 1765, the colonists had been extremely vocal in their denial that the English Parliament had any right to tax their property without their consent. Although Great Britain repealed the Stamp Act, it continued to declare the right to tax the colonists. After the repeal of the Townshend Acts, taxing glass, lead, paper, and tea, the British government issued an extraordinary series of Royal Instructions that, Richard Frothingham tells us,

> *required the dissolution of assemblies…negatived arbitrarily the choice of speakers; provided for the maintenance of local officers; and thus entirely ignored the local legislation for the support of government.*[24]

Arbitrary Laws Supplant Local Self-Government

This attempt to supplant local self-government with arbitrary rule aroused great indignation throughout the colonies. The Colonial leaders stressed the dangers to liberty if they consented to being governed by these tyrannical Royal Instructions. Frothingham records:

> *Among these leaders, Samuel Adams was pre-eminent. He had been steadily rising in reputation in Massachusetts and abroad…. He gave to the cause the whole of his time…. [His] masterly state papers attest his intelligence, industry, and influence.*[25]

A devout Christian of the highest character, Samuel Adams sacrificed much for the cause of liberty. Historian George Bancroft describes him as a "statesman of a clear and logical mind…. His will resembled well-tempered steel, which may ply, but will not break."[26] His untiring efforts on behalf of the cause of liberty in the colonies—he was among the first to see the need for independence from the Mother Country—earned him the title "Father of the Revolution." In 1772, Samuel Adams produced one of America's great state papers:

"The Rights of the Colonists as Men, as Christians, and as Subjects"

There is a strong resemblance between this document by Samuel Adams, the Declaration of Rights of the First Continental Congress in 1774, and the great Declaration of Independence of 1776. The document's first terse sentence under the heading of "The Rights of the Colonists as Men" is:

> *Among the Natural rights of the Colonists are these: First, a right to life; Secondly, to liberty; Thirdly, to property; together with the right to support and defend them in the best manner they can.*[27]

Because Adams saw liberty as the gift of God, he said that man could not "voluntarily become a slave."

> *In short, it is the greatest absurdity to suppose it in the power of one, or any number of men, at the entering into society, to renounce their essential natural rights, or the means of preserving those rights; when the grand end of civil government...is for the support, protection, and defence of those very rights; the principal of which...are Life, Liberty, and Property.*[28]

In the centerpiece of his paper, "The Rights of the Colonists as Christians," Adams says:

> *These may be best understood by reading and carefully studying the institutes of the great Law Giver and Head of the Christian Church, which are to be found clearly written and promulgated in the New Testament.*[29]

In the section, "The Rights of the Colonists as Subjects," Adams maintains that the legislative branch of government

> *has no right to absolute, arbitrary power over the lives and fortunes of the people; nor can mortals assume a prerogative not only too high for men, but for angels, and therefore reserved for the exercise of the Deity alone.*[30]

Nor can the legislative rule by "extemporary arbitrary decrees." On the contrary, the rights of subjects are to be decided by "standing and known laws."

When he comes to discuss property specifically, he asserts that "the supreme power cannot justly take from any man any part of his property, without his consent in person or by his representative." And he challenges the right of the English House of Commons "at pleasure to give and grant the property of the Colonists."[31]

In the very next sentence, Adams voices the grievance of the colonies, with a righteous wrath that must have electrified those who read it or heard it read: "Now what liberty can there be when property is taken away without consent?" Here he touches the vital connection between the individual's property and his liberty. For his property not only sustains his life but is the bulwark of his liberty and his ability to support God's work. If it can be taken away from him without his consent, then he has lost his liberty. The Russian novelist and patriot Alexander Solzhenitsyn warned of the dangers of allowing the government to determine jobs and property in his book *From Under the Rubble*. The Soviet Union starved and enslaved tens of millions of their citizens, including Solzhenitsyn, for seventy years. Let us remember how huge segments of our population are being thrown into poverty or worse by the government theft of their jobs under the cover of disease, climate, or even just one's religious or political views.

Liberty or Death

After the Boston Tea Party in December 1773, Great Britain resolved to punish Massachusetts by blockading the Port of Boston and abolishing local self-government. But, instead of intimidating the other colonies, these acts only united them behind Massachusetts. Virginia called for the First Continental Congress, which convened in Philadelphia on September 5, 1774, and drew up a Declaration of Resolves and Grievances. Events began to gather momentum. English statesmen William Pitt and Edmund Burke, in the English Parliament, counseled moderation in dealing with the colonies, but neither the majority in Parliament nor the king was in the mood to redress the grievances of the colonists.

One of the delegates to the first Continental Congress was Patrick Henry, who urged that the colonies unite in their opposition to Great Britain, forgetting distinctions between Virginians, Pennsylvanians, and New Englanders in their determination to stand for their God-given rights to life, liberty, and property. Henry's love of liberty had been nurtured from his childhood when his mother took him week after week to hear the great Presbyterian minister Dr. Samuel Davies, a staunch defender of religious and political liberty and an eloquent preacher. Young Henry absorbed not only something of Davies's oratorical style, but also his ideas of religious liberty, and his early career as a lawyer was notable for his defense of Baptist ministers and other religious dissenters from persecution by the state-supported Episcopal Church in Virginia.

Upon adjournment of the Continental Congress in October 1774, Henry returned to Virginia. Here, on March 20, 1775, he made his most famous speech before the Virginia Convention assembled at Richmond in St. John's Episcopal Church. Henry was convinced that reconciliation with England was no longer possible, and events at Lexington and Concord were soon to prove him right.

Henry proposed resolutions putting Virginia into an active military defense posture, but others at the Convention opposed him. Finally, in his great speech that turned the tide in favor of independence, he delivered a series of searching questions that reveal how the colonists had followed a very distinct, peaceful, and Biblical pattern for resolving conflicts, whether in the home, church, or state. (See *Lex Rex*, by Samuel Rutherford, for details on the Christian rights of resistance.) At the end of his speech, he gave the only answer for a man of courage and principle:

> *What...has there been in the conduct of the British ministry for the last ten years to justify hope? Are fleets and armies necessary to a work of love and reconciliation? These are implements of subjugation.... And what have we to oppose to them? Shall we try argument? We have been trying that for the last ten years.... In vain may we indulge the fond hope of reconciliation.... An appeal to arms and to the God of Hosts is all that is left us!... Three millions of people, armed in the holy cause of liberty...are invincible.... We shall not fight alone. A just God presides over the destinies of nations.... Is life so dear, or peace so sweet, as to be purchased at the price of chains and slavery? Forbid it, Almighty God! I know not what course others may take; but as for me, give me liberty, or give me death.[32]*

The Shot Heard around the World

On April 18, 1775, General Gage, the military governor sent out from England to subdue the rebellious colony of Massachusetts, secretly planned a raid on the patriots' ammunition stores at Concord. He also hoped to arrest Samuel Adams and John Hancock, who were rumored to be in nearby Lexington. Providentially, patriot Dr. Joseph Warren got wind of the plot and sent Paul Revere and William Dawes through the countryside that night sounding the alarm. Revere arrived at the home of Rev. Jonas Clark, where Adams and Hancock were staying, just in time to warn them to make their escape.

Rev. Clark was one of New England's great patriot pastors. For years, he had been preaching on the basic Biblical principles under-girding righteous government: that the people's rights to their life, liberty, and property came from God; the people had the right to form their governments by sacred covenant before God. In his book *Orators of the American Revolution*, E. L. Magoon records Clark's achievements:

> *The town records of Lexington contain many important docu-ments which discussed the great questions involved in the national struggle for Independence. In 1765, the citizens vindicated the popular movement in respect to the Stamp Act.... In 1768, they argued...against the right of Great Britain to tax America. In 1772, they resolved...to seek redress for daily increasing wrongs; and in 1774, they took measures to supply themselves with ammunition, arms, and other requisites for military defense. What hero drew those masterly papers, defended their principles, and fired the people at all hazards to defend them? History has recorded the fact, the Reverend Jonas Clark was their author and chief defence.*[33]

On April 19, 1775, the British detachment of soldiers arrived at Lexington Green to find the town's militia assembled and ready to defend their community. Only eighty men stood their ground, defend-ing their town from the British confiscating their firearms. They faced a force of nine hundred British Regular soldiers. The British officer ordered the militia to disperse. According to Rev. Clark, who saw all that happened that day from his church on the Green, the British began to fire on the militia even as it was dispersing. Only then did the men of Lexington return the enemy's fire. Eight of them were killed.

This conduct is in character with their pastor's teaching that only a defensive war could be just. The Battle of Lexington, brief as it was, gave the patriots at Concord the time they needed to collect their arms and ammunition and hide them carefully, as well as to muster their militia. These arms were their property, obtained to ensure their means of defense and should not be taken by the British for use against them. Here, too, at Concord, the patriots were not the first to fire. Frothingham relates that the British posted a guard of a hundred men at the Old North Bridge.

About ten o'clock, as a body of militia were approaching this bridge, the guard fired upon them, when more citizens were killed and wounded.[34]

The Minute Men defended themselves well. They forced the British into a disorderly retreat. By the time the British reached Charlestown, they were on the run and only narrowly missed being defeated by seven hundred militia bearing down on them just as they reached the shelter of the British fleet. On that day, the British lost 273 men, the American militiamen ninety-three. But if the Lexington farmers had not made their stand, thus buying time for Concord—if Revere had not reached Hancock and Adams in time to warn them—in short, if Providence had not intervened several times, the day would have been a total disaster for the Americans.

Connecticut's Day of Prayer

One thing the people of Lexington probably did not realize was that on that very day, the Colony of Connecticut held a day of prayer and fasting for all the colonies. Note that the Governor's declaration does not target England as the real enemy of freedom for the colonists. Through this declaration, he points to the first cause of "ruin" for any people: their own "iniquities." Here we see the first step in restoring America's covenant: humble, personal repentance. Our political enemies, foreign and domestic, are not the central problem. He called the people "to take the logs out of their own eyes" if they wanted the Lord's protection and blessing.

Likewise, when Governor Trumbull proclaimed April 19, 1775, as a day of prayer, fasting, and repentance, he could little dream what momentous events would be taking place at Lexington, just north of Connecticut that very morning! His proclamation asked

> that God would graciously pour out His Holy Spirit on us to bring us to a thorough Repentance and effectual Reformation that our iniquities may not be our ruin: that He would restore, preserve, and secure the Liberties of this and all the other British American colonies, and make the Land a mountain of Holiness, and Habitation of Righteousness forever.[35]

Attempting Peaceful Reconciliation

When the Congress reconvened on May 10, 1775, the war with the Mother Country had begun. Still, some members of Congress hoped for reconciliation, despite Lexington and Concord. Congress drew up another petition and sent it to England, hoping against hope that the king would listen to their plea for redress of grievances. Instead, the British monarch cut off all trade with the colonies and declared them to be in rebellion. The king of England had gone rogue, breaking England's long-held covenants and agreements with the colonies. The king had lost his right to rule. He had to be resisted before all Colonial rights and liberties were crushed forever. Now many Colonial leaders began to see that independence must be declared.

Note that the colonists did not resort to riots or murders of the king's troops or governors. For over a decade, they had been pursuing peace following the established, Biblical rights-of-resistance strategy reasoned by Christian leaders like Samuel Rutherford. Rutherford, author of the *Westminster Confession of Faith*, had written the book *Lex Rex (The Law is King)*. The colonists were serious students of this Biblical defense of the right to stand for God's Law if a king crushed the people and their rights. Unlike most of the riots and revolutions of the modern world, beginning with the French Revolution, the

Founders went peacefully into their assemblies and designated "lesser magistrates" to take over the responsibilities of the mad monarch.

The Virginia Declaration of Rights

Nevertheless, it was not until a year later, on May 14, 1776, that Virginia took the step of convening its House of Burgesses as a free convention of delegates—the royal governor having fled—and voted for independence. George Mason was then asked to draw up a Declaration of Rights which was to have a twofold importance: first, it was used subsequently by many of the colonies as the basis of their declarations; second, it was undoubtedly one of the documents that influenced Thomas Jefferson as he wrote the Declaration of Independence.

On June 12, 1776, the Convention approved Mason's great declaration, which states in Section 1:

> That all men are by nature equally free and independent, and have certain inherent rights, of which, when they enter into a state of society, they cannot, by any compact, deprive or divest their posterity, namely the enjoyment of life and liberty, with the means of acquiring and possessing property, and pursuing and obtaining happiness and safety.[36]

Here is an acknowledgment of the sanctity of natural rights, which men have no moral authority to relinquish, because they come from God. No decision by any majority could be valid against these God-given rights.

Historian Richard Frothingham says of the Declaration of Independence,

> It includes far more than it expresses; for by recognizing human equality and brotherhood, and the individual as the unit of society, it accepts the Christian idea of man as the basis of political institutions.[37]

Daniel Elazar, a distinguished contemporary scholar, refers to the Declaration as "the founding covenant of the American people." Such scholars as Elazar and Andrew C. McLaughlin recognize the covenant roots of our nation. Just as the Mayflower Compact united the

Pilgrims in their shared Biblical vision of the body politic, so now the Declaration united a whole people in a solemn covenant.

It is true that Thomas Jefferson's draft of the Declaration included only a reference to "nature's God," but when it was revised in committee by John Adams, Robert Livingston, Benjamin Franklin, and Roger Sherman, they added the important words, "They are endowed by their Creator with certain unalienable rights." Then, when the Declaration was debated on the floor of Congress, the phrase "appealing to the Supreme Judge of the World, for the rectitude of our intentions" was added, as were the eloquent words, "with a firm reliance on the protection of divine Providence." This brought the Declaration into complete harmony with the Christian consensus of Congress.[38]

The Pursuit of Happiness

But why did Congress allow Jefferson to change the commonly used phrase "Life, liberty, and property" to "Life, liberty, and the pursuit of happiness"? Did not this diminish their stated conception of the rights they had undertaken to defend?

It is true that the Resolution adopted by Congress in 1774 stated simply that the colonists had a right to "life, liberty, and property." But the use of the word *happiness* by Jefferson (and also by Mason in his Declaration of Rights) was not considered as a curtailment of the idea of property, but, rather, as an enlargement of it. A popular treatise on the "Principles of Natural Law" had been written by a Swiss writer, Jean Jacques Burlemaqui, in 1774, in which the author used this phrase. Certainly, the Founders knew that the protection of property—internal or external—was vital to the pursuit and achievement of happiness.

John Dickinson wrote in his "Letters from a Pennsylvania Farmer":

> *We cannot be happy, without being free—that we cannot be free, without being secure in our property—that we cannot be secure in our property, if without our consent, others may, as by right, take it away.*[39]

His words take us right back to the individual's right to the fruits of his own labors that he has been commanded by God to perform.

Both the Declaration of Rights and the Declaration of Independence stand as examples of the Christian idea of man and government. Rosalie Slater reminds us:

> As the words of the Declaration of Independence resound down the years, we can remember that "the price of liberty is eternal vigilance." Because the American Revolution is a Christian revolution for individual freedom—or salvation—it is never over.[40]

Sacrifices of the Founding Fathers

It is humbling to consider the great price the Founding Fathers were willing to pay to secure the rights we enjoy today. Our Founders were willing to sacrifice their lives and all they owned in order to preserve these rights for their posterity. Of the fifty-six signers of the Declaration, nine died in the war; five were captured and suffered severely at the hands of the British, and the homes of twelve were either burned to the ground, looted, or defaced by occupying troops.

Thomas Nelson, Jr.

A planter from Yorktown, Nelson succeeded Thomas Jefferson as governor of Virginia, put up his own property as collateral, and raised almost two million dollars to help the new nation fight the War of Independence. When the notes came due, he was unable to pay and lost those properties. At the final battle of Yorktown, Nelson personally directed the cannon fire that destroyed his own home, which had been appropriated by the British as field headquarters for General Cornwallis.

Robert Morris

Known to historians as "the Financier of the American Revolution," Morris became a strong patriot as early as the days of the Stamp Act crisis in 1765. As a prosperous Philadelphia merchant, he patriotically supported the nonimportation agreement (by which the colonies refused to import any more British goods until their grievances were redressed), even though he knew this would mean significant financial losses for his business. In November 1775, the Pennsylvania

Legislature chose him as a delegate to the Continental Congress, where he was put to work to provide naval armaments. This was the beginning of many outstanding services to the Congress and the people of the United States.

So great was his conviction that the war must be won, that when the Continental Army was experiencing serious reverses at the end of 1776 and had just been forced to retreat across New Jersey, Morris raised ten thousand dollars upon his personal credit. Without his help at this crucial moment, historians point out that Washington would not have been able to hold his starving troops together or to recross the Delaware and win a much-needed victory at the Battle of Trenton.

In 1781, Congress appointed Morris General Financial Agent of the United States (i.e., Secretary of the Treasury). He had such a high reputation as a businessman that he was able to raise tens of thousands of dollars at a time when Congress could not even raise a thousand. But more greatly to his honor is the fact that, according to official records, the great campaign of 1781 at Yorktown, which virtually won the war, could not have taken place without the aid of Robert Morris. This conclusive campaign was waged solely on his financial credit. Robert Morris unhesitatingly risked his property and his reputation in order to secure the rights of all of his fellow Americans. Never let it be said that one man can do nothing significant to turn the tide of history![41]

George Washington

But perhaps the greatest sacrifices were made by George Washington. On his own insistence, he served throughout the war without salary and sacrificed the years he so much wanted to spend as a farmer on his estate at Mount Vernon. He felt called by divine Providence to serve his country for the better part of forty-five years. It was only at the age of sixty-six that he was finally able to retire to the peace of Mount Vernon. Within three years, he was dead. He, like so many others, gave up the life he loved in order to ensure the liberty we now enjoy.

Christian Social Responsibility

Do contemporary Christians need to make sacrifices of time and money in order to solve today's many pressing social and economic problems? Or should we be content to relinquish control over the fruits of our labor to an all-powerful State and allow it to become the provider of the poor? Or do we perhaps desire to hold on to all we have earned and give only token amounts to help those in need? Is there an alternative to either self-centered *laissez faire* or the welfare state? What can we do when, as government spending at every level is curtailed, taxes are reduced, and budgets balanced—as they should be—the needs of the poor, the handicapped, and the aged become more pressing?

The books *The Tragedy of American Compassion* and *Tithing and Dominion* historically document the proven answers that were lived out in America for three hundred years. They acknowledge that a free nation such as ours cannot exist without "a vast network of social institutions which require financing and support."[42] But it is because of the failure of American Christians that such financing is not forthcoming from the private sector. "If a Christian concept of social financing is lacking, then the State moves in quickly to supply the lack and gain the social control which results."[43]

This is exactly what has happened through our falling away from the Bible's commands. For, as these authors point out, the Bible provides the tithe as the foundational law for society. In the early days of our nation, the tithe supported not only churches, but church schools and colleges, and it provided for a variety of other social needs. The book *Revolt Against Maturity* discusses how one New England town coped with radical population changes wholly by the use of the tithe. Salem, Massachusetts, saw a population boom between 1795 and 1845, doubling its population several times over until it had grown from a village into a city. There was a flood of foreign immigrants, and one would think that the town's character would have been completely changed and that the burden of such an influx of people would have caused a complete dislocation of its social fabric. But, as a matter of fact, the needs of the immigrants—as well as of the town's own citizens—were met through a variety of tithe-supported agencies that cared for the poor and provided education, job training, children's education, Bible courses, and English-language instruction. Salem is just one example of our nation when it was still actively obedient to God's Scriptural laws. Salem shows what conscientiously tithing Christians can accomplish in the field of social welfare. "Conscientious and intelligently administered tithing by even a small minority can do much to reconstruct a land."[44]

Our Responsibility as God's Stewards

If we act upon our knowledge of God's principles of property, stewardship, and economy, then we can present to the world a positive example of the benefit of living in covenant with God. If we desire a reduction in taxation, expenditures, services, and control by the Federal government—and more local autonomy—we must be weaned from our dependency on government largesse. We must also influence our families and our churches to be self-governing. If we are going to cut back on government services and welfare, then private charity and personal care for the truly needy will need to be met through the private sector.

We must end our own deficit spending and obey the Biblical admonition to be debt free and live within our means ("owe no one anything, except to love each other"[45]). We must also guard our motives so that our desire to preserve private property is not just a desire for selfish gain, but that it is truly a desire to preserve the sovereignty of God and the stewardship over all that God has given us to do.

We the people must take our principles, our loving charity, and our finances back into the public square—into the political arena—beginning with our local towns. Then we, working from the ground up, living out the love of God, can require that our "national government" shrink to its constitutionally restricted responsibilities.

Then we must be prepared to educate our own children with our own money, care for those in need, and stop our own personal deficit spending. If we do not do these things and other actions that our principles will dictate, then we have very little hope or right to expect a restoration of our liberty. Benjamin Franklin summarizes this thought with his famous words, "Those who would give up essential

Liberty, to purchase a little temporary Safety, deserve neither Liberty nor Safety."[46]

Our economic and political future rests not in the hands of foreign powers or governmental bureaucrats in our land, but in our own hands through our obedience to God. As we, the Christian community, renew our American Covenant with God and with each other, then truly our best days and centuries are ahead!

For FREE bonus material & in-depth study on a variety of topics beyond what you find here in *The American Covenant,* visit WorldHistoryInstitute.com/free-downloads.

Chapter 6 Study Questions

1. What do human rights include, and who grants them?

2. Who owns us, and to whom are we accountable for our property?

3. What is the Biblical authority for the individual's right to property?

4. What property does every person in the world possess?

5. Why does no one but you have the right to the fruits of your labor?

6. Our Founding Fathers thought of property as internal and external. Give some examples of internal property.

7. What is external property? Give some examples.

8. What is the most sacred of all property?

9. Was collective ownership of property part of God's intention for man?

10. What is morally wrong about the Marxist system that takes from each according to his abilities and gives to each according to his needs?

11. Shouldn't the government tax the affluent in order to provide for the needy?

12. If not, who should provide for the needy, and how should it be done?

13. What were the three elements of a man's property discussed by John Locke and the Founding Fathers?

14. What happens to religious and civil liberty when you lose economic liberty—i.e., the right to your property?

15. Why are most Christians today not active politically in defending their property rights?

16. The Declaration of Independence speaks of men's rights to life, liberty, and the pursuit of happiness. What did the Founding Fathers feel was necessarily included in happiness?

Chapter 6 Notes

1. Jacob M. Braude, *Lifetime Speaker's Encyclopedia* (Englewood Cliffs, NJ: Prentiss Hall, 1962), I:326.

2. "Jefferson's Draft," *The Papers of Thomas Jefferson*, vol. 30: *1 January 1798 to 31 January 1799* (Princeton University Press, 2003), 536–43.

3. "Madison Debates," July 11, 1787, *The Avalon Project*, avalon.law.yale.edu.

4. First Timothy 6:16; Hebrews 2:14.

5. John 12:31; Colossians 2:15.

6. First Corinthians 6:20 KJV.

7. Ephesians 2:10.

8. Verna M. Hall, *The Christian History of the Constitution of the United States of America: Christian Self-Government*, (San Francisco: Foundation for American Christian Education, 1975, 160.

9. Ibid., 161.

10. Ibid., 162.

11. Ibid., 163.

12. Ibid.

13. Ibid., 300.

14. Ibid., 91, emphasis added.

15. Ibid., 58.

16. Ibid., 63–64.

17. Ibid., 64.

18. Ibid., 64.

19. Ibid., 65–66.

20. Ibid., 248A, emphasis added.

21. Matthew 12:35.

22. Alice M. Baldwin, *The New England Clergy and The American Revolution* (New York: Frederick Ungar Publishing Co., 1958), 129.

23. Verna M. Hall, *The Christian History of the American Revolution: Consider and Ponder* (San Francisco: Foundation for American Christian Education, 1976), 41.

24. Hall, *The Christian History of the Constitution*, 317.

25. Ibid., 318.

26. Rosalie J. Slater, *Teaching and Learning America's Christian History* (San Francisco: Foundation for American Christian Education, 1975), 251–52.

27. Hall, *The Christian History of the Constitution*, 365.

28. Ibid., 367.

29. Ibid., 367.

30. Ibid., 368.

31. Ibid., 369.

32. Ibid., 346A.

33. Slater, *Teaching and Learning*, 49.

34. Hall, *The Christian History of the Constitution*, 346.

35. Hall, *American Revolution*, 407.

36. Andrew C. McLaughlin, *Foundations of American Constitutionalism* (New York: New York University, 1932; Fawcett World Library, 1961), 78.

37. Hall, *The Christian History of the Constitution*, 359.

38. Frank Donovan, *Mr. Jefferson's Declaration* (New York: Dodd, Mead, & Co., 1968), 96.

39. Hall, *The Christian History of the Constitution*, 445.

40. Slater, *Teaching and Learning*, 254.

41. See Benjamin Lossing, *Signers of The Declaration* (New York: J. C. Derby Publisher, 1856). See also the article on Morris in the Spring issue of *The Restoration Press*, published by Restore America Institute, P. O. Box 23343, Columbus, Ohio 43223.

42. Edward A Powell and Rousas John Rushdoony, *Tithing and Dominion* (Vallecito, CA: Ross House Books, 1979), 1.

43. Powell and Rushdoony, *Tithing and Dominion*, 1.

44. Ibid., 4.

45. Romans 13:8.

46. "Pennsylvania Assembly: Reply to the Governor," 11 November 1755.

Chapter 7

The Genius of
the American Republic

For to us a child is born, to us a Son is given; and the government shall be upon His shoulder.... Of the increase of His government and of peace there will be no end.

Isaiah 9:6–7

SIGNING OF THE CONSTITUTION (DETAIL)
BY HOWARD CHANDLER CHRISTY

*Just as the heart of the covenant of ancient Israel consists of two parts,
the Decalogue or Ten Commandments with its electrifying statement
of fundamental principles and the Book of the Covenant with its more
detailed framework of basic laws of the Israelite Commonwealth, so
too does that of the American covenant consist of two basic documents
serving the same purposes—the Declaration of Independence and the
Constitution.*

— Daniel J. Elazar

Chapter 7

The Genius of the American Republic

*H*ow can America be a Christian republic when, under our Constitution, there is supposedly a separation of Church and State?

As we discussed in chapter 1, the Founders were intent upon preventing any one denomination from imposing its views on the self-governing individual through the power of civil government. As we saw in chapter 6, they viewed conscience as the most sacred of all property, to be carefully protected by the government. When they wrote in the First Amendment to the Constitution, "Congress shall make no law respecting an establishment of religion, or prohibiting the free exercise thereof," they made it clear that they would not live under a nationally established Church that could demand their membership and financial support. It was the tyranny of religious conformity that they opposed.

But to say that they intended a secular State in which religion would play no part flies in the face of all evidence to the contrary. They never envisioned a secular State where God's moral laws would be systematically and deliberately flouted. Yet this has come to pass.

The Spirit and the Letter

Our state governments and the federal government were built largely upon principles that the Founders derived from their study of the Scriptures. The form of our republic still remains, but the spirit—which is Christianity—has been stifled. Without this animating spirit, the letter is dead.

To understand the American Christian Constitution as the Christian form of government, it is necessary to consider its two spheres—the spirit and the letter—the internal and the external. Both spheres must be active in order that the Constitution function to preserve the basic republican spirit of individual liberty. Today we still have the letter of the Constitution. That is, we still go through most of the legal processes of the structure of the Constitution in enacting legislation, and in the executive and judicial branches. But the spirit which was intended and understood by our Founding Fathers is missing—and has been for the last one hundred years. That spirit was the Christian foundation of our Constitution—the Faith of our Fathers—and as our nation has fallen away from its foundations—the essence of that faith—our Constitution has become a hollow shell.[1]

As Americans have forgotten the Biblical foundation of their government, they have allowed a subtle transformation of the doctrine of separation of Church and State into separation of religion and State, so that now Christianity can no longer receive a hearing in the schools; prayer and Bible reading are prohibited. The rights of Christian pastors to express their convictions on governmental matters in the pulpit—as our Colonial pastors did—are curtailed and penalized in an attempt to prevent all meaningful criticism of the secular State.

Our Founders Established a Republic, Not a Democracy

Because our form of government is derived in all its parts from Biblical principles, it cannot be understood without comprehending those principles, nor can it be made to work as our Founding Fathers intended.

FOUNDING FATHERS ESTABLISHED:	TODAY WE HAVE:
1. Republican government representing *each individual's* rights.	1. A majoritarian democracy representing the will of the majority—even when it tramples on the rights of the individual.

2. Separation of powers—legislative, executive, and judicial—in order to protect the individual against the tyranny resulting from concentration of power.	2. Balance of powers upset by a) increasing predominance of the presidency, b) the Supreme Court usurping the rights of the legislative branch, c) the most important branch, the representative, greatly weakened.
A. A legislative power to respect the individual's rights to his own life, liberty, and property and to his Christian self-government.	A. A legislative branch that passes laws encroaching upon the individual's right of self-government and his rights to his own life, liberty, and property.
B. Specifically limited powers for the presidency.	B. Presidential powers frequently bypassing Congress through executive orders.
C. The Supreme Court as the interpreter of law in accord with the Constitution, which is undergirded by Biblical Law.	C. The Supreme Court flouting Biblical Law in many of its rulings and often usurping the rights of the legislative branch.
3. A dual system of government: a) the states retaining most powers, b) the federal government having only those powers necessary for its sphere of authority.	3. A strong unitary government with powers being absorbed by Washington, the states steadily losing their local self-government and sources of revenue to the federal government.

This decline would never have come to pass if American Christians had not stepped aside from the political arena and retreated into purely personal religion, leaving the field of civil government largely to the secular humanists. Of course, if we had known the distinctively

Christian nature of the elements of our government, we would not have turned our backs on our heritage.

The Biblical Perspective of our Founders

What is it that identifies America as a Christian nation? What elements in our form of government are distinctively Biblical? Every American should be able to answer this question. Contrary to common belief today, most of our Founders were serious Christians and, in contrast to the everyday person today, understood that every nation has a theological and philosophical basis. Were they here today, they would not find it difficult to understand that even atheistic Marxist cultures are religious to the core—preaching by force the doctrine of man as the measure of all things. In their day, our Founders had the example of the failed French revolutionaries who were preaching much the same thing. But our Founding Fathers, with few exceptions, were diametrically opposed to the atheistic path chosen by the French revolutionaries.

Although quite true, it is important to remember that our nation was established as a Christian nation, not because all the Founders or all the people were Christian, but because it was founded on the *Christian view of man and government* that prevailed at that time. Those who try to dismiss the historical evidence that ours is a Christian republic often point to two or three unbelieving Founding Fathers as if they were representative of all the rest. But the contrary is true, and these few individuals had to bow before the prevailing Christian perspective that surrounded them. The main elements of our government sprang from this perspective.

President Harry Truman laid out the case for America's Biblical foundations in a speech in 1950. He stood against the redacted, anecdotal, revisionist histories sweeping into America's schools from John Dewey and the progressive, socialist academics of the time. He foresaw what could happen if we forgot our covenant with the Almighty. He said,

> *The fundamental basis of this nation's laws was given to Moses on the Mount. The fundamental basis of our Bill of Rights comes*

from the teachings we get from Exodus and St. Matthew, from Isaiah and St. Paul. I don't think we emphasize that enough these days. If we don't have a proper fundamental moral background, we will finally end up with a totalitarian government which does not believe in rights for anybody except the State.[2]

The First Pillar of the Constitution:

The Principle of Representation

One of the fundamental elements of our new political system was a new phenomenon in the world: the American representative system of government. This system may justly be called the first pillar of the Constitution. In 1783, the Rev. Dr. Ezra Stiles, then president of Yale University, said in a speech:

> *All the forms of civil polity have been tried by mankind, except one, and that seems to have been reserved in Providence to be realized in America…. A democratical polity for millions, standing upon the broad basis of the people at large, amply charged with property has not hitherto been exhibited.*[3]

Setting the Stage

Before a representative system could be implemented that would hold down the power of tyrants, a whole chain of events had to bring about the miracle that was America. As we have seen in chapter 3, the Bible must get into the hands of individuals. This gave them not only the desire for liberty, but the ability, skills, and wisdom needed for self-government, which, in turn, safeguards liberty. Second, a land had to be provided that was separated from the Old World despotism of monarchs and separated, too, from the religious skepticism which was to arise during the Enlightenment. Third, a people had to be prepared who shared a Biblical worldview of the nature of man and government. The Biblical view of man drove them to develop a form of government that would neither depend blindly upon the will of the masses nor give absolute power to one man. They knew that, as

Lord Acton succinctly stated, "Power tends to corrupt and absolute power corrupts absolutely."

Why did they understand the corrupting nature of power so well? Because they shared the Biblical view of the sin nature of man. Therefore, they could not share the view of the French philosopher Jean Jacques Rousseau that man is naturally good and able to perfect himself. Nor could they share his enthusiasm for the "general will." The general will could be dead wrong; it could trample on the God-given rights of the individual. But neither did they believe what King George had tried to tell them—that they must bow to the decrees of the sovereign as a leader by divine right.

A Balanced, Biblical Outlook

The balanced, Biblical outlook of our Founding Fathers is exemplified in both the Old and New Testaments and produced a new view of the body politic beginning with representative government. For example, Moses's father-in-law Jethro encouraged Moses to choose qualified judges or representatives to help him guide and direct Israel. "Look for able men from all the people, men who fear God, who are trustworthy and hate a bribe, and place such men over the people as chiefs of thousands, of hundreds, of fifties and of tens."[4] The New Testament churches were admonished to choose elders and deacons (representatives) based upon the qualifications laid out in First Timothy 3 and Titus 1:6–9. Because they understood the Biblical view of government, the American republics and the great Federal republic they created were quite different from all the republics that had preceded them.

What then is a republic? The word is from the Latin and means simply "public affairs." Noah Webster, in his 1828 *Dictionary*, defines it as

> *A Commonwealth; a state in which the exercise of the sovereign power is lodged in representatives elected by the people. In modern usage, it differs from a democracy or democratic state, in which the people exercise the powers of sovereignty, in person. Yet the democracies of Greece are often called republics.*

Tyrannical Greek Democracies

Let us survey the nature of these so-called republics, comparing them with the American model.

These Greek democracies were turbulent, easily swayed assemblies of the whole people, who came under the influence of silver-tongued orators. Hannah More, English writer and philanthropist, writes of the Athenians:

> *This unsettled government, which left the country perpetually exposed to the tyranny of the few, and the turbulence of the many, was never bound together by any principle of union, by any bond of interest, common to the whole community. The restraint of laws was feeble; the laws themselves were often contradictory; often ill administered.*[5]

James Madison, known as the Father of the Constitution, thoroughly studied both Greek and Roman history and understood government from the Christian perspective, having studied theology and ethics under the Reverend Dr. John Witherspoon at the College of New Jersey. Dr. Witherspoon prepared Madison and many other young men for distinguished public careers. As a signer of the Declaration of Independence, Witherspoon was a devoted supporter of the patriot cause and served as a delegate to the Continental Congress for seven years. From him, James Madison absorbed the Christian view of man as a sinner who could not be trusted with unlimited power. Sharing this view of life, as did most of the Founding Fathers, Madison saw the dangers of unrestrained majority rule, remarking that a society made up of those

> *who assemble and administer the government in person, can admit of no cure for the mischiefs of faction. A common passion or interest will, in almost every case, be felt by a majority of the whole...and there is nothing to check the inducements to sacrifice the weaker party or an obnoxious individual. Hence it is that such democracies have ever been spectacles of turbulence and contention; have ever been found incompatible with personal security and the rights of property; and have in general been as short in their lives as they have been violent in their deaths.*[6]

Defect of the Roman Republic

But if the Greek democracies did not hold the key to political wisdom, what about the great Roman republic? Historian John Fiske saw that Rome had been unable to protect personal liberty because of a fundamental defect:

> *Now if we ask why the Roman government found itself thus obliged to sacrifice personal liberty and local independence to the paramount necessity of holding the empire together, the answer will point us to the essential and fundamental vice of the Roman method of nation-making. It lacked the principle of representation.... Its senates were assemblies of notables.... There was no notion of such a thing as political power delegated by the people to representatives who were to wield it away from home and out of sight of their constituents.... When, therefore, the Roman popular government...had come to extend itself over a large part of the world, it lacked the one institution by means of which government could be carried on over so vast an area without degenerating into despotism.[7]*

When Julius Caesar seized the reins of power, this is exactly what happened. In his study of the ancient republics, Madison saw that a truly representative principle would solve this very problem because it acted,

> *to refine and enlarge the public views, by passing them through the medium of a chosen body of citizens, whose wisdom may best discern the true interest of their country, and whose patriotism and love of justice will be least likely to sacrifice it to temporary or partial considerations.[8]*

While Madison hoped that the men chosen to office would be godly men who would act from the highest motives, he was under no illusion as to the sin nature of man. He knew that unless their powers were limited,

> *Men of factious tempers, of local prejudices, or of sinister designs, may, by intrigue, by corruption, or by other means, first obtain the suffrages, and then betray the interests, of the people.[9]*

Madison's Political Presuppositions

Throughout his career, Madison was always acutely aware of "the mischiefs of faction," which he was convinced could only by handled effectively through a separation of powers. His college mentor, Dr. Witherspoon, had long held this view. Indeed, in order to understand Madison's political principles, it is necessary to understand his theological roots. As scholar James H. Smylie writes: "Madison's theological orientation is of paramount importance."[10] The source of his political presuppositions lies in the Calvinism he learned from Witherspoon during his formative years. While Madison came under many influences throughout his life, it was Witherspoon's that was of critical importance.

What did he learn from Witherspoon that would affect his view of political power?

> *Interpreting Scripture and the script of human experience, Witherspoon spoke often about human nature.... His view of human nature must be seen in relation to his view of the "Dominion of Providence." On the basis of this dependence, Witherspoon could emphasize human depravity as universal and inevitable without excluding or minimizing man's obvious potential for good. The latter possibility was evidence of the preserving Providence of God, who was continually working to fulfill His promises and purposes.*[11]

Because Madison gained a realistic Christian view of the nature of man from Dr. Witherspoon, he had far less confidence in the people than Jefferson did—far less confidence in political majorities.

> *He steered clear of that optimism in human nature which almost always leads to anarchy, and thus he helped to modify the least desirable aspects of Jefferson's political thrust.*[12]

Virtue Essential

It is not too much to assert, as Smylie does, that "Madison translated the views of Witherspoon on the nature of man into a political instrument."[13]

Because godly men like Madison and Witherspoon created our system of representative government, it needs the leavening of godly men and women to make it work—whether acting as voters or as those elected to office. This is not to say that men must be perfect in order to have good government. Such a hope would be unrealistic. But men and women who understand and support the Biblical view of man and government are needed to represent the people at all levels of government. As Samuel Adams observed:

> *He therefore is the truest friend to the liberty of his country who tries most to promote its virtue, and who, so far as his power and influence extend, will not suffer a man to be chosen into any office of power and trust who is not a wise and virtuous man.... THE SUM OF ALL IS, IF WE WOULD MOST TRULY ENJOY THIS GIFT OF HEAVEN, LET US BECOME A VIRTUOUS PEOPLE.*[14]

The Second Pillar of the Constitution:

The Separation of Powers

Because our Founding Fathers realized that trusting too much authority to any one man or group of men was dangerous, they opposed concentration of power and favored its distribution or dispersion. The second pillar of the Constitution, therefore, is the separation of powers.

Our Founders really did not need the French philosopher Charles de Montesquieu to tell them that "in every government there are three sorts of power," for they already knew the source of these three powers. "For the LORD is our judge; the LORD is our lawgiver; the LORD is our King."[15] They knew that human government should seek God's model for these three aspects of political power. But they were impressed by this eminent French philosopher's analysis of the need for a separation of powers and of the divine origin of all law and power in his *Spirit of Laws*.

> *God is related to the universe, as Creator and Preserver; the laws by which He created all things are those by which He preserves*

them. He acts according to these rules, because He knows them; He knows them because He made them; and He made them, because they are in relation to His Wisdom and power.[16]

Scriptural Guidelines and Limitations of Power

Certainly, God knew what frame of government would best suit the frame of man. That is why He limits the power of civil government by His own authority. Throughout Scripture, there are numerous guidelines and limitations upon civil authorities. The absolute power and control God exercises over all spheres of government were never given by Him to any finite man or group of men, who by their very nature would be incapable of exercising such awesome power justly.[17] Reasoning from this Biblical perspective, our Founders agreed with Montesquieu that

> *When the legislative and executive powers are united in the same person, or in the same body of magistrates, there can be no liberty. There is no liberty, if the judiciary power be not separated from the legislative and executive. Were it joined with the legislative, the life and liberty of the subject would be exposed to arbitrary control; for the judge would be then the legislator. Were it joined to the executive power, the judge might behave with violence and oppression.*[18]

Consequently, in the federal government, we find a careful separation of the three powers of government, none of which constitutionally has any right to encroach on the other. But, as Rosalie J. Slater reminds us:

> *Can we expect these three governmental actions to operate correctly if we, as individual Christians, do not know the source from which they are derived, and what was their purpose? In our ignorance today we are tempted to believe that the power of the judicial, executive, and legislative branches of our government resides in those individuals who staff these offices. Yet, upon consideration of the Biblical base and purpose, we can see that the power or control resides not in the staffing but in the electorate*

which these offices represent. It resides in each individual Christian as he allows Christ to rule his life.[19]

The Capacity of Mankind for Self-Government

Americans have journeyed far from the principles of our Founding Fathers. No longer understanding our Constitution, we have allowed the human desire for unchecked power to circumvent constitutional law through executive orders, judicial activism, and legislation that intrudes on the legitimate rights of the people. Today, most of our people believe that the federal government is an inevitable intruder into most areas of their lives simply because of the complexity of modern global politics. Some even say we are no longer capable of self-government.

Our Founders knew that the sin nature of man required society to be protected from concentration of power in a few hands. But they also knew that man had been created in the image and likeness of God and that, with the aid of divine Providence, he was capable of self-government. Thus, James Madison wrote concerning the plan of government finally agreed upon at the Constitutional Convention:

> *The first question that offers itself is whether the general form and aspect of the government be strictly republican. It is evident that no other form would be reconcilable with the genius of the people of America; with the fundamental principles of the Revolution; or with the honorable determination which animates every votary of freedom, to rest all our political experiments on the capacity of mankind for self-government.*[20]

So it is that the integrity of all three powers of government depends upon the integrity of the self-governing individual and on what he acknowledges to be the foundation of the body politic—the laws of God, or the laws of men.

The Third Pillar of the Constitution:

A Dual Form of Government

The third pillar of the Constitution, our unique dual system of government, is America's solution to the age-old philosophical question: How can unity and diversity exist in harmony? How can there be individual liberty and also cultural and governmental unity without one destroying the other? Our Founders concluded that only through the application of a balanced, Biblical perspective could they arrive at a form of government that allowed both form and freedom, unity and diversity. It was a difficult concept to grasp. John Fiske ascribes to "the great mind" of James Madison the honor of being the first

> *to entertain distinctly the noble conception of two kinds of government operating at one and the same time upon the same individuals, harmonious with each other, but each supreme in its own sphere.*[21]

As we mentioned before, in both the Old and New Testaments, civil government is always limited, and accountability is demanded of representatives who exercise strictly delegated authority.[22] From the Biblical perspective, all human authority is delegated because God is sovereign. The concept of different spheres of authority acting upon the same individuals—or rather, proceeding from the same individuals—could only work in a Biblically-based society. In order to avoid the eventual usurpation of power by the strongest institution, there must be a recognition that God has delegated certain "unalienable rights" and responsibilities to specific institutions: the home, Church, school, and State.

The Issue of Slavery

From the time of the fall of man, slavery has existed in all major civilizations on every continent and in virtually every culture. All of the ancient civilizations, such as Babylon, Egypt, Greece, Rome, and China, all practiced slavery on a mass scale.

"By the time of Christ, slaves made up an estimated 75% of the population in Athens [in Greece], and well over half of the Roman population.... With few exceptions, kings, priests, and philosophers approved of it [slavery]. Aristotle, the influential Greek philosopher, saw it as natural, expedient, and just (Politics 1. 1255)."[23] Aristotle is known for his "human slave theory," in which most are born to serve as slaves and only a few to rule.

When Christ came into the world, He stated His purpose and fulfilled it. He said He came to "set the captives free." So He did through His death, resurrection, and ascension. He sent out His army of compassion, which has brought liberty increasingly to all peoples, nations, and races. The apostle Paul, speaking to the Galatian Christians, said that they were "neither Jew nor Greek,... slave nor free, there is no male and female, for you are all one in Christ Jesus."[24] True believers, especially those who had the Word of God to read, played the central role in practically eliminating slavery from Europe in the Middle Ages.

"It is important to note, that although by the fourteenth century, slavery had essentially come to an end in Europe, including England [slavery still continued unabated on all other continents], it was revived by the British in the seventeenth century, especially in England's colonies."[25] This evil of slavery was then forced by England upon the American colonies.

> *Many of the Founders vigorously complained against the fact that Great Britain had forcefully imposed upon the Colonies the evil of slavery.... Many of the Founders started and served in anti-slavery societies. Franklin and Rush founded the first such society in America, in 1774. John Jay was president of a similar society in New York. Other Founding Fathers serving in anti-slavery societies included: William Livingston (Constitution signer), James Madison, Richard Bassatt, James Monroe, Bushrod Washington, Charles Carroll, William Few, John Marshall, Richard Stockton, Zephaniah Swift, and many more.*[26]

Thomas Jefferson, although he owned slaves, believed that slavery was wrong and that it should be abolished. He heavily criticized that

British policy of the importation of slaves. Jefferson continued his condemnation of the practice in a paragraph in the first draft of the Declaration of Independence:

> *He [King George III] has waged cruel war against human nature itself, violating its most sacred rights of life & liberty in the persons of a distant people who never offended him, captivating & carrying them into slavery in another hemisphere, or to incur miserable death in their transportation thither.... Determined to keep open a market where MEN should be bought & sold, he has prostituted his negative for suppressing every legislative attempt to prohibit or restrain this execrable commerce.*[27]

But the Founders faced a few state delegates, led by South Carolina, who would walk out if slavery were abolished. The above paragraph was not included in the final draft of the Declaration of Independence. So, the men in Philadelphia made a compromise on the issue, so that they could maintain their fragile unity necessary to defeat the English king who had perpetuated the trade. They made a tragic compromise as they pushed the issue of the abolition of slavery back to 1808.

The Prophetic Warning of George Mason

Like many of the other Founders, George Mason knew that the price of putting off this issue would be dire. He said,

> *Every master of slaves is born a petty tyrant. They bring the judgment of heaven upon a country. As nations cannot be rewarded or punished in the next world, they must be in this. By an inevitable chain of causes and effects, Providence punishes national sins by national calamities.*[28]

The handling of the slavery issue was unquestionably a tragic blot on the work of the Constitutional Convention, which opened itself to divine direction in so many other ways and accomplished so much of enduring worth. It should serve as a reminder to us of what Madison and Witherspoon understood so well: the sin nature of man often prevents him from accomplishing all that God would have him do. But God is not mocked. Although it took a disastrous Civil War, His

Providence achieved through blood what could so easily have been achieved by the pen. This episode is also a reminder that God did not bless our Founding Fathers merely because they were brilliant thinkers, but only to the extent that they relied upon Him—and in regard to slavery, they did not. Nevertheless, our remarkable Constitution came into being owing to His Providence.

Phillis Wheatley, World Changer (1754–1785)

Even though she would never live to see the emancipation of her people as a race, Phillis Wheatley was certainly a forerunner of the Christian liberty that would come.

At age seven, Phillis was bought at a slave auction by John Wheatley of Boston in 1761. The Wheatley family loved her dearly and helped educate her mind, rather than merely giving her menial duties. Within five years, she was writing poetry comparable to the finer poets of her day.

Trained as a devout Christian, she wrote most of her poems about her faith. She was freed by her former owners and, as the war approached, began to write poems in support of American liberty. She wrote her poems directly to leaders, like the Earl of Dartmouth, who came as the king's secretary to America in 1772. She called on him to release America from its tyranny under the foot of England and used her own painful brush with tyrants, as a black child snatched from her parents, to drive the point home:

> *What pangs excruciating must molest,*
> *What Sorrows labour in my parents' breast?*
> *Steel'd was that soul and by no misery moved*
> *That from a father seized his babe beloved:*
> *Such, such my case. And can I but pray*
> *Others may never feel tyrannic sway?*

After a poem written to encourage General George Washington, he wrote her back and invited her to visit his headquarters at Cambridge.

But as the war dragged on, John Wheatley died, and Phillis married a free Black named John Peters. He was a hard man and broke the young poet physically and financially. Phillis Wheatley died at the age of thirty-one. But she had helped inspire the patriot cause and forwarded the cause of her African American race, as she testified of her faith in Christ and helped set the stage for the world to acknowledge that all men and women are created equal.

In the same year that Phillis died, God converted an English Parliamentarian three thousand miles to the east, who then labored continually for twenty-two years to abolish the slave trade, against incredible odds. His name was William Wilberforce. On February 23, 1807, Parliament abolished the slave trade forever, and the U.S. followed suit the same year. God hears the cries of His people in bondage.

Beware of "Chronological Snobbery"

"Historical presentism," the practice of imposing our present views of the moment on people of centuries past, is a strategy to destroy the character of individuals and the history of nations. C. S. Lewis calls this practice "chronological snobbery." Why study the past, since some of the Founders owned slaves, and this makes them unworthy of mention. It is cancel culture in action. "However, if we were to cut ourselves off from the history of nations who had slavery in the past, we would have to have nothing to do with any people, because almost every society has had slavery."[29]

Americans of all races and political persuasions should be aware that the above-mentioned strategy is a well-laid plan of erasing the constitutional liberties of all our people. That strategy is called "critical race theory." Charlie Kirk of Turning Point USA says:

> The "critical race theory" is extremely dangerous. CRT came from a philosopher from the Frankfurt School who came to America by the name of Herbert Marcuse, who brought it into the academy. And it is neo-Marxist. But what makes this philosophy different—and it has many different manifestations—is that it is not economic in nature.... What makes CRT so different is that it is a power struggle, in their own estimation, between races. Everything is actually racist. [CRT teaches] that the entire American system is a by-product of a white-supremacist experiment.

Kirk concludes, "This is the death of traditional American values. CRT is in the military, in the civil service, in the universities. It's in every single school system across the country."[30]

There is only one force strong enough to combat tyrants within and without and to help us heal the racial and cultural divides that are engulfing us. That force is the self-governing Christian who loves God and his neighbor. The true history of man's enslavement of his fellow man is ample evidence of the above hypothesis.

The Bill of Rights

The Constitution almost failed to be ratified by the states because of another fundamental defect: there was no Bill of Rights. George Mason and others at the Convention were sure that without careful spelling out of the individual's basic rights to his liberties, the central government would encroach on the rights of the individual. Madison promised to do all in his power to secure a Bill of Rights in exchange for ratification of the Constitution. He kept his promise. With ratification, America produced a unique political system: a dual form of government, the central government supreme in its sphere, and the state governments supreme in their spheres.

Rosalie J. Slater sees the Biblical basis of this dual form of government as derived from the two Commandments of our Lord:[31]

> Our national sense, as AMERICANS, is predicated upon our willingness to be God-governed—the first commandment. This is the basis for Christian Self-Government. Our FEDERAL sense, as Californians, Washingtonians, Oregonians, etc.—is predicated upon the second commandment. The individual's relation to God and to man are hereby stated, and for the Christian, there must be consistency in his behavior—whether he is dealing with one neighbor—or two hundred million.[32]

Christianity Astonished the World

The representative system, the separation of powers, the dual form of government—these three great pillars of the American system of government—were the inspired means to a great end: the world's first Christian republic. As Verna Hall remarks:

> *Each religion has a form of government, and Christianity aston-ished the world by establishing self-government. With the land-ing of the Pilgrims in 1620, Christian self-government became the foundation-stone of the United States of America. "The stone which the builders refused is become the head stone of the corner" (Ps. 118:22; Matt. 21:42).*[33]

In an election sermon in 1799, Dr. Jedediah Morse reminds us of our part in the preservation of our Christian form of government:

> *To the kindly influence of Christianity we owe that degree of civil freedom, and political and social happiness which mankind now enjoy. In proportion as the genuine effects of Christianity are diminished in any nation, either through unbelief, or the corrup-tion of its doctrines, or the neglect of its institutions; in the same proportion will the people of that nation recede from the blessings of genuine freedom.... Whenever the pillars of Christianity shall be overthrown, our present republican forms of government, and all the blessings which flow from them, must fall with them.*[34]

Today, we have the awesome but exhilarating task of repairing these pillars of Christianity, which are also the pillars of our Constitution, that the structure shall not fall.

Colonizing Ideas

As we repair our own nation and put it in order, we shall then be in a position to do what we were meant to do originally—to "colonize ideas"—specifically, the Christian idea of man and government, so they do not stop on these shores, but go on to cover the globe. Our historians used to believe that it was part of our mission to colonize America's unique political ideas, but as we have forgotten what our Founding Fathers achieved—forgotten the source of our freedom and affluence—we have failed to do this.

This does not mean that we can export our structure and system of government to other countries and expect it to make sense to them without an understanding of the Christian principles of self-government that underlie the structure. We have learned that self-government begins first with the individual aligning himself with the will of God, then caring for himself and others and applying Biblical principles to all areas of his life. A limited, representative civil government will not long survive without what George Washington called the pillars of America in his Farewell Address: "Of all the dispositions and habits which lead to political prosperity, religion and morality are indispensable supports."[35]

All merely external forms of democratic structure which we may attempt to promote in other lands are doomed to failure. Such attempts will inevitably bring cries of "American imperialism!" or cries of an attempt to exercise external control over other nations. Each nation, in covenant with their citizens and God, must choose God's ways voluntarily. Then their free institutions can be grounded on truth and prosper.

Attempts to throw money at the acute problems in other nations when there is little understanding of Christian self-government is a tragic waste of resources. A major problem in expanding lasting liberty in the world is the Christian community. In recent generations, many of our missionaries have not been taught the wonderful scope of their kingdom task. We must not only bring the verbal Gospel of salvation, which is primary. We must also communicate and exemplify the Biblical principles of a Christian nation.

Our political ideas, under the Providence of God, have achieved more civil and religious liberty and more self-government and genuine prosperity than the world has ever known before. We need to recapture the vision of the great American historian Charles Bancroft, who wrote:

> America stands a model which other nations will carefully copy, in due time, as they can adapt themselves and change their institutions. There may be no literal copy or close formal imitation; but there is little doubt that the spirit and true sense of our Declaration of Independence will finally mold the structure and control the workings of all governments.[36]

Bancroft, writing in the nineteenth century, was optimistic about spreading the essence of our liberty. But he could not foresee that the American people would lose "the spirit and true sense of our Declaration of Independence." He, like our Founding Fathers, understood that our form of government can only be communicated from the spirit of one people to the spirit of another. Good government— Biblical government—cannot be forced from without but rises from within the hearts of a people dedicated to God's will.

Chapter 7 Study Questions

1. What did the Founding Fathers hope to achieve by the First Amendment to the Federal Constitution?

2. What are the three pillars of the American constitutional form of government?

3. What are some Biblical references to describe each form?

4. In what ways have the three pillars deteriorated?

5. What caused their deterioration?

6. Why is Christian character necessary to the maintenance of the American republic?

7. How is our republic different from those of Greece and Rome?

8. Why is the election of godly people as our representatives vital to the preservation of our unique republic?

9. What necessary qualities should our representatives possess?

10. What is the purpose of the separation of power?

11. Where does power lie—in us or in our representatives?

12. What will happen to our nation's form of government if its Christian foundation continues to be undermined?

13. How can we "colonize" the Christian idea of man and government?

Chapter 7 Notes

1. Rosalie J. Slater, *Teaching and Learning America's Christian History* (San Francisco: Foundation for American Christian Education, 1975), 240.

2. Harry Truman at Attorney General's Conference, 1950, quoted in William Federer, *Change to Chains* (St. Louis, MO: Amerisearch, 2011), 59.

3. Verna M. Hall, *The Christian History of the Constitution of the United States of America: Christian Self-Government*, (San Francisco: Foundation for American Christian Education, 1975, 382.

4. Exodus 18:21.

5. Slater, *Teaching and Learning*, 161.

6. James Madison, *Federalist*, no. 10, in Alexander Hamilton, James Madison, and John Jay, *The Federalist* (New York: Tudor Publishing Co.,1937), 67.

7. Hall, *The Christian History of the Constitution*, 13.

8. Hamilton, Madison, Jay, *The Federalist*, 67–68.

9. Ibid., 68.

10. James H. Smylie, "Madison and Witherspoon: Theological Roots of American Political Thought," *The Princeton University Library Chronicle* 22 (Spring 1961): 119.

11. Ibid., 121.

12. Ibid., 131.

13. Ibid., 131.

14. Slater, *Teaching and Learning*, 247, emphasis added.

15. Isaiah 33:22.

16. Hall, *The Christian History of the Constitution*, 134.

17. See Genesis 9:1–6; Ezekiel 45:9; Romans 13:1–5; Revelation 1:5.

18. Hall, *The Christian History of the Constitution*, 134–35.

19. Slater, *Teaching and Learning*, 242.

20. James Madison, *Federalist*, no. 39, in Hamilton, Madison, Jay, *The Federalist*, 256.

21. John Fiske, *The Critical Period of American History: 1783–1789* (Boston and New York: Houghton, Mifflin & Co., 1898) 239.

22. See Deuteronomy 1:13; Exodus 18:21; Luke 20:25; Acts 1:19–20.

23. Alvin J. Schmidt, *Under the Influence: How Christianity Transformed Civilization* (Grand Rapids: Zondervan, 2001) 272.

24. Galatians 3:28.

25. Alvin J. Schmidt, *How Christianity Changed the World*, repr. of *Under the Influence* (Grand Rapids: Zondervan, 2004), 276.

26. David Barton, "The Founding Fathers and Slavery," *Patriot Press,* patriotacademy.com/founding-fathers-slavery/; "The Bible, Slavery, and America's Founders," *WallBuilders*, December 31, 2016, wallbuilders.com/bible-slavery-americas-founders/.

27. Julian P. Boyd, ed., *The Papers of Thomas Jefferson, Volume 1: 1760–1776* (Princeton, NJ: Princeton University Press, 1950), 423–28.

28. Robert A. Rutland, ed., *The Papers of George Mason*, 3 vols. (Chapel Hill, NC.: The University of North Carolina Press, 1970), 3:1787.

29. David Barton, "The Bible, Slavery, and America's Founders."

30. Charlie Kirk interviewed by Mark Levin, *Fox News*, Feb. 12, 2021.

31. Matthew 22:37–40.

32. Slater, *Teaching and Learning*, 242–43.

33. Hall, *The Christian History of the Constitution*, iii.

34. Ibid., v.

35. George Washington, "Farewell Address," 19 September, 1796, *National Archives*, Founders Online, founders.archives.gov/documents/Washington/05-20-02-0440-0002.

36. Hall, *The Christian History of the Constitution*, 6.

Chapter 8

A Strategy for Success

This Book of the Law shall not depart from your mouth, but you shall meditate on it day and night, so that you may be careful to do according to all that is written in it. For then you will make your way prosperous, and then you will have good success.

Joshua 1:8

"THE SURRENDER OF YORKTOWN" (OCTOBER 19, 1781)
(DETAIL) BY LOUIS VAN BLARENBERGHE

I take a particular pleasure in acknowledging that the interposing hand of Heaven, in the various instances of our extensive Preparation for this Operation [Yorktown], has been most conspicuous and remarkable.

— George Washington to Thomas McKean,
President of Congress,
November 15, 1781

Chapter 8

A Strategy for Success

*A*s we have seen, the American Covenant is not one document but a traceable chain of individual, church, and government agreements between the God of the Bible and the American people. We believe the American Covenant is the fundamental reason for the successful rise of our constitutional republic. The beguiling "father of lies" has for too long taken the day of battle, as his messengers have distorted the facts of our history and omitted the reason for America's greatness. God told His people that they "are destroyed for lack of knowledge,"[1] and so it is today, especially in the strategic battle for the American republic.

Throughout this book, many reasons have been given for the decline of our nation. But the purpose of this unveiling has not been to detail the failures of our modern secular state and its educational institutions. Ample material exists documenting the bankruptcy of the various secular alternatives that claim to have the solution to the crises of our time.

The blame for our current perilous condition must fall upon those of us who say we believe in God and share the legacy of our Founders' vision. We have forfeited the institutions bequeathed to us by our forefathers. They have not been forcibly taken away from us by some overwhelming conspiracy, but we and our fathers simply stopped teaching the Bible's nation-building principles to ourselves and our children.

Now a new day is dawning. Americans are once again studying the power of God in our history. As a result, many are renewing their faith for the saving of our nation and are believing once again the words of our Lord: "The gates of hell shall not prevail against it [My Church]."[2]

Instant Replay

To this point, we have outlined what America once was and what principles undergird the structure of our republic. We have shown how the individual, once the Bible was in his hands, desired to be free from external dominance by either king or pope. That individual then became self-governing in all areas and formed institutions—churches, schools, government—to protect the individual in order that he might serve God. ("Let My people go, that they may serve Me."[3])

In chapters 6 and 7, we illustrated how our Founders reasoned our economic and governmental establishments from a Biblical worldview that was commonly shared. Now, in this final chapter, let us analyze an historically proven strategy for success that can lead to the rebirth of our nation.

Planning to Win

Several major ideologies, or religions, are dedicated to spreading their worldview to cover the whole world. Communism and its manifestations, such as cultural Marxism, are perhaps the most systematic and brutal in their schemes to dominate the world. They butchered and enslaved tens of millions of people throughout the twentieth century and continue to do so in such places as China.

Another powerful religious ideology is that of radical Islam. The history of its attempts to dominate the world is an epic tale of woe. From the seventh century until today, militant Islam has invaded, conquered, and dominated much of the Middle East, Asia, and parts of Africa.

But the truth of history and the declaration of Scripture is that Jesus Christ and His Army of Compassion—the *Ecclesia*—is permeating and reconciling the world to God. "God…through Christ reconciled us to Himself and gave us the ministry of reconciliation; that is, in Christ God was reconciling the world to Himself, not counting their trespasses against them, and entrusting to us the message of reconciliation."[4] Just since WWII, more people have become Christians than in all of the centuries before combined. Dinesh D'Souza writes of this global reach of Christianity. He says, "For the first time in history, Christianity has become a universal religion. It is in fact the only religion with a global reach."[5]

One of the above philosophies, or religious worldviews, will dominate our culture. It is surely the ultimate irrationalism to believe that a do-your-own-thing America will survive through the twenty-first century. A self-centered, materialistic democracy is no match for well-defined, war-tested, revolutionary ideas.

It has been the presupposition of this study that a proper understanding of Biblical Christianity, lived out in the lives of individuals and institutions, has brought the greatest degree of liberty, prosperity, creativity, and peace that the world has known. There have been aberrations of this truth, as men, desiring to hide themselves behind the religious symbol of the cross, have pillaged nations on so-called Crusades, put men in slavery, and persecuted Jews. But a perusal of history, as seen in this volume, shows that these atrocities do not represent the philosophy or methodology of Jesus and the apostles or of true Christianity. The authentic Founder of Christianity never called for an external theocracy but offered freely an internal transformation of life that would lead to external transformations of society and to a better life for all.

Our ancestors knew that they were living out a great drama in America that was orchestrated by the Almighty. George Washington said that we are all on the stage of history and that our task is to play our role well. Our Founders, who were students of the Bible, perceived that when they walked in covenant with the Lord, they could expect, even through trials, that God would bless them and their posterity. They took seriously the covenantal promises of God in Deuteronomy 6 to bless them and their posterity to a thousand generations.

But they also knew the inescapable reality that if they broke their covenant with God instead of voluntarily walking in His loving ways, God's favor would be withdrawn, and personal and national calamity would naturally befall them.

We, for several generations in America, have been ignoring our covenants with God, both personal and national. We have taken for granted the blessings of liberty and prosperity, heaped upon ourselves the wealth of the nations, and failed to prepare our children to repair and renew our broken national and personal covenants.

President Abraham Lincoln understood America's deep dependence upon these covenants with God. He said, "Those who fight the purpose of the Almighty will not succeed. They always have been, they always will be, beaten."[6]

George Washington expressed the same Biblical understanding that the life of a nation and an individual rests upon our covenantal relationship with our Creator. In President Washington's Inaugural Speech, he said:

> The propitious smiles of Heaven can never be expected on a nation that disregards the eternal rules of order and right, which Heaven itself has ordained.[7]

In this speech, our first president warns us that the success of our one-of-a-kind experiment in liberty rests upon our obedience to the "Eternal Rules of Right." He is saying that the world has eternal laws. Some of these are scientific laws such as the law of gravity. But others are the unchanging moral laws of the universe, that likewise cannot be violated without consequences.

In other words, I may be free to jump from the Empire State Building expecting to fly like a bird, breaking the law of gravity. But my flight will only last for three seconds, till I hit the concrete below. Then I will know, "You don't break the law of gravity, it breaks you." The same is true regarding all of God's precepts that guide us in developing a blessed society. If we leave our Biblically based government of a decentralized, constitutional republic and adopt the model of the atheist socialists, which is happening now, we are fighting against the very way the world is structured by God.

I was in the audience in 1984 when President Ronald Reagan gave a speech to the National Religious Broadcasters. Proving his legendary ability as the "great communicator," the president summarized the great decisions that confront us. He fully embraced the covenantal language of our forefathers, always alluding to our responsibility to be "a city on a hill." Then he declared, "If we ever forget that we are One Nation under God, then we will be a nation gone under."

Now, a generation later, the torch of the covenant has passed to us. It is barely flickering under a relentless assault by a committed contingent of power-hungry humanists, who are lovers of power. But, as we have documented throughout our study, God is working His plan to liberate men and nations. And we—those who love Him—are His Army of Compassion. Now, let us address the proven strategy for success—what we must do if we are to restore "liberty and justice for all" under His protection.

In order to restore the American Covenant, it is up to us, as the inheritors of the Founders' Biblical worldview, to return that worldview to the public forum. Although this worldview is the only hope for the restoration of our institutions, we should not expect to be invited to the debate. We must be prepared to enter the fray with compassionate, persuasive ideas and explanations in order to gain a hearing. America's success is the result of its covenant with God, and few things are as persuasive as success.

Explaining the significance of worldviews and the superiority of the Biblical worldview is the first step for us to take in repairing the devastating breach in the wall of the American Covenant.

What Is a Worldview?

Everyone—including teachers and textbook writers—has a set of conscious or unconscious presuppositions that guide all thoughts and actions. Dr. Francis Schaeffer, the major twentieth-century Christian apologist, defines *presuppositions* this way:

> *By presuppositions we mean the basic way an individual looks at life, his basic world view, the grid through which he sees the world.... Presuppositions also provide the basis for [his] values, and therefore the basis for [his] decisions.*

An individual's presuppositions make up his or her worldview. Professor Ron Jenson emphasizes the importance of developing the proper worldview when he says, "Our worldview may be conscious or unconscious, but it determines our destiny, and the destiny of the society we live in."

Worldviews are not inherited; they are learned. If a parent does not reinforce a Biblical worldview at home, students will probably absorb a secular worldview from the classroom. Many modern historians, scientists, philosophers, and educators have attempted to claim objectivity in their chosen field of study. Most Americans have adopted this myth of neutrality. They have been convinced that basic education skills and facts can be taught without a religious or philosophical bias. This has resulted in the unspoken but ironclad separation of a Christian worldview from education. R. L. Dabney explained the impossibility of neutrality in education:

> *The instructor has to teach history, cosmogony [study of origins], psychology, ethics, the laws of nations. How can he do it without saying anything favorable or unfavorable about the beliefs of evangelical Christians, Catholics, Socinians [Unitarians], Deists, pantheists, materialists, or fetish worshipers, all who claim equal rights under American institutions? His teaching will indeed be "the play of Hamlet, with the part of Hamlet removed."*

A person's worldview will shape every conclusion he draws. A Marxist historian will choose and interpret the facts of history to portray religion as the "opiate of the people." An unbelieving scientist will welcome a theory such as spontaneous evolution to avoid his accountability to a holy God and His immutable laws. And a Christian will (or should) interpret life based upon the Word of God and Jesus Christ. One worldview is right, and other worldviews are wrong. But no worldview is neutral.

What Is the Impact of a Biblical Worldview?

A Christian worldview is at the core of the great accomplishments of Western civilization. Christian historian Philip Schaff illuminates the significance of Christ and Christianity:

> *Jesus of Nazareth, without money and arms, conquered more millions than Alexander, Caesar, Mohammed, and Napoleon; without science and learning, He shed more light on things human and divine than all the philosophers and scholars combined; without the eloquence of the school, He spoke words of life such as*

were never spoken before, nor since, and produced effects which lie beyond the reach of orator or poet.

Without writing a single line, He has set more pens in motion and furnished themes for more sermons, orations, discussions, works of art, learned volumes, and sweet songs of praise than the whole army of great men of ancient and modern times. Born in a manger and crucified as a malefactor, He now controls the destinies of the civilized world and rules a spiritual empire which embraces one-third of the inhabitants of the globe.

Not a Theocracy

Perhaps a note of clarification is needed at this point. The misconception is widespread that those, like ourselves, who believe that a return to Biblical principles in our society and government is imperative are at the same time calling for a legalistic theocracy that would destroy liberty and dictate religious views to the people. The source of such fears is somewhat understandable, since there have been power-hungry leaders throughout history who have used the Church as their excuse to persecute men (e.g., the so-called divine right of kings).

What we are calling for is a simple return to the principles laid down by our Founding Fathers in the Declaration of Independence and the Constitution. These documents, following the genuine Christian philosophy of freedom of choice, allowed the individual to determine his own faith and practice without governmental interference. Conscience was not to be compelled. The individual was to be left free to choose his faith or to have none at all. Nevertheless, this was not an invitation to hedonism. There had to be a basic code of law and societal standards, and that code was found in the Bible. It acted not to repress the individual in his constructive activities but to liberate him as never before. Nineteenth-century historian Charles Bancroft summarized the positive impact of the early American republic upon all men:

As the heart in the human body receives the current of blood from all parts of the system, and, having revitalized it, returns it with fresh elements of strength, so America adopts the children of all lands only to return a manhood ennobled by a sense of its own dignity through the practice of a system of self-government which improves the condition and promotes the interest of each while it produces harm to none.[8]

No other nation in history has accepted those of varying faiths and creeds as has the United States of America. Coercion is not the Biblical way, but persuasion and love ("Come now, let us reason together"[9]). Our warning is to the Christian community, for if we do not persuade our fellow Americans through our loving words and actions that reveal the need for maintaining our nation's Biblical roots, all of us—both believers and unbelievers—will be led down the well-traveled path to slavery.

Winning the War, Not Just a Battle

If we are to avoid misconceptions mentioned above and succeed in restoring our nation, we must proceed carefully. Remember that only a very small minority of Americans (approximately 5 percent) "makes things happen" in our country. Mr. James Halcomb, the master planner of the Alaska pipeline, who is one of the finest Christian strategic planners in America, gives some invaluable insights concerning reaching a goal. Here are three aspects of that planning strategy:

1. We Must Know Our Goal!

As Christians, we should be in general agreement as to our goal, since we have the infallible Word of God to guide us in fulfilling God's will. But after helping many Christian organizations, Mr. Halcomb has found that this is not always the case. Many, he says, have no observable goal and so reach no observable objective.

Now is a good time to reflect upon whether we have set our life goals in line with God's ultimate purpose to be glorified in all things.[10] In the past century, Christianity often encouraged a self-centered goal relating to personal fulfillment rather than a God-centered goal that accomplishes His cosmic purpose of redeeming His world. We have too often been subtly caught by the "me-oriented" worldview and therefore have not seen ourselves as a vital part of His loving Army of Compassion, marching through history with a common commission.

As mentioned in the Introduction to this book, a few socialists shared the ideal of a "perfect socialist state" and were nearly able to derail the "prodigal nation of America" by offering the people a goal of sorts.

If an historically disastrous scheme can gain such influence, what will be the impact when millions of Americans reaffirm the American Covenant "to the glory of God and the advancement of the Christian faith"? The slowdown in the cultural impact of Christianity in this century is not because other philosophies are better or stronger, but because God's people have forgotten and not pursued His goal with a passion to see it accomplished!

2. We Must Know Our Assets

Jesus said that before we embark upon any venture, we should count the cost and see that we have the needed materials to carry out the task.[11] The most powerful asset for accomplishing God's purpose that has ever been known to the world is the self-governing Christian in covenant with his God.

We have seen how God set the stage for the full functioning of this world-changing individual, and how Jesus Christ died to set the individual free from the burden of sin. He told His disciples, "Greater works than these will he [the one who believes in Him] do, because I am going to the Father."[12]

Then we recalled how He gave to His new creation His Spirit and a completed Word to guide him into all truth. We traced how the individual was set free from the bondage of statism when the Bible made its way to the everyday person so that he could express his Christian self-government in every area of life, without the State dictating his every move. We saw how a nation was prepared that protected the rights of the individual so that each person could accomplish God's purpose for them.

As we enter this critical stage in the battle for the Gospel of Christ, are most American Christians aware of the great assets that have been given to them as a result of the faith of millions of persecuted believers over two thousand years? Is it not our responsibility—more than that of those who have never shared such a heritage—to use and preserve what God has given us? Jesus said that to everyone to whom much is given, much is required.[13]

During our study, we have discovered that our Founders were Biblicists who believed that the Word of God was the foundation for success in all areas. Let us illustrate the art of building a successful nation that they left for us, and then let us compare it with the humanist model.

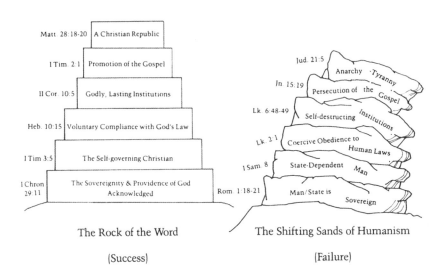

The Rock of the Word   The Shifting Sands of Humanism

(Success)   (Failure)

Comparing the two diagrams above and their techniques of building nations, which of them do you think is more likely to succeed? We live in a day in which many Americans cower in fear, believing the unbiblical and ungodly system shown above is going to sweep over the world, while, in reality, it is doomed to eventual self-destruction. If we determine to restore our nation's Biblical foundations, we may not have to follow the path of communist nations worldwide into judgment and cultural disintegration.

In order to reach our goal of reestablishing self- and civil government, should we spend our priority time combating the collapsing tent of humanism or rebuilding our godly system? Our critiques of the humanist system can accomplish little beyond awakening the people. But an example of a positive Christian alternative will have assured results, because light always dispels darkness. Building upon our assets, which requires knowing our true history, we can once again be a light on a hill, becoming an example to other nations rather than a reproach.

3. We Must Know the Critical Path

In strategic planning, "the critical path" is a term often used to describe the chain of critical or important events that must take place to accomplish a goal. For example, the building of a guided missile involves hundreds of steps and processes. If someone forgets to place a decal on the side of the missile, it may be somewhat inconsequential. But if, while constructing the missile, a fuel line is not included, then the billion-dollar nose cone will never get off the ground.

Most people do not follow a critical path to accomplish their life goal. The "urgent-" or "emergency-path" method is much more common (e.g., answering every telephone call, putting out fires in the office, etc.) This technique abandons planning to circumstance and focuses upon the so-called "urgent" issue of the moment without regard to what is important in the long run.

Jesus taught the method to be used to accomplish His great goals. His was not the "emergency-path" method. He had a critical path that He followed throughout His life, not allowing Himself to be sidetracked by circumstances.[14]

He knew the kingdom of heaven would grow in the hearts of men and then would influence all of society, but it was not to be a bloody revolution of the flesh,[15] but an infiltrating or leavening from within. (See the parables on the kingdom in Matthew 13.) The method, or critical path, of Jesus was to make right the internal (change the hearts of men)—then the external results (liberty, justice, love) would follow.

You may have noticed that this book does not focus mainly upon the issues of the day, but upon the principles behind them. For from the heart comes the issues of life.[16] Ideas have consequences. If Christians in America will learn to reason from principles (ideas) to the issues of life (consequences), then they will be ready for battle and for victory.

Unfortunately, today, millions of Christians are hurtling into the issues of the day without a firm foundation of principles or understanding of history. Their efforts are frustrated because they have left God's critical path.

God's critical path for the rebuilding of our nation begins with the self-governing Christian. A godly nation is not simply prayed for and received; it is built "line upon line,... precept upon precept."[17] The self-governing Christian is God's building block for a Christian nation.

In Scripture, the Christian is seen as more than a person who does good and avoids evil. He has within him all the power necessary to bring all areas of life into submission to God, which is his ordained purpose.[18] United with the Word of God and faith, he will accomplish all that His Lord has commanded.[19]

Timeless Biblical Blueprint: The Shema

In our media world of fantasy and hype, becoming a celebrity is the dream of millions. But the real world-changing occupation—and the most satisfying—is being a parent and preparing one's children to serve God in the next generation. "Behold, children are a heritage from the LORD, the fruit of the womb a reward. Like arrows in the hand of a warrior are the children of one's youth."[20]

The Bible makes it clear that the authority and responsibility to educate children rests with parents. We may have assistance in the form of teachers or a curriculum, but we are accountable to train and point God's "immortal arrows" into the next generation. Obedience to this task brings great reward. "Train up a child in the way he should go; even when he is old he will not depart from it."[21]

What is the Bible's strategy for successful child training? Most Biblical scholars, both Jewish and Christian, would agree that the most powerful statement in all the Bible concerning children's education is the five-step strategy of Deuteronomy 6:4–12. This passage is called the Shema, and it relates God's strategy of blessing to the Hebrew people as they prepared to enter the Promised Land. God begins His vital declaration with the wake-up call: "Hear [Shema], O Israel!" It means, "Listen! Attention! Wake up!"

It is not an overstatement to say that obedience to the principles laid down in the Shema is pivotal to the success of any family, education program, and ultimately, the success of any nation. Here are those principles.

Know God: His Character and Attributes

Hear, O Israel: The LORD our God, the LORD is one.[22]

A knowledge of the true character and nature of God is the first and most important truth to be comprehended by any parent or child. Without this knowledge of our Creator from the Bible, we would be left groping for false gods and idols like much of the world. The *Westminster Catechism* is an ideal means of educating children about the nature of God.

Love the Lord: Personal Relationship and Faith

You shall love the LORD your God with all your heart and with all your soul and with all your might.[23]

As parents, we must do more than teach an intellectual knowledge of God. We are admonished to love the Lord with all of our heart, our soul, and our might, as well as our mind. In doing so, we are responding in obedience to the love God has already displayed for us: "But God shows His love for us in that while we were still sinners, Christ died for us."[24] Christian educator Douglas Wilson says,

> *The command to teach children all the time is not limited to religious instruction. If our children do not think like Christians when they study history, math, or science, then they are not obeying the command to love God with all their minds.*

As a result of obedience to the first two commands of the Shema, parents themselves are prepared to share God's view of the world, and through their sincere love for Him, exhibit a real faith to their children.

Teach God's Truth to Your Children

These words that I command you today shall be on your heart.
You shall teach them diligently to your children, and shall talk of
them when you sit in your house, and when you walk by the way,
and when you lie down, and when you rise.[25]

This commandment tells us that God's Word and truth should be in
our memory so that as parents, we can naturally take advantage of
every opportunity, throughout the day or night, to teach our children.
Here we see the importance of consistent training. We are told in
Isaiah 28:10, "For it is precept upon precept, precept upon precept,
line upon line, line upon line, here a little, there a little." Even fifteen
or twenty minutes of consistent daily teaching can transform a child.

Mark Yourself, Your Home, and Your Business with Obedience to God's Law

You shall bind them as a sign on your hand, and they shall be as
frontlets between your eyes. You shall write them on the doorposts
of your house and on your gates.[26]

Like the Hebrews, who visibly displayed their obedience to God
on their persons and homes, we should show our obedience to the
world—first in our own lives, then in our homes, and then through
the works of our hands. This command graphically documents God's
internal-to-external strategy for changing His world from the heart,
to the home, to the society. The Bible affirms this strategy in both
the Old and New Testaments: "This is the covenant that I will make
with them after those days, declares the Lord: I will put my laws on
their hearts, and write them on their minds."[27] This is how the New
Testament believers were able to permeate and eventually subdue the
pagan Roman Empire.

Expect Blessings for You and Your Children for One Thousand Generations

And when the Lord your God brings you into the land that He
swore to your fathers…to give you—with great and good cities that

you did not build, and houses full of all good things that you did not fill, and cisterns that you did not dig, and vineyards and olive trees that you did not plant,... take care lest you forget the LORD.[28]

Here we see the promise of blessing that follows obedience to the Shema. Those who by faith obey God can be the greatest optimists because they know God is going to reward them regardless of their temporary situation.

Later in Deuteronomy, God details how long this generational blessing can reach: "Know therefore that the LORD your God is God, the faithful God who keeps covenant and steadfast love with those who love Him and keep His commandments, to a thousand generations."[29]

We know that God's plan centers on the fulfillment of the Shema, for He blessed the nations through Abraham, who trained his children and his household:

> *The LORD said, "Shall I hide from Abraham what I am about to do, seeing that Abraham shall surely become a great and mighty nation, and all the nations of the earth shall be blessed in him? For I have chosen him, that he may command his children and his household after him to keep the way of the LORD by doing righteousness and justice, so that the LORD may bring to Abraham what He has promised him."*[30]

Passing the Torch to a New Generation

The stability of Christian civilization has always been based on the family and the passing of the torch of truth from one generation to the next. Each of us stands at the apex of an unfolding generational drama. We are heirs to the past, and ancestors to the future. We were mentored by our grandparents, parents, and key influential people. We now have the opportunity to pay it forward to others in a lineage of covenantal purpose that touches back over two hundred years and includes parts of four centuries of our American history.

From its inception, Christianity has been a religion of ideas and learning. Oxford historian Robin Lane Fox documents that Christianity became the marvel of the world because it was spread by ordinary people who, despite a lack of formal education, were able to explain the mysteries of God more effectively than the educated elite of the pagan world.

Christians became a people of the Book and started schools of learning that civilized a barbarian Europe. The educational legacy left to us by the Reformers and our forefathers is unsurpassed. Luther's training spawned the universities of Germany. Calvin's Geneva was an international center of scholarship and the cradle of civil and religious liberty for the world. Knox enlightened and trained a whole generation of Scots, bringing them from tribal passions to a powerful, Biblical view of life and government, all within a twenty-year span. These early saints of the Reformation fought State tyranny, epidemic illiteracy, and poverty that rival any of our problems today. Our Founders carried on this tradition of Christian education, seeing the home as the foundation for its propagation. They left us a great legacy to replicate.

This legacy of educational excellence is a Christian inheritance. Jesus tells us that much is required of him to whom much is given. In our generation, we, as believing families, have the mandate to revive the great tradition of Christian learning. By accepting and fulfilling this responsibility, we will be taking a bold step toward reasserting our rightful leadership in the education of our children. Our entire nation will be blessed by the godly, intelligent young believers who will emerge from such homes.

The Expanding Spheres of Influence

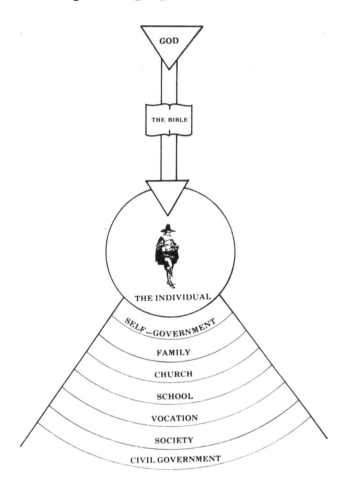

The above graph details God's way of reconciling His world to Himself.[31] It starts with the individual in covenant with Him and then moves to the family, to the Church, and then out to restoring the nation.

Daniel Webster explains the strategy of our ancestors:

Finally, let us not forget the religious character of our origin. Our fathers were brought [here] by their high veneration for the Christian religion. They journeyed by its light, and labored in its hope. They sought to incorporate its principles with the elements of their society, and to diffuse its influence through all their institutions, civil, political, or literary. Let us cherish these sentiments, and extend this influence still more widely, in the full conviction, that that is the happiest society which partakes in the highest degree of the mild and peaceful spirit of Christianity.[32]

As we go about accomplishing this task, we must build a firm foundation for the reformation of the structure of society. External changes based on power politics or heated rhetoric will be short lived.

The Self-Governing Individual

Proverbs 25:28 says: "A man without self-control is like a city broken into and left without walls." If we cannot rule ourselves, our cities will certainly break down and will, in their chaos, eat up our liberty.

In 1654, Hugo Grotius, a Dutch diplomat and theologian, beautifully stated the pattern of societal rule, beginning with the rule of God in the individual:

He knows not how to rule a kingdom that cannot manage a Province; nor can he wield a Province that cannot order a City; nor he order a City that knows not how to regulate a Village; nor he a Village that cannot guide a Family; nor can that man Govern well a Family that knows not how to Govern himself; neither can any Govern himself unless his reason be Lord, Will and Appetite her Vassals: nor can Reason rule unless herself be ruled by God, and (wholly) be obedient to Him.[33]

Our Pilgrim fathers and our Colonial forefathers both understood that dependence upon God was the only true insurance that the sin nature of man could be restrained and his great potential for good unleashed. If you do not know the God of our ancestors, my hope is that you will come to know Him through faith in His Son Jesus Christ. "If the Son sets you free, you will be free indeed."[34]

The Self-Governing Christian Family

The most important institution for the saving and preserving of the world is the family. The destruction of the family, as we are witnessing in this generation, is a sure sign of impending cultural collapse.

The self-governing home was the major institutional cornerstone of early America. The American Christian home is the engine of godly dominion and the hope for the future of our nation.

God ordained the family institution in Genesis chapter 1, and throughout the Bible He enumerates the responsibilities of this unit for the care of its members,[35] the education and training of its children,[36] and the stewardship and tithing to God's work on earth.[37]

The home has become little more than a revolving door for millions of Americans. Money, food, and media time are provided by the parents, but the civil government is the dominant teacher controlling the minds of our youth. We must recapture the importance of the Christian home as the foundation of our children's lives.

The first area to reclaim is the education of our youth. Over the last century or so, we have been misled into believing that the public school is as innately American as the flag, Mom, and apple pie. As parents, we must face the facts that tell us that "public schools" have become "statist schools" where the philosophy and the religion of the State are promoted. The uniqueness of America was, and should be again, that parents can educate their children in the religious and moral values of their choice. This is only possible, however, through privately controlled and funded schools where parental control can be maintained.

If we, the Christian parents in America, would make the sacrificial decision to send our children to quality Bible-based private schools or home schools, the battle for our nation would be well on the road to victory. We know this is a challenging task, especially since many Christian schools are not at the level of quality they should be. But there is no alternative. We as families must encourage the development of Christian schools. We who have the means must develop scholarship funds to help those who cannot afford private education. Churches should use their facilities to either start Christian schools or host home-school co-ops.

To enable this godly movement to fulfill its purpose, parents should insist that these schools not only provide Christian teachers and chapel services but a Bible-based curriculum in all subjects. (Many times, schools unwittingly use secular-humanist textbooks and methodology.) That curriculum should reflect the godly educational philosophy of our Founding Fathers and should train our youth to be self-governing citizens of this great land.

Along with education and care of our children, the home must become—if it is to follow the Biblical pattern—the place of hospitality, care, and evangelism once again. Only when the American home and pocketbook open to the needs of the elderly, handicapped, and orphaned will the burden of federal taxation be lifted from our necks. Welfare is a Family and Church responsibility, and so it was in the United States well into the twentieth century.

A final suggestion for our homes is to see them as training centers for our own personal study and for others in our communities. In early America, almost every home had a well-used library.

Many of us may say, "How can I find the time? This sounds too difficult." *We have no choice.* We have passed the buck for too long. If we do not *read* and *think* governmentally, educationally, economically, etc., someone else will do our thinking and decision making for us! God's dominion (or cultural) mandate is for individuals—you and me, not the government.[38]

We are encouraging the development of home study groups throughout America. These groups should focus on training family and friends in our own homes. This training does not need to take place only in school classrooms or online classes.

We must teach our children the sacrifice of our fathers that ensured our liberty and the Providence of God in the founding of our nation in order to give them hope for the future. Out of homes that are willing to take the above suggestions seriously can come the future leaders of America who will more closely resemble the great statesmen of our Founding Fathers' generation.

The Self-Governing Church

The believing Church in America makes up hundreds of thousands of individual organizations. Churches of many different denominations were once the mainstay of every community and its activities. Now there is a growing realization that these local fellowships are the key to rebuilding our nation and reaffirming our covenant with God.

The beginning of any action emanating from the local church should be a training of the congregation for their task in the world. Many fine churches are doing this and are encouraging study groups or Sunday school classes in our Christian heritage and its Biblical base. This book is being used in hundreds of churches for that purpose.

Self-Governing Charitable Free Enterprise

We mentioned at the beginning of this chapter that the self-governing Christian is more than a person who is self-controlled. When seen in the sphere of economics, the self-governing individual is in reality neither an economic unit, as Marx called man, nor a creature of self-interest, as Adam Smith postulated. When properly prepared with God's principles of property and stewardship, the Christian believer is the most productive resource in the world. In past history, he has been the driving force behind the Industrial Revolution, the rise of modern science, and the great American prosperity that flowed from Reformation principles. This miracle of productivity is called the "Biblical work ethic"—a sense of duty to God to do honest work and to pursue excellence in work.

Today, the Christian believer's role is more important than ever, for as he obeys God's principles of economics and learns how to be a godly entrepreneur, wisely investing what God has given him, he can provide the financial base needed to restore our land and take the Gospel to the world.[39]

Here, we must escape the tendency to think that the government, big tech, or the Federal Reserve control our economic destiny. It is up to us to restore economic sanity to our nation through our example, as we look to Biblical principles concerning deficit spending, the graduated income tax, loaning our money to our nation's enemies, government regulation of business, etc. Then, we need to band together with others to promote godly answers that will give us assured economic success.[40] We must resist governmental efforts to control business, steal our property, and drive us to dependence upon its "merciful" handouts.

The COVID catastrophe revealed something more destructive even than our vulnerability to targeted viral attacks, whether accidental or planned. It showcased that, as of today, Americans can be silenced and will submit passively to the destruction of their rights by out-of-control governors and mayors who can shut down their lives and businesses without their consent.

When he came to America in the 1830s, Alexis de Tocqueville said he saw very little evidence of external government, but that the nation seemed to be run by voluntary associations. Most of these associations that cared for the needs of society were tithing associations (Christian ministries), either related to a church or started by some Christian and supported by tithing Christians. Average voluntary giving to charity is way down today. Instead of giving 10 percent or so to God, we now give almost one-half of our income to the government. Until we have made up our giving to God, we should expect to carry this double burden.[41]

If even a fraction of today's one hundred million or so church-goers begins to tithe to godly causes, in and out of the church, then billions of dollars will be released to show forth the love of God, and the role of the federal government will immediately begin to shrink to its proper size. Christian schools, hospitals, businesses, and social agencies can offer real examples of Christian love. Christian think tanks or study centers can use historically proven principles to develop solutions to society's problems. The impact of applying the above ideas will overwhelm the secular humanist—through love, not criticism—and proven facts, not reactionary emotionalism, showing to the world in humility what God can do through individuals committed to Him.

Our Self-Governing Republic

There is an increasing sense of urgency in the hearts of millions of Americans today to restore our self-governing republic. The only possible way for this desire to become a reality is to follow God's unchanging strategy for success. The reality we must face is that the basic structure of government will not conform to its original constitutional model until the people become self-governing in their homes, churches, schools, and businesses.

As we humbly reclaim our rights and responsibilities to educate our children privately and care for the truly needy, we must immediately become involved in the political process. We must provide and elect the godly leaders of the future who will work to restore godly government.

For example, God will not long tolerate a nation whose laws allow for the killing of tens of millions of unborn children. We have inherited peaceful and lawful means of reform. We have no right to speak of civil disobedience when we have not used our constitutional means of redressing grievances.

It is a fatal mistake to forget that the godly way of building a nation presupposes as its foundation godly character and intelligent self-governing people. This is the reason we are failing in our current attempt to set up republics in foreign lands. It does little good to give a copy of the Constitution and plans for popular elections to a people who do not know how to govern themselves. We have allowed the government to become a nanny state because of our apathy and complacency. The battle must be won from the *internal* to the *external*, from content to form, from character to its full expression as a Biblically based republic.

Scripture clearly teaches that God is sovereign over all. But He has delegated limited authority to His ordained institutions: the Family, the Church, and the State (civil government). The government, because it holds the power of the sword, has through the ages tended to usurp and dominate by force the God-given responsibilities of the Family and the Church.

The governmental applications for the principles in this book are many. One basic theme that should be driven home through letters, phone calls, discussion, social media, and political pressure is that civil government in America must shrink to its Biblical and Constitutional function—i.e., to protect the lives, liberties, and estates of the citizens, "that we may lead a peaceful and quiet life, godly and dignified in every way."[42]

Many of us need to train for public service, in this way ensuring that the God-intended purpose for magistrates is limited to its God-ordained purpose. We cannot expect ungodly men and women to lead our nation toward our Founders' perception of a republic. If humanists maintain leadership, Christians will soon be the outcasts of society, and civil liberty will be but a memory. "When the righteous are in authority, the people rejoice: but when the wicked beareth rule, the people mourn."[43]

Is There Real Hope?

Even after seeing the potential means of restoration, the well-informed reader may rightly ask at this point, "Is there a real hope for meaningful cultural change?" We have traveled far down the road from our Biblical origins. Certainly, short-term, pragmatic measures to reform the economy, halt our moral decline, and reverse the flood of government incursion into our lives will not stop the tide of totalitarianism that is sweeping our world.

Alexander Solzhenitsyn, in his acceptance speech for the Templeton Prize for Progress in Religion (May 1983), summarized our present state well when he said:

> We are witnesses to the devastation of the world, be it imposed or voluntarily undergone. The entire twentieth century is being sucked into the vortex of atheism and self-destruction. This plunge into the abyss has aspects that are unquestionably global, dependent neither on political systems, nor on levels of economic and cultural development, nor yet on national peculiarities. And contemporary Europe, seemingly so unlike the Russia of 1913, is today on the verge of the same collapse.... Different parts of the world have followed different paths, but today they are all approaching the threshold of a common ruin.

Today's world has reached the stage which, if it had been described in the preceding centuries, would have called for the cry: "This is the Apocalypse!"

So what hope is there? To be honest, if we live in a world without God, there is very little hope. But if, as we declare in this book, a loving God "presides over the affairs of men," great reformation can and usually does occur in times of great distress.

Speaking as a Christian, Solzhenitsyn ends his sobering address in London by challenging us to remember God and reform our world.

Instead of the ill-advised hopes of the last two centuries, which have reduced us to insignificance and brought us to the brink of nuclear and non-nuclear death, we can only reach with determination for the warm hand of God, which we have so rashly and self-confidently pushed away. If we did this, our eyes would be opened to the errors of this unfortunate twentieth century and our hands could be directed to set them right. There is nothing else to cling to in the landslide: all the thinkers of the Enlightenment can give us nothing.

Our five continents are caught in a whirlwind. But it is during such trials that the highest gifts of the human spirit are manifested. If we perish and lose this world, the fault will be ours alone.

Success in "The Worst of Times"!

Throughout our historical survey, we have highlighted the fact that real world changers are not defeated by bleak circumstances but overcome them. Our patriot forefathers were such men, and their example can be a great lesson for us on the way of success—even in the worst of times.

On January 1, 1781, things looked bleak in the patriot cause. The Pennsylvania line troops had revolted for lack of pay and short enlistments. The reason for no pay was that the continental paper money had collapsed and was "not worth a continental." The army had to live off the land and barter for its needs. Washington, who took no salary for his efforts, did not even have sufficient funds to entertain foreign dignitaries when soliciting their help. This war with one of the great world powers had gone on for eight full years by the beginning of 1781. It was the worst of times.

But let us now survey the events that brought the American cause from defeat to victory in the War of Independence. The final battle that brought victory was at Yorktown, Virginia, on October 19, 1781.

From Defeat to Victory

Led by George Morgan, the Americans defeated Colonel Tarleton's entire detachment at the Battle of the Cowpens, January 17, 1781. Lord Cornwallis, leading the large British army in the south, was infuriated by this defeat. Destroying his heavy baggage, he headed for the Catawba River to cut off the retreat of the small American army.

Cornwallis reached the Catawba River just two hours after General Morgan had crossed. Confident of victory, the British general decided to wait until morning to cross. But during the night, a storm filled the river, detaining his troops. Twice more in the next ten days, Cornwallis nearly overtook the American Army. On February 3, he reached the Yadkin River in North Carolina, just as the Americans were landing on the eastern slopes. But, before he could cross, a sudden flood cut off the British troops again!

On February 13, the Americans reached the Dan River that would lead them into friendly Virginia territory. They crossed, and a few hours later, when Cornwallis arrived, rising waters once again stopped him from defeating the American Army. Even Clinton, the commander-in-chief of Lord Cornwallis, acknowledged that divine Providence had intervened. He wrote: "Here the royal army was again stopped by a sudden rise of the waters, which had only just fallen (almost miraculously) to let the enemy over, who could not else have eluded Lord Cornwallis' grasp, so close was he upon their rear."[44]

The significance of the Battle of Cowpens and the safe retreat of the patriots that followed is that our small army in the south was saved by God's Providence so that it could harass General Cornwallis and drive him to the sea, which set the stage for the final defeat of the British at Yorktown in October 1781.

Interposing Hand of Heaven

The above providential account is but one of many events that converged like parts of a well-laid cosmic plan to defeat the British. For example:

1. If General Washington had not decided to leave New York and march to Yorktown when he did, Cornwallis would have been reinforced.

2. If Robert Morris, the generous and capable merchant, had not used extraordinary means to raise money to pay Washington's troops, they would have gone home rather than to Yorktown.

3. If France had not sent a fleet from the West Indies (unknown to Washington), which arrived just in time to defeat the British fleet sent to relieve General Cornwallis at Yorktown, Cornwallis could have escaped. In this battle, the French fleet, under Admiral de Grasse, soundly defeated the British, cutting off all sea routes.

4. If a sudden tornado-like storm had not stopped Lord Cornwallis in his last-minute attempt on October 16, 1781, to cross the York River and escape to New York, the war would have dragged on.

After the surrender at Yorktown, General Washington acknowledged the many Providential events of the war. He declared the day after the surrender to be a day of Thanksgiving, and his troops were directed to attend religious services. On November 15, 1781, Washington wrote to the president of Congress:

> *I take a particular pleasure in acknowledging that the interposing hand of Heaven, in the various instances of our extensive preparations for this operation, has been most conspicuous and remarkable.*[45]

If Then, Why Not Now?

The "interposing hand of Heaven" should be just as obvious to us today as it was to our Founders. They consistently declared church, town, state, and national days of prayer, humiliation, and fasting. They knew that the nations were being sifted by the hand of God. They understood periods of calamity, hardship, war, or pandemic as important times to align themselves with the will of God. Through personal repentance and the acknowledgment of God's Providence in their history, our ancestors reaffirmed the American Covenant over and over. What is to keep us from such a reaffirmation? Only if we are willing to have the faith of our fathers will we be able to restore the nation they built. Trusting in Him who is Master of all, we can follow His strategy for success.

Conclusion

The untold story of the American Covenant began with a group of Christians who met together off the coast of New England, covenanting with their God to form a nation that would glorify Him and spread His Gospel. They were followed by many others, most of whom reaffirmed and restated their initial compact. Out of their covenant with God and their willingness to apply His Word to all areas of life came a Biblically based republic that has promoted the greatest expansion of the Gospel in the history of man. We must now realize that we can no longer live off the heritage and covenant of our fathers. We must reaffirm their covenant and move ahead to become the pilgrims of the twenty-first century, bearing the cross if we intend to wear the crown.

Our Founders did not claim to have all the truth. They did not have the Biblical study aids we have. They did not have a Biblically based republic upon which to base their efforts. They did not have hours every day free from toil to use for study. But they did have a vision—a future orientation. They saw themselves standing upon the shoulders of faithful believers through the ages. They knew there were greater things yet to come. Their faith aligned with that of Samuel Adams, the father of the American Revolution, who said at the signing of the Declaration of Independence:

> We have this day restored the Sovereign to Whom all men ought to be obedient. He reigns in heaven, and from the rising to the setting of the Sun, let His kingdom come.

Pilgrim Edward Winslow relates what Pastor John Robinson shared in his farewell address to the Pilgrims, just before the *Mayflower* set sail from England for the New World:

> Here also he [Pastor Robinson] put us in mind of our church covenant, at least that part of it whereby we promise and covenant with God and one another to receive whatsoever light or truth shall be made known to us from His written Word; but withal exhorted us to take heed what we receive for truth, and well to examine and compare it and weigh it with other Scriptures of truth before we receive it. For saith he, it is not possible the Christian world should

come so lately out of such thick anti-Christian darkness, and that full perfection of knowledge break forth at once.[46]

God surely has given us further light. Let us take His Word and truth to the four corners of the world so that we may hasten the day when "the earth shall be full of the knowledge of the LORD as the waters cover the sea."[47]

Our rededication to the American Covenant is the only hope for the survival of our republic. By trusting in the Almighty, Who is Master of all, we can walk with Him in covenant, following His strategy for success.

For FREE bonus material & in-depth study on a variety of topics beyond what you find here in *The American Covenant*, visit WorldHistoryInstitute.com/free-downloads.

Chapter 8 Study Questions

1. How should Christians determine their life goals?

2. What are some of the responsibilities of parents in the education of their children?

3. How can your church be more effective in meeting society's social problems?

4. Why is tithing so important?

5. What was the original source of American prosperity?

6. What values should be reflected by the Christian's vocation and lifestyle?

7. What can we do to restore the structure of the American Christian republic?

8. Why do we need to focus on principles before issues?

9. What is the Biblical position on "deficit spending" and taxation?

10. What kind of voluntary associations should we institute and support?

11. Why do we need to reaffirm the American Covenant?

Chapter 8 Notes

1. Hosea 4:6.
2. Matthew 16:18.
3. Exodus 9:1.
4. Second Corinthians 5:18–19.
5. Dinesh D'Souza, *What's So Great about Christianity* (Carol Stream, IL: Tyndale House Publishers, 2007), 9.
6. William J. Federer, *America's God and Country Encyclopedia of Quotations* (St. Louis, MO: Amerisearch Inc., 2000), 377.
7. George Washington, *Writings of George Washington*, Lawrence B. Evans, ed. (New York: G. P. Putnam's Sons, 1908), 324.
8. Verna M. Hall, *The Christian History of the Constitution of the United States of America: Christian Self-Government*, (San Francisco: Foundation for American Christian Education, 1975, 8.
9. Isaiah 1: 18.
10. First Peter 4:11.
11. Luke 14:28.
12. John 14:12.
13. Luke 12:48.
14. Luke 13:31–33.
15. Matthew 26:51–54.
16. Proverbs 4:23.
17. Isaiah 28:10.
18. First Corinthians 10:31; Second Corinthians 10:5.
19. Psalm 8:3–6.
20. Psalm 127:3–4.
21. Proverbs 22:6.
22. Deuteronomy 6:4.
23. Deuteronomy 6:5.
24. Romans 5:8.
25. Deuteronomy 6:6–7.
26. Deuteronomy 6:8–9.
27. Hebrews 10:16, after Jeremiah 31:33.
28. Deuteronomy 6:10–12.

29. Deuteronomy 7:9.

30. Genesis 18:17–19.

31. Second Corinthians 5:19.

32. Hall, *The Christian History of the Constitution* , 248.

33. Rosalie J. Slater, *Teaching and Learning America's Christian History* (San Francisco: Foundation for American Christian Education, 1975), 69.

34. John 8:36.

35. First Timothy 5:8.

36. Proverbs 22:6.

37. First Corinthians 16:2.

38. See chapter 1.

39. Luke 19:12–27.

40. Deuteronomy 28.

41. Malachi 3.

42. First Timothy 2:2.

43. Proverbs 29:2 KJV.

44. William Hosmer, "Remember our Bicentennial—1781," *Foundation for Christian Self-Government Newsletter* (June 1981): 5.

45. Washington, *Writings*, 23:343.

46. Hall, *The Christian History of the Constitution,* 184.

47. Isaiah 11:9.

Appendices

A Deeper Dive into the Impact of the Covenants

APPENDIX 1

PANDEMIC, PLAGUE, AND PESTILENCE

*T*he greatest victories in history have most often occurred during times of great catastrophes. Americans are enduring a series of devastating trials, including the recent pandemic. History provides hope that Americans can prevail against the spiritual, economic, and cultural challenges ahead.

The Army of Compassion vs. the Roman Pandemics

Two of the great pandemics of history swept through the Roman Empire in the second and third centuries. The first plague lasted for fifteen years, killing up to a fourth of the population of the empire. An even greater pandemic struck a century later. Rome's failed response to these plagues contributed to the total collapse of the Roman Empire. However, during these tragedies, a new faith, Christianity, emerged in the empire. The new Army of Compassion became the greatest healing and liberating force in history.

Rome and other cities in the empire "were far more crowded, crime-infested, filthy, disease-ridden, and miserable than are the worst cities in the world today."[1] One can only imagine the depth of despair brought on by a plague in these places. Rome's pagan gods and priests provided no solace to the suffering people. Their gods were brutal and had no interest in the plight of human beings. Their emperors were especially cruel and demanded to be worshipped. Life for the individual was of little value. "The individual was regarded as of value only if he was a part of the political fabric and able to contribute to its uses, as though it were the end of his being to aggrandize the State."[2]

During the third-century pandemic, Bishop Dionysius was a leading pastor in Rome. He described how the pagan Romans treated their sick: "At the first onset of the disease, they pushed the sufferers away and fled from their dearest [family members], throwing them into the roads before they were dead, and treated unburied corpses as dirt.... In the pagan world, and especially among the philosophers, mercy was regarded as a character defect and pity as a pathological emotion."[3] Without the hope of heaven or the fear of judgment, people of the empire lived their entire lives in a culture of death. Murder, suicide, and infanticide permeated the empire.

Into this dying world, an Army of Compassion appeared, which held a high view of the sanctity of human life. They represented a new kingdom with a new King. They were persecuted by emperors and often thrown to the lions in the Coliseum. Many took refuge in the Roman catacombs beneath the city. This army was not armed with swords but armed with mercy and love for all people, as they followed their Lord's admonition to "love your neighbor as yourself." Their character and bravery became legendary throughout the empire. Entire cities, such as Antioch, began to embrace the Christian faith.

In times of plague, the Christians not only nursed their own families and those of the faith but cared for anyone in need or sick. These believers endured ten major persecutions over 250 years. Yet, they continued to grow in number and influence throughout the empire.

In the midst of the pandemic, Christianity provided an island of mercy and security. Bishop Dionysius observed the Christian response: "Most of our brethren were unsparing in their exceeding love and brotherly kindness. They held fast to each other and visited the sick fearlessly, and ministered to them continually, serving them in Christ. They died with them most joyfully."[4]

One of the leaders of this new force faced off with the governor of Rome during the second pandemic. Lawrence was the leading pastor of the church that met in the catacombs beneath the city. The church had a powerful ministry, especially to the poor and downtrodden. Lawrence recorded a list of 1,500 needy people fed and cared for with the voluntary gifts of Christians. The Roman governor heard of the gold and silver vessels that were said to have been used in the services of the church. His plan was to seize this wealth for the empire. He had Lawrence arrested and dragged before him. The governor demanded that Lawrence give him the riches. The pastor replied, "In three days I will bring before you the greatest treasures of the church." With this assurance, the governor released Lawrence.

After three days, the governor came back to Lawrence. "Are the treasures collected?" The pastor replied, "They are, my lord. Will you enter and view them?" He opened a door and displayed, to the astounded gaze of the governor, the poor pensioners of the church, a chosen number—a row of the lame, a row of the blind, orphans and widows, the helpless and weak. The governor turned fiercely upon Lawrence, saying, "What mean you by this mockery? Where are the treasures of gold and silver you promised to deliver up?" "These that you see before you," replied Lawrence, "are the true treasures of the church. In the widows and orphans, you behold her gold and silver, her pearls and precious stones. These are her real riches. Make use of them by asking for their prayers; they will prove your best weapons against your foes."

The governor, enraged at not securing the gold, commanded his guards to seize Lawrence and have him burned. The saint triumphed over the tyrant to the last. He did not cry out in the flames, but in his dying breath prayed for the conversion of the entire empire. Witnessing his great faith, the executioner was converted at that moment and was also martyred.[5]

Pandemics in Rome exposed the cruelty of pagan religion but also showcased the compassion and unconditional love of Christians. The people of the Roman Empire began to turn from their pagan ways to the God of Christianity. Just sixty years after Lawrence's death, Constantine became the first emperor to bow the knee to the compassionate, all-powerful Christ. He legalized the faith. The old empire would soon die. But a far more compassionate and advanced Christian civilization would arise.

The Black Death: The Greatest of All Plagues (A.D. 1345–1349)

In 1345, the Black Death, a bubonic plague, became the greatest pandemic in recorded history. It first ravaged Asia then descended upon

Europe in 1345 and swept into England in 1348. The deadly bacteria were carried by flea-infested rats on ships from Asia. The plague killed up to 50 million people—roughly 60 percent of the entire population of Europe. Life came to a standstill, except for the mass burials of the dead.

Like the headless horseman, the Black Death marched up the Thames River in England, killing one hundred thousand people in London alone. When the plague reached Oxford University, half of the students and professors were struck down. A young student, John Wycliffe, saw his friends die agonizing deaths, with raging fevers and black boils covering their bodies. It seemed that the end of mankind was at hand.

Wycliffe "passed days and nights in his cell groaning…and calling upon God to show him the path he ought to follow."[6] He threw himself on the mercy of God as he studied Scripture. John was transformed as he learned that salvation came only as an unearned gift of grace from his Savior. This brilliant scholar poured all his energies into the work of translating the Word of God from Latin into English.

For decades, Wycliffe was under constant attack from royal tyrants and church prelates. Yet undaunted, he trained an army of "poor preachers" to teach everyday people to read—especially to read the Bible. The Bible was a forbidden book during the Middle Ages.

Throughout the fifteenth century, Wycliffe's disciples, called "Lollards," reached much of England with the liberating truths of Scripture. Although many were persecuted and martyred, these Christians changed the future of England and the world. This transformative movement was launched by one young college student who was brought to Christ in the middle of the greatest plague in world history.

The Pilgrim Pestilence (1620–1621)

In November of 1620, four hundred years ago in 2020, the Pilgrims arrived in New England. They soon became victims of a deadly epidemic that took the lives of half their number within a few months. They had been transformed by the love of God and learned from the Scriptures the sacred value of each human life. As Jesus taught: "Do to others as you would have them do to you.... Love your neighbor as yourself.... Greater love has no one than this: to lay down one's life for one's friends."[7]

On Christmas Day, 1620, the Pilgrims began constructing their first building. Soon they were challenged to obey the words of their Lord. During the deadly sickness that winter, all but six or seven of the 102 settlers were bedridden and writhing in pain. William Brewster was their spiritual leader and the eldest among them. He was among the few who worked tirelessly to save his fellow settlers.

The disease began to take the lives of the sailors still aboard the *Mayflower*. About half of the crew were sick and dying, including the ship's officer, who was among those who had cursed and mocked the Pilgrims during the voyage. But the officer now praised the Pilgrims who were nursing him. He said, "You...show your love like Christians indeed to one another, but we let one another lie and die like dogs."[8]

By winter's end, half of the settlers had died. They were buried in a common grave. But these Pilgrims, as well as the Jamestown settlement in Virginia, became the first pioneers of the Army of Compassion in the New World.

The surviving Pilgrims became friends with King Massasoit of the neighboring Wampanoag tribe. When the king became deathly ill, the Pilgrims nursed him back to health. They signed a peace treaty of mutual assistance with the Wampanoags. The treaty was upheld for fifty years.[9]

When the *Mayflower* returned to England in the spring of 1621, not one of the surviving Pilgrims chose to return. However, the testimony of the Pilgrims' brave compassion reverberated throughout England. The word spread that America could be settled in peace.

In 1630, thirteen hundred English settlers arrived in Boston. They contracted the same deadly illnesses the Pilgrims had endured. The Pilgrims sent their doctor, Dr. Fuller, and others to nurse the new settlers back to health. Dr. Fuller died in his efforts. The Boston settlers, coming from the higher classes of English society, had mocked the "Separatist" Pilgrims when they were in England. But in the New World, they came to love them and even emulated their form of representative government. This event changed the course of history. It set

America on the path towards a self-governing, representative republic rather than continuing the tyrannical, monarchial system of Europe.

Catastrophes to Great Awakenings

In 1720, there was a stock market collapse in London that led to a great depression in England and the American colonies. It was a time of spiritual apathy and decay in both places. The mighty French threatened to annihilate the colonies. At the same time, filth, disease, and death ravaged the workers in the coal mines of Wales and the child sweatshops of London.

But in the 1730s, a new wind blew across the English-speaking world. John Wesley and George Whitefield began their preaching throughout the British Isles as the people flocked to hear the transforming Gospel. The revival of faith spread to America. Whitefield joined with men like Jonathan Edwards of Connecticut to spark America's First Great Awakening.

This awakening of repentant hearts toward God was not an escape from the world. These new believers did not separate from their civil duties but now dedicated themselves to reforming first themselves and then their society. Dr. Marvin Olasky says that the revived Americans "emphasized God's sovereignty over all.... They strove for holiness in government as well as in their own lives." It is estimated that one-half of the people in the south and one-third of those in the north came to faith in Jesus Christ just before the War of Independence. John Adams, Father of the American Revolution, said that the real war was fought and won before the British invaded. He said, "What do we mean by the American Revolution? The war? That was no part of the Revolution; it was only an effect and consequence of it. The Revolution was in the minds of the people,... a change in their religious sentiments [convictions]."[10]

Wall Street Awakening

In 1857 in New York City, another Great Awakening was birthed. It began with a pastor and a prayer meeting of six men. They prayed for a revival in Manhattan, as most people had drifted away from the faith. Suddenly, another stock market crash occurred on Wall Street. The prayer meeting grew from six men to hundreds and then thousands of men. Within a few months, ten thousand men had taken over the Broadway theaters at lunch for two-hour prayer meetings. The awakening spread from New York to England, Scotland, and then around the world.

When the Civil War began two years later, an epidemic of infectious disease began to decimate the ranks of both the North and the South. Over six hundred thousand men died in the Civil War. More than half of those men died of disease, not in battle. As the awakening spread, pastors were asked to preach in the battle camps. Untold tens of thousands of soldiers on both sides committed their lives to Christ. After the war, the nation slowly healed, as Christian forgiveness and compassion soothed and comforted the people.

President Abraham Lincoln's words in the dark days of the Civil War speak to us today:

> *We have been the recipients of the choicest bounties of Heaven. We have been preserved these many years in peace and prosperity. We have grown in numbers, wealth, and power as no other nation has ever known. But we have forgotten God. We have forgotten the gracious hand which preserved us in peace and multiplied and enriched and strengthened us; and we have vainly imagined, in the deceitfulness of our hearts, that all these blessings were produced by some superior wisdom and virtue of our own. Intoxicated with unbroken success, we have become too self-sufficient to feel the necessity of redeeming and preserving grace, too proud to pray to the God that made us! It behooves us then to humble ourselves before the offended Power, to confess our national sins and to pray for clemency and forgiveness.*[11]

"Blessed is the nation whose God is the LORD" (Psalm 33:12).

Appendix 1 Notes

1. Rodney Stark, *The Triumph of Christianity* (New York: Harper Collins, 2011) p. 102.

2. Richard Frothingham, *The Rise of the Republic of the United States* (Boston: Little, Brown, 1910), 6.

3. Stark, *The Triumph of Christianity*, 112–15.

4. Alvin J. Schmidt, *How Christianity Changed the World* (Grand Rapids: Zondervan, 2001) 152.

5. John Foxe, *Christian Martyrs of the World* (San Antonio, TX: Mantle Ministries, 1986), 84–86.

6. J. H. Merle d'Aubigné, *History of the Reformation* (Grand Rapids: Baker Book House, 1976), 703.

7. Luke 6:31; Matthew 22:39; John 15:13 NIV.

8. William Bradford, *The Plymouth Settlement* (San Antonio, TX: American Heritage Ministries, 1988), 78.

9. Ibid., 79.

10. Dinesh D'Souza, *What's So Great About Christianity* (Carol Stream, IL: Tyndale House, 2007), 72.

11. Abraham Lincoln, Proclamation of a National Fast Day, March 30, 1863.

APPENDIX 2

THE FRENCH VS. THE AMERICAN REVOLUTION

Vital Lessons to Benefit Us Today

*W*e, the American people, are facing a day of decision. Our choice was stated well by President Ronald Reagan: "You and I are told we must choose between a left or right, but I suggest there is no such thing as a left or right. There is only an up or down. Up to man's age-old dream—the maximum of individual *freedom* consistent with order, or down to the ant heap of *totalitarianism*."

Two landmark revolutions, the American Revolution (1776) and the French Revolution (1789), are commonly taught as revolts against tyrannical kings for the benefit of the people. But the truth of history presents a very different picture. Yes, each country did face tyranny. But how they dealt with it made all the difference. The French Revolution repeated the same errors of hundreds of failed rebellions throughout history. The American Revolution was a war of self-defense and unique in history. It defended the Biblical truth that "All men are created equal, that they are endowed by their Creator with certain unalienable rights, that among these are Life, Liberty, and the pursuit of Happiness."

The following stories are examples of two great nations: one chose the well-worn path to totalitarianism, and the other chose the path to freedom under law with dependence upon divine Providence. The choices of these two nations have shaped the modern world.

The French Revolution

Much myth has been written about the French Revolution. Many have been taught to believe the revolt was a spontaneous uprising of the everyday people to end discrimination and monarchy. In reality, the revolt was a diabolical anti-Christian horror. The motto of the revolution was "Liberty, Equality, Fraternity, or Death." The only promise fulfilled in this motto was "Death." Not only did forty thousand people lose their heads under the blade of the guillotine in Paris alone, over three hundred thousand French citizens were publicly executed in the countryside through mass murder, including firing squads and drowning. Ultimately, many millions of young Frenchmen were slaughtered in the twenty-five years of foreign wars that emanated from this reign of terror.

How did this atrocity occur? Lord Acton, in his *Lectures on the French Revolution*, said, "The appalling thing in the French Revolution is not the tumult but the *design*. Through all the fire and smoke we perceive the evidence of *calculating organization. The managers* remain studiously concealed and masked; but there is no doubt about their presence from the first." It was not spontaneous. *It was planned.*[1]

The plan for the revolution unfolded in France, the world's most prosperous nation at the time. But this country was ripe for chaos. France by the eighteenth century had made a hard turn away from its Christian heritage. Its kings and corrupt clergy had carried out a century-long wholesale genocide or exile of at least one-fifth of the population who had chosen to become Christians of the Reformation. These intelligent, productive citizens who were persecuted were called Huguenots. This fatal cleansing of Christianity from French culture virtually eliminated the once-thriving literate and productive middle class of the nation.

Generations of illiterate Frenchmen grew up without any Biblical knowledge. They became easy prey for beguiling Enlightenment philosophers like Jean-Jacques Rousseau and the atheist Voltaire. Rejecting the Bible and God's sovereignty, these thinkers enthroned human reason and the dream of man's "progressive" liberation without God. Denying the sin nature of man, Rousseau propounded his theory of the "naked savage," unpolluted by the restrictions of "moral law" and "civilization." He lived out his philosophy of unfettered hedonism. He had twenty-three children and abandoned them all to poor houses, where they all died of starvation and neglect. His motto was: "Do away with the family."

Rousseau died in 1789, the year the French Revolution began, but his character and wicked philosophy were stamped on the ensuing disaster. A small cadre of "enlightened" radicals, such as Jean Paul Marat, George Danton, and Maximilien Robespierre railed against the French monarch King Louis XVI and the rich nobles who congregated at the castle at Versailles. Using class warfare and identity politics, these libertines promised the peasants freedom and bread for all. The people believed the lies of these politicians, and on June 14, 1789, a mob was incited to storm the Bastille, an ancient prison and symbol of the monarchy. The conspirators hired mobs and agitators to stage "spontaneous" riots in Paris. Business owners, shopkeepers, nobles, and finally the king and his family were targeted. They all suffered the loss of their heads under the guillotine.

For the central goal of the revolution—that is, totalitarian control—to be achieved, all vestiges of Christian heritage had to be destroyed. Ancient Rome, with its worship of emperors, was their model. Robespierre declared himself the high priest of their "Cult of Reason" with its satanic roots. Over two thousand churches were turned into "Temples of Reason," as hundreds of priests were drowned in the Seine River. The press and theaters were turned into instruments of State propaganda to ridicule anything Christian. Great festivals were staged to pacify the masses. At the festival at the Notre Dame Cathedral, an actress (actually a prostitute), was enthroned as the goddess of France.

Then, in 1793, the infamous Reign of Terror swept the nation. The "Committee for Public Safety"—i.e., the execution squad led by Robespierre—determined each day who would die. They began to butcher tens of thousands of citizens of Paris, regardless of their rank. Individuals were paraded through the streets and then beheaded before the multitudes under the guillotine. Their bloody heads were held up for all to see and cheer. Who were these people being beheaded? Anyone who fell out of favor with the "Committee"—which is to say, anyone who was not "politically correct." It was a celebration of death. Without the moral constraints of a higher law, the leaders' political enemies list soon degenerated into the mass murder of all dissenters. By the time the Reign of Terror was over in 1793, forty thousand citizens in Paris alone had lost their heads. Modern Marxism, the heir of this revolutionary ideology, has practiced this same debauchery on steroids.

The plan of the revolutionaries included the deceptive use of elections as a tool against political opposition. They asked for everyone to vote on their new revolutionary constitution for their faux "republic." Over one and a half million people voted. What the people didn't know is that 44,000 members of the Committee of Vigilance (secret police) were taking down the names of anyone who voted against the revolution. Then they rounded up 150,000 Frenchmen who dared to vote against the radical constitution and shot them to death, or beat them to save ammunition.

The Reign of Terror finally ended after Robespierre himself fell out of favor and was beheaded, as well as his fellow conspirator George Danton, before the people of Paris. The French Revolution collapsed, leaving the nation in ruins. Not only did it fail, but it led to a radical backlash that carried France into a military despotism under Napoleon Bonaparte a few years later. He declared himself emperor and plunged all of Europe into twenty years of war. Millions of Frenchmen were slaughtered in Napoleon's drive for world conquest. France, even after two hundred years, has never fully recovered.

The French Revolution was the first of the modern, secular, socialist revolutions. It was followed by a second French revolt called the Revolution of 1848—the first avowed Marxist revolution. The German, Russian, and Chinese communist revolutions of the twentieth century followed the French strategy, killing over one hundred and fifty million people. And today, the rebellious spirit of the French Revolution and its fatally failed experiment in governance has permeated all of America's institutions.

Cultural Marxists and atheist globalists in our generation are following the same strategy seen in the French Revolution. "The tools of the French Revolution were disinformation, propaganda, the subversion of language (changing the meanings of words), malice, envy, hatred, anger, jealousy, mass murder, and foreign military adventurism [foreign wars] as a DIVERSION to distract the masses from the failure of government."[2] These same devises have been used by modern revolutionaries such as Lenin, Stalin, Mao Zedong, Fidel Castro, and now the socialists in control of many of America's institutions.

The true history of America's War of Independence stands in stark contrast to that of the French Revolution. By learning that history, we can, by God's grace, recover America's "holy cause of liberty" and avoid another anti-Christian holocaust in the coming years.

The American War of Independence

The American Revolution was an act of self-defense and was not an offensive war to disobey legitimate, lawful authority. It was fought to defend the colonists' wives, children, lives, and property from an out-of-control tyrant abusing his power. The colonists were upholding the rule of law and the charters agreed to with English rulers since the earliest colonies. Colonists were guaranteed all the rights of English citizens. But in the mid-eighteenth century, King George decided to crush the American colonies into submission, ignoring the law and 150 years of precedent.

England had become drunk with the power of an ever-expanding, worldwide empire. The English, especially the king and Parliament— awash in wealth—disregarded their centuries-long march toward liberty. In the seventeenth century, the English had fought their own wars against the lawless dynasties of Charles I and James II. From these revolutions, the people, who were at that time committed to Biblical liberty, created the English Bill of Rights and the "Glorious Revolution" of 1688. The English and continental reformers, including Martin Luther, John Calvin, and eminent ministers like Samuel Rutherford, had clearly taught the Biblical rights to resistance to tyranny. Tyrants were to be removed by lesser magistrates—the peoples' representatives—not by mobs or individuals. This Biblical doctrine is called "interposition."

Increasingly in the eighteenth century, the English became envious of the colonists' growing power and wealth. By 1764, the king had decided to take dictatorial control over the colonies. He ignored the mutual agreements—covenants between the colonies and their monarch that had been in effect for five generations.

The king began his unlawful crackdown on the colonists with acts such as the Stamp Act, meant to control all media and printing among the colonists. Much like media giants today, King George attempted to control all written communication. He wanted to censor all opposing thought by forcing his stamp of approval to be placed on all printed matter. The colonists forced the repeal of the Stamp Act, but Parliament then immediately passed the Declaratory Act. It stated that they, the Parliament, could pass any act to control the colonists without their consent, effectively destroying their freedoms. Then the king attacked and occupied Boston in 1774 with an army of four thousand men. He ordered that the private weapons of the colonists be confiscated. In the "shot heard around the world," on April 19, 1775, nine hundred British soldiers opened fire on seventy-six militiamen in Lexington, intent on disarming the citizenry. English warships then bombed Norfolk, Virginia, into oblivion. In the summer of 1776, the king sent 130 ships with 33,000 men to enslave New York City and crush all of the colonies.

The Colonial leaders of the resistance to England's growing tyranny in America were nearly all Protestant Christians. They were highly literate students of both history and Scripture. The Colonial pastors were the most powerful, intellectual, political, and spiritual influence on the colonists. Yale professor Harry Stout says: "The New England sermon had a topical range and social influence so powerful in shaping cultural values, meanings, and a sense of corporate purpose that even television pales by comparison." Stout says that the average colonist in New England listened to about seven thousand sermons in a lifetime. Many of these treatises were Biblical expositions of the "just-war theory" reasoned through the centuries. So, the Founders of America followed the Biblical plan to resist despotic rulers as written in such documents as the Magna Carta, Vindiciae Contra Tyrannos (the Defense of Liberty against Tyrants), and *Lex Rex* (*The Law Is King*). All of these works were widely studied in the colonies at this time.

Samuel Adams, the father of the American Revolution, is often caricatured as a rabble-rousing brawler. In fact, he was a devout Christian who committed his life to Christ while a student at Harvard during the Great Awakening led by George Whitefield. He spent most of his life teaching the principles of Biblical liberty to his fellow colonists. His *Committees of Correspondence* were created for the colonists to communicate with each other in the 1770s. They were as pervasive a tool for education as the media is today. Adams led his compatriots to reason from the Scriptures, teaching his fellow colonists to be self-governing and law abiding. Samuel led his compatriots to reason and plead with the king in formal letters of reconciliation. But when the king denied all their lawful appeals and began to attack and murder the colonists, Adams was a powerful force calling the people to stand and fight for their liberty under God. And so they did.

Just days before the first shots of war were heard in Lexington, Patrick Henry gave his "Give Me Liberty or Give Me Death" speech. In that speech, he rehearsed for the legislators of Virginia how they had followed the peaceful strategy of reconciliation with the king. Patrick said, "Sir, we have done everything that could be done to avert the storm which is now coming on. We have petitioned; we have remonstrated; we have supplicated; we have prostrated ourselves before the throne.... Our petitions have been slighted; our remonstrances have produced additional violence and insult; our supplications have been disregarded; and we have been spurned, with contempt, from the foot of the throne! In vain, after these things, may we indulge the fond hope of peace and reconciliation. There is no longer any room for hope. If we wish to be free...we must fight! I repeat it, sir, we must fight! An appeal to arms and to the God of hosts is all that is left to us."

The Declaration of Independence is America's founding document. It is in the form of a covenant, like the Mayflower Compact. It is an agreement between God and the people who have been created equal, to form a new nation. They defend their right to do so by listing dozens of felonies committed by the king of England against his citizens in the colonies. Based on these facts, they declared him to be a tyrant—a renegade ruler. Unlike the French Revolution, with its riots, destruction of property, and mass murder, the American defensive war shunned the pillaging of private property and generally was fought avoiding civilian casualties. We won against all odds.

The leaders of the colonies had every right and responsibility to interpose themselves between the king and the people. Unlike the

French Revolution, which worshipped false gods, the American Revolution acknowledged a "firm reliance upon divine Providence." Samuel Adams gave his American Independence speech shortly before the fifty-six Founders signed the Declaration. Adams said, "We have explored the temple of royalty, and found that the idol we have bowed down to has eyes which see not, ears that hear not our prayers, and a heart like the nether millstone. *We have this day restored the Sovereign, to whom alone men ought to be obedient.... From the rising to the setting sun, may His kingdom come.*"

The American War of Independence resulted in the creation of the Biblically based constitutional republic that has brought more freedom to the world than any other nation in history. Our democratic republic has lasted almost two and a half centuries. The Founders built safeguards into our Constitution so that we would be able to peacefully prevent small minorities of power-hungry rebels from seizing dictatorial powers over the people. Neither the French nor the Americans had those safeguards back in the eighteenth century.

We have no right to talk of rebellion or violence at this time. We have a Biblical and constitutional procedure that must be followed. Never is their justification for personal vengeance or taking the law into our own hands. That is vigilante justice, and the rotten fruit of the French Revolution reveals the consequences of such action.

I encourage my fellow Americans, however, to make careful study of the Founders' humble but brave stand for liberty. We, at this moment especially, must be fully invested in our civic duties, our private charities, and the education of our children in the Bible and the Constitution. We must support our local and state "lesser magistrates," governors, mayors, and sheriffs in upholding the rule of law. Then, as "we the people" stand together in covenant, trusting in God, no tyrant will be able to enslave us. If they do try, then, and only then, are we bound by God to stand in the "shield wall," as did the American Founders, and declare "with firm reliance upon the protection of divine Providence," that we, like our forebears, "pledge our lives, our fortunes, and our sacred honor." If that day comes, we must say with Patrick Henry: "I know not what course others may take, but as for me, *give me liberty or give me death!*"

Today, America is more dangerously divided than at any time since the Civil War. Many fear the republic will not survive. But let us remember that the odds against the Founders succeeding against the most powerful empire since Rome were nearly impossible. Yet, by depending upon divine Providence, they pledged their "lives, their fortunes and sacred honor" and were victorious.

But in our hour of decision, we cannot rest upon the sacrifice of those who have come before. Ronald Reagan wisely warned us:

> *Freedom is never more than one generation from extinction. We didn't pass it to our children in the bloodstream. It must be fought for, protected, and handed on to them to do the same. Or one day we will spend our sunset years telling our children and our children's children what it was once like in the United States when men were free.*

Now is the time to stand for the Truth that will set us free! Abraham Lincoln saw beyond the conflict and division of his time. He said, "Freedom is the natural condition of the human race, in which the Almighty intended men to live. Those who fight the purpose of the Almighty will not succeed. They always have been, they always will be, beaten."

Appendix 2 Notes

1.   Colin Newman, "Bastille Day and Why Christians Should Not Celebrate the French Revolution," *ReformationSA.org*, July 11, 2016, reformationsa.org.

2.   Ibid.

APPENDIX 3

THE SPEECH THAT SAVED THE U.S. CONSTITUTION

*I*n 1776, the American patriots had just broken free from the tyrannical pattern of nations throughout history. In the Declaration of Independence, they pledged their "firm reliance upon divine Providence" as they formed their new nation. Eleven years later, fifty-six delegates were sent from the states to Philadelphia. They hoped to create a lasting Constitution that would cement their union yet maintain their freedom as states. For accountability, power was not to be centralized (at the top) but was to be in the hands of *We, the People* at the local level.

After the long, hot summer of 1787, the delegates emerged with a proposed Constitution. But to be implemented, the document had to be ratified by three-fourths of the states. But what would cause the diverse and independent states to unite behind this Constitution? They had won their freedom from England and the tyrant King George. They did not want to create another all-powerful national government.

Their fears of falling back into tyranny were well grounded, because when America began, dictators ruled nearly all the world. For five thousand years, citizens everywhere in the world were born into iron-clad caste systems, condemning them to lifelong bondage, poverty, and hopelessness.

Because of these legitimate concerns, a battle ensued regarding the approval of the new Constitution. This battle would divide fellow patriots like Patrick Henry and George Washington. However, by the fall of 1788, eight states had voted to approve the Constitution. One more state was needed for approval. It would be up to New Hampshire, as the ninth state, to determine its fate.

At this critical turning point, the New Hampshire legislature chose Dr. Samuel Langdon, former president of Harvard and esteemed clergyman, to address the representatives. America's future hung in the balance. Langdon's intelligent, powerful speech helped turn the tide in favor of the new Constitution.[1] He lifted the argument above the rancor of partisan politics.

Calling the Founders Back to the Covenants of Scripture

How did Dr. Langdon encourage a skeptical New Hampshire legislature to ratify the Constitution? He reminded them that the new U.S. Constitution was patterned after the divine constitution of Moses and the decentralized republic of the ancient Hebrews (1400–1000 B.C.). He said that this liberating form of accountable and just (fair) government is "a pattern to the world in all ages" for any nation desiring freedom and prosperity.

The Israelites, he said, were transformed from a band of disorderly families coming out of bondage in Egypt into self-governing, orderly tribes. He said there was no example in history of a people making "this quick progress of the Israelites, from abject slavery, ignorance, and almost total want of order to a national establishment perfected in all its parts far beyond all other kingdoms and states!"

Langdon detailed how the Hebrews formed their successful republic. First, before the Hebrew tribes arrived at Mt. Sinai, Moses instructed them to elect character-filled leaders at the local level. These rulers were to be competent, godly, and honest, and they would refuse bribes.[2] These local elections decentralized power in their new republic.

Second, at Mt. Sinai, God graciously gave His people few concise but perfect laws that would protect life, families, personal freedoms, private property, and personal reputations without partiality: the Ten Commandments and other laws.[3]

Langdon described the Lord's compassion: "God did not leave a people, wholly unskilled in legislation, to make laws for themselves: He took this important matter wholly into His own hands.... Had the unexperienced multitude been left to themselves to draw up a system of civil and military government, it would have been entirely beyond their abilities to comprehend so complicated a subject; they must have committed innumerable mistakes." The Lord lovingly created a representative constitutional republic with maximum freedom and no need for an earthly king. Through the centuries, this plan has liberated hundreds of millions of people from bondage.

Third, Langdon detailed the basic structure of this Hebrew republic. He said:

> A SENATE was constructed, as necessary for the future government of the nation, under a chief commander [EXECUTIVE BRANCH].... The people were consulted, the whole congregation [HOUSE OF REPRESENTATIVES] being called together on all important occasions: the government therefore was a proper republic.
>
> Moreover, to complete the establishment of civil government, courts were to be appointed...and elders most distinguished for wisdom and integrity were to be made judges [JUDICIAL BRANCH].

These courts were a safeguard to ensure that the laws would be applied on an equitable basis without class distinction or partiality. Appeals were allowed to a Supreme Court.

After detailing all of the obvious similarities between the proposed U.S. Constitution and the structure of the Hebrew republic given by God to the Hebrews, Langdon ended his speech calling the representatives to aspire to the example set by the ancient Hebrews.

Langdon explained that the proposed U.S. Constitution mirrored the divinely inspired Hebrew republic and would maximize freedom and limit tyranny. He called the legislature to approve the proposed Constitution. With their approval, the new Constitution would become law.

"A Republic, If You Can Keep It"

After Rev. Langdon's speech, the New Hampshire legislature voted to approve the Constitution, assuring that it would become the foundational document of America, along with the Declaration of Independence. It is universally considered by freedom-loving peoples from around the world to be the best and longest-lasting freedom document in modern history. The obvious reason for this is that it mirrors the divine pattern given by Moses to the Hebrew people.

Langdon's final charge to the legislature gives us a great challenge for our generation as well. He said:

> *The best constitution, badly managed, will soon fall and be changed into anarchy or tyranny.... ON THE PEOPLE, therefore, of these United States it depends, whether wise men or fools, good or bad men shall govern them; whether they shall have righteous laws, a faithful administration of government and permanent good order, peace and liberty; or, on the contrary, feel unsupportable burdens and see all their affairs run to confusion and ruin.*

The issue that confronts us now, nearly two and one-half centuries after the Constitution was established, is not only whether socialism will take over America. There is always some form of tyranny threatening to descend upon a free people, whether from communists, fascists, or globalist elites. As Langdon clearly stated, no constitution will save us if we the people lose our character and ability to choose wise leaders. It is in the hands of *We the People*, under God, to become voluntarily self-governing followers of the Great Liberator, Jesus Christ.

Statesman Daniel Webster's immortal words challenge us with the very strategic decision we face for ourselves and the world. He said:

> *Hold on to the Constitution and to the republic for which it stands. Miracles do not cluster, and what has happened once in 6,000 years may not happen again. Hold on to the Constitution, for if the American Constitution should fail, there will be anarchy throughout the world.*

We still have our precious freedom documents ascending from a bombproof vault every morning in the National Archives. We, of all people, have been blessed with the finest Christian heritage of liberty in history, going back to Moses.

Benjamin Franklin was approached by a lady as he was leaving the Constitutional Convention. She asked him, "What form of government have you given us?" Franklin's reply summarizes our challenge.

The wise sage told the lady, "A republic, if you can keep it." The hopes for the freedom of our children and the children of much of the world are resting upon those of us who will sacrifice to restore America's covenant with God. May we make the right choice.[4]

Appendix 3 Notes

1. Ellis Sandoz, ed., *Political Sermons of the Founding Era* (Indianapolis: Liberty Press, 1991), 943–67.

2. Exodus 18.

3. Exodus 20ff.

4. Rev. E. C. Wines authored a masterpiece volume entitled *Commentaries on the Laws of the Ancient Hebrews* in 1850. His book fully documents Langdon's sermon. Those interested in the Biblical roots of our Constitution are encouraged to study this text.

APPENDIX 4

A PEACEFUL REFORMATION

*A*s hard times are descending on America, what hope is there? Can one individual impact the world for good? Can a small group—around a dining room table, facing a hostile culture—ignite a peaceful reformation? The following story is one of the many powerful examples in history of a small group of believers in covenant with God transforming their nation.

Like America today, England in the eighteenth century was facing an empire collapsing from within. The similarities between England then and America today are described by author Herbert Schlossberg. He says, "The empty religiosity coexisting with open contempt for the Christian heritage of the nation, the widespread hypocrisy, the general lawlessness, and the political corruption were similar."[1]

Both the English people and the clergy had become spiritually dull and committed to blatant materialism. Few people read the Bible, and even church leaders ridiculed Biblical faith as a myth and hindrance to hedonism. England had slid into a morass of immorality. It became unsafe to go out after dark. Gangs roamed the streets—attacking, robbing, and murdering. The Industrial Revolution (birthed through Biblical principles a century before) became disconnected from its Christian roots and morality. England's lower classes, including their women and children, worked sixteen-hour days in dark and dangerous factories. They buried their sorrows in a sea of cheap gin. The higher classes and politicians were addicted to Madera, prostitution, and amusements, such as gambling.

Suddenly, an Awakening!

But suddenly, a peaceful revolution began. The preaching of men like George Whitefield and John Wesley ignited a spiritual fire that exploded upon English society. The spiritual fire grew, as Schlossberg explains, "recreating in tiny villages or in isolated parishes the promise of a Gospel that had atrophied from neglect and self-interest. As the movement spread, it coalesced around academic leaders in Cambridge and then political leaders in Clapham [South London]; it spawned publications and societies almost beyond number; it attracted the allegiance of many millions of people who accepted its claim upon them."[2]

The Clapham Group, a small collection of wealthy and influential leaders, was radically converted to Christ. They settled on a goal that dwarfed the self-centeredness of their times. Their objective was no less than the total transformation of a decadent, godless England and the abolition of the horrific slave trade, the empire's biggest source of revenue. Who were these leaders? Their inspirational leader was William Wilberforce, a member of Parliament who led the fight in Parliament for abolition of slavery for forty-two years.

Another Clapham leader was Henry Thornton, a financial genius whose practical business advice was indispensable. He gave away more than one-third of his fortune to their cause. Other Clapham leaders included powerful business leaders, politicians in Parliament, a banker, a Colonial governor, a brilliant lawyer, authors, educators, the governor-general of India, and clergymen. They were, for the most part, wealthy and influential. But they were up against all the power, institutions, and wealth of the greatest empire since Rome.

Before he died, Wilberforce spoke about this group of believers who laid their fortunes, reputations, and even their lives before a hostile, nearly pagan England. He said that the Clapham Group "challenged the whole moral climate of their times and changed their world! Their efforts ranged across a wide spectrum of issues, including slavery, missions, prison reform, public immorality, the needs of the poor." Professor Richard Pierard says that British Christians "between 1780 and 1844...founded at least 223 national [private] religious, moral, educational, and philanthropic institutions and societies to alleviate child abuse, poverty, illiteracy, and other social ills."[3]

The Army of Compassion

The English renewal took place because the Christians refused to limit their faith to personal piety. They set out to liberate entire institutions and cities from debilitating paganism. Schlossberg said of these reformers:

> *A veritable army was marching through England doing good.... Multitudes supported them with their labor and money. They rejected the view that serious Christianity concerned only the individual, not the society.... They banded together in huge numbers to form societies for helping the poor, evangelizing among an amazingly diverse array of groups, reforming morals, suppressing vice, improving the lot of prisoners, rescuing prostitutes from their economic distress, distributing religious literature, and promoting foreign missions....*
>
> *This brief sketch of the main elements of the religious revival leaves out the most important part of it. The ignorant became readers, writers, and leaders; the indigent began working and learning to excel at their work; housewives raised their children to be good family people, citizens, and neighbors; paupers and drunks began to earn a living, to save and invest [for their children and grandchildren].... An often brutal society in which a woman walking alone on the street could expect to be at least verbally molested, in which the highways were unsafe for the unarmed, in which political corruption was common, in which sexual promiscuity was the norm, had by the early years of the new century become kinder, more loving, and, "dare we say it?" more Christian.*[4]

Author Mark Galli said of English Christians in the 1800s, "Nearly everything they touched had improved: prisons, medical care, education, [working] conditions, slums.... They made life bearable for millions and saved the lives of millions more. That is no small legacy. And it is a legacy that history shows we hand on to our children, and to our children's children."

Speaking of the Clapham Group, Schlossberg challenges us to raise our spirits and raise the bar of our Christian commitment: "Full of hope, they did their duty to God and man as they were given light, braved the setbacks, and did not seem amazed at their great successes. It was as if they believed that God was ultimately in charge, and they had only to be faithful to their charges. There is no reason that experience could not be repeated today, despite the widespread pessimism."[5]

If a collapsing England can be revived by a small minority believing God to restore England to its covenant with God, why can't that happen in twenty-first-century America?

Peaceful Restoration

Fast-forward to our day. Democratic socialism has failed. The god of the secular State cannot be our provider anymore. It has, as Margaret Thatcher put it, "Run out of other people's money." But Christ's Army of Compassion, His Church, armed with His love for the spiritual and physical needs of men and nations, is awakening once again in America. And Americans have the advantage of having a constitutional republic that by its very words and structure demands the decentralization of power away from the national government and down to the "states and the people thereof." (See the Tenth Amendment to the Constitution.)

Do you have a few friends in your community who could gather, pray, and believe God to reach your community with the Gospel, to restore private welfare for the truly needy, and to educate the people once again in God's ways of living? It is beginning to happen in communities throughout the land.

The peaceful restoration of our nation lies before us. Kirk Cameron, in his movie *Monumental*, explains where the reformation of America must begin. He says the reformation of America "begins at your house, not the White House." We must vote wisely for the most Biblically sound candidates, and it may require that we ourselves run for office. But we must never lose sight of our role. We are the light of the world, the salt of the earth. We know that private Christian charity (love) can save our bankrupt civil institutions. If then, why not now?

Appendix 4 Notes

1. Ted Baehr, Susan Wales, and Ken Wales, *The Amazing Grace of Freedom* (Green Forest, AR: New Leaf Press Inc., 2007), 51.
2. Ibid., 50.
3. Ibid., 38.
4. Herbert Schlossberg, "How Great Awakenings Happen," *First Things* (October 2000).
5. Baehr, *Amazing Grace*, 51.

APPENDIX 5

SCOTLAND'S GIFT TO AMERICA

*T*he brave people of Scotland reasoned, prayed, and fought for the cause of Christian liberty for over a thousand years. The spirit of "bravehearts" like William Wallace, Robert the Bruce, and John Knox still runs deep in the American soul. In order to recover freedom and prosperity in America today, it is vital to understand the Scottish fight for liberty and their covenant documents.

As the fourteenth century neared, the English King Edward I, known as Edward Longshanks, was brutally tyrannizing the Scots, including men like William Wallace. The king's hypertaxation, land theft, and wholesale murder without trial broke all the rules of the Magna Carta (the heart of the English constitution) and common law. Longshanks even passed laws giving his nobles *prima nocta* (first rights of nobles to rape Scottish brides on their wedding day).

After his wife was brutally ravaged and killed by the English, William Wallace raised a citizen army of Scots to throw off English oppression. He became Scotland's greatest patriot by inspiring his men to fight for liberty based upon their God-given rights guaranteed in the Magna Carta and English common law—all of which rights were derived from the Scriptures. Wallace was eventually defeated and martyred. But in 1314, Robert the Bruce, King of the Scots, picked up the torch of freedom. He defeated the English oppressors at the battle of Bannockburn, obtaining liberty for Scotland for two hundred years.

Soon after, the Scots wrote the Declaration of Arbroath. This was the first of their Biblically based covenants, or freedom documents. Their words cry out to us through the ages and inspire millions even today:

> *For as long as but a hundred of us remain alive, never will we on any conditions be brought under English rule. It is in truth*

not for glory, nor riches, nor honors that we are fighting, but for FREEDOM—for that alone, which no honest man gives up but with life itself.

But over the next two hundred years, the government abuse under the so-called "divine right of kings" almost wiped out freedom again. The kings of England were burning Scotland's most sincere believers in the streets.

Then, gloriously, in the sixteenth century, the original document of freedom, the Bible, was unleashed in the language of the people in Scotland. In 1558, after centuries of semi-pagan barbarity, the Scottish people were led to the Savior and His Word by a former bodyguard and galley slave, and then powerful preacher, John Knox. With their new Biblical understanding, they were the first nation to put limits on the power of government with checks and balances. Within a decade, the Scots succeeded in dethroning their tyrannical queen.

The struggle for liberty against big government oppression continued for another century. But the Scots created a number of precious freedom documents—covenants—during this time of trial in Scotland. These freedom documents set the stage for America's Declaration of Independence.

English King Charles I attempted to destroy true Biblical faith in Scotland by forcing his warped religious training upon all the children of Scotland. The Scots were enraged at this violation of the Biblical mandate to train their children. They met in the Greyfriar's churchyard in Edinburgh and signed their National Covenant of 1638. Many Scots signed the document in their own blood, swearing never to compromise their faith or allow anyone to educate their children against their understanding of God's Word.

The Christian Scots were declaring to the world that their rights came from God, not from the king or any government leader, court, or legislature. Therefore, a ruler could not force his arbitrary laws upon the people and expect them to passively follow. Note that the Scottish believers were ready to die rather than allow the king (or government of any kind) to teach their children things contrary to the Word of God. The main issue of the National Covenant was not taxes or property, but the internal character development of their children.

Would we be willing to die to protect our children today from the anti-Biblical teachings of the government schools?

To understand this bold National Covenant, we must realize that these Scottish believers in kilts were not just playing war games. They did not promote anarchy, as have most modern revolutions up to our time. They were Biblically and intellectually prepared by men like the eminent Professor Samuel Rutherford to stand against oppression, even unto death. Rutherford's book, *Lex Rex*, written in 1644, stands even today as the premier defense of the Biblical rights and responsibilities of people to resist tyranny (out-of-control government) and to restore the rule of law (God's Law).

For hundreds of years, the people of Europe had been erroneously taught by ruler and prelate alike that the king was God's "absolute authority" on earth and was always to be obeyed. Rutherford unraveled this argument Biblically. He powerfully defended, from Scripture, the right of the people to resist, with force if necessary, a ruler who abuses his trust and his people, just like an abusive father or husband may be removed from leadership of his family. Rutherford made it clear from Scripture, as did Calvin and others, that the people have no right to riot. Rather, they must act formally through their representatives, publicly naming the wrongs the ruler has committed. America's Declaration of Independence directly parallels the principles delineated in *Lex Rex*.

The leaders of the Covenantors, those who signed the National Covenant, were the pastors of the nation. James Guthrie pastored at his church in Stirling, until the king's troops dragged him from his pulpit in 1660. After a mock trial, Pastor Guthrie was paraded before a huge crowd to be hanged, drawn, and quartered. He encouraged the crowds of Scots to stand strong in their liberty. He said with his last breath, "The covenants! The covenants shall yet be Scotland's reviving."

It took another forty years and the martyrdom of tens of thousands of courageous ministers and those in their churches until the brutal Stuart kings were swept from power. In 1688, England and Scotland experienced true freedom under William and Mary, the Glorious Revolution, and the English Bill of Rights. Again, the revival of liberty can be traced to brave defenders of God's justice who remembered the covenants—documents of freedom.

Two hundred years later, liberty was again at risk. English King George III had chosen to brutally oppress his colonies in America. Defying eight hundred years of English law and the blood-bought freedom documents going back to the Biblically based law code and common law of Alfred the Great, King George taxed without representation and boarded his troops in American homes (giving them the right to steal and rape), taking entire cities captive.

But the Scots—900,000 of them—had immigrated to America during the eighteenth century. They made up almost a third of the population of the American colonies during the American Revolution and were the heart of America's Army Officer Corps. They led in a historic remembrance, calling the colonists back to the documents of freedom. The Declaration of Independence was a restatement of the Scottish and English Biblical resistance-to-tyranny documents of the past thousand years! The Founders rose up, stood on principle, and created the finest constitutional republic in history.

We can see from this brief history that the brave Scots who came to America planted the tree of liberty, and we in America have eaten its fruit. Now, two hundred years later, we have once again forgotten the freedom documents—the sacred covenants that have been the only safe and secure anchor of liberty throughout history. Like America's Founders, the Scots and the English before us, we must turn humbly back to our God, remember the essential lessons of history, and work diligently to restore true freedom and prosperity again.

How One Scotsman Prepared America's Founders for Freedom

Prior to the founding of America, John Witherspoon, a devout pastor and descendant of John Knox, was forced to leave Scotland. He accepted the invitation to become president of the College of New Jersey (Princeton University). In the 1760s, the colonies were being pressed toward war with England. They were determined to create the world's first constitutional republic rather than fall back into the European model of divine-right kings and impoverished commoners. If the colonists were to succeed, they would need political, military, and spiritual leaders that would surpass any in history.

John Witherspoon, as the head of the College of New Jersey, became the teacher of those future leaders. He combined a deep faith in the Biblical Christianity of the Reformation with an understanding of how to apply that faith to every academic discipline, including nation building. During his tenure, there were 478 graduates of his college. With only three professors, including himself, John was able to mentor all who came to his school, using the tutorial method in six academic fields. He was then able to preach to them each Sunday in the campus chapel. Until 1902, every president of Princeton was a minister. America's youth were largely mentored by ministers like Witherspoon until the twentieth century.

Of his graduates, at least eighty-six became active in civil government and included: one president (James Madison), one vice-president (Aaron Burr), ten cabinet officers, twenty-one senators, thirty-nine congressmen, twelve governors, a Supreme Court justice, and one attorney general.

Nearly one-fifth of the signers of the Declaration of Independence, one-sixth of the delegates of the Constitutional Convention, and one-fifth of the first Congress under the Constitution were graduates of the College of New Jersey. It can truly be said that John Witherspoon discipled his new nation by training its leaders, just as his ancestor John Knox had done in Scotland two hundred years before.

Along with leading a college and serving in the Presbyterian Church, Witherspoon threw his efforts into the political drive for freedom. He was elected to the Continental Congress and sat on one hundred different committees. As the debate over independence raged in Philadelphia on July 2, 1776, John stood to his feet and declared, "We are ripe for independence and in danger of becoming rotten for want of it, if we delay any longer!" He was the only formal minister to sign the Declaration of Independence (twenty-two others had ministerial training.) The next year, the British took out their revenge on him, ravaging his college and burning his personal and college libraries. He also lost two of his sons in the War for Independence.

John Witherspoon was an indispensable leader used by God to help found this freest and most blessed of all nations. His words on the National Day of Prayer in 1776 still ring with the spiritual power of his forebear John Knox, the fiery reformer of Scotland: "While we give praise to God, the supreme disposer of all events, for His interposition on our behalf, let us guard against the dangerous error of trusting in or boasting of an arm of flesh [human power]....If your cause is just, if your principles are pure, and if your conduct is prudent, you need not fear the multitude of opposing hosts."

John Witherspoon's words and life speak to us from the "great cloud of witnesses." This is our day on the stage of history. God is orchestrating world events and our lives, because He "causes all things to work together for good to those who love God, to those who are called according to His purpose."

I believe that around our kitchen tables are seated the "Knoxes" and "Witherspoons" of our day who will be used to disciple the nations in our time. May God give us the eyes to recognize them and the commitment to train them while they are still in our sphere of influence!

For FREE bonus material & in-depth study on a variety of topics beyond what you find here in *The American Covenant,* visit WorldHistoryInstitute.com/free-downloads.

Selected Bibliography

Ames, Bobbie. *The Land that I Love: Restoring Our Christian Heritage.* Ventura, CA: Nordskog Publishing Inc., 2020.

Arber, Edward, ed. *The Story of the Pilgrim Fathers, 1606–1623, A.D., as Told by Themselves, Their Friends and Their Enemies.* London: Ward & Downey Limited; Boston, New York: Houghton, Mifflin & Co., 1897; repr., New York: Klaus Reprint Co., 1969.

Baldwin, Alice M. *The New England Clergy and the American Revolution.* New York: Frederick Ungar Publishing Co., 1958.

Bartlett, Robert Merrill. *The Pilgrim Way.* Philadelphia: United Church Press, 1971.

Billington, D. W. *Patterns in History.* Downers Grove, IL: InterVarsity Press, 1979.

Bradford, William. *The History of Plymouth Plantation.* 2 vols. New York: Russell & Russell, 1968, repr. of Massachusetts Historical Society, 1856.

Brown, Alexander. *The Genesis of the United States.* Boston and New York: Houghton Mifflin & Co., 1890.

Brown, John. *The Pilgrim Fathers of New England and Their Puritan Successors.* Pasadena, TX: Pilgrim Publications, 1970.

Burgess, Walter. *The Pastor of the Pilgrims: A Biography of John Robinson.* New York: Harcourt, Brace & Howe, 1920.

Burrage, Champlin. *The True Story of Robert Browne (1550?–1633), Father of Congregationalism.* London: Henry Frowde, 1906.

Campbell, Douglas. *The Puritan in Holland, England, and America.* New York: Harper & Bros., 1893.

Campbell, Norine Dickson. *Patrick Henry: Patriot and Statesman.* New York: The Devin-Adair Co., 1969.

Clark, Jonas. *The Battle of Lexington: A Sermon and Eyewitness Narrative.* Ventura, CA: Nordskog Publishing Inc., 2007.

Cornelison, Isaac A. *The Relation of Religion to Civil Government in the United States of America, a State without a Church, But Not without a Religion.* New York and London: G. P. Putnam & Sons, 1895.

Craig, Whitney Hobson. *John Brown of Priesthill.* Ventura, CA: Nordskog Publishing Inc., 2017.

d'Aubigné, J. H. Merle. *The Reformation in England,* vol. 1. Carlisle, PA: The Banner of Truth Trust, 1977.

Dexter, Henry Martyn and Morton Dexter. *The England and Holland of the Pilgrims*. Boston: Houghton, Mifflin & Co., 1905.

Dimitrov, Nikola D. *The Four in One Gospel of Jesus: Chronologically Integrated According to Matthew, Mark, Luke, and John*. Ventura, CA: Nordskog Publishing Inc., 2017.

Donovan, Frank. *Mr. Jefferson's Declaration*. New York: Dodd, Mead & Co., 1968.

Elazar, Daniel J. *From Biblical Covenant to Modern Federalism: The Federal Theology Bridge*. Philadelphia: Workshop on Covenant and Politics of the Center for the Study of Federalism, Temple University, 1980.

Eidsmoe, John. *Historical and Theological Foundations of Law*. 3 vols. Ventura, CA: Nordskog Publishing Inc., 2016.

Fiske, John. *The American Revolution*. 2 vols. Boston and New York: Houghton, Mifflin & Co., 1898.

———. *The Beginnings of New England or The Puritan Theocracy in Its Relations to Civil and Religious Liberty*. Boston and New York: Houghton, Mifflin & Co., 1900.

———. *The Critical Period of American History: 1783–1789*. Boston and New York: Houghton, Mifflin & Co., 1898.

Green, J. R. *A Short History of The English People*. New York and London: Harper & Bros., 1898.

Grimstead, Jay. *Rebuilding Civilization on the Bible: Proclaiming the Truth on 24 Controversial Issues*. Ventura, CA: Nordskog Publishing Inc., 2014.

Hall, Verna M. *The Christian History of the American Revolution: Consider and Ponder*. San Francisco: Foundation for American Christian Education, 1975.

———. *The Christian History of the Constitution of the United States of America: Christian Self-Government*. American Revolution Bicentennial edition. San Francisco: Foundation for American Christian Education, 1975.

———. *The Christian History of the Constitution of the United States of America: Christian Self-Government with Union*. San Francisco: Foundation for American Christian Education, rev. ed., 1979.

———. *George Washington: The Character and Influence of One Man*. Chesapeake, VA: Foundation for American Christian Education, 1999.

Hall, Verna M., Rosalie J. Slater, and Carole Adams. *The Bible and the Constitution: A Primer of American Liberty*. San Francisco: Foundation for American Christian Education, 2012.

Hamilton, Alexander, John Jay, and James Madison. *The Federalist.* New York: Tudor Publishing Co., 1937.

Henry, Matthew. *Commentary on the Whole Bible.* 6 vols. Old Tappan, NJ: Fleming H. Revell Company. Repr. of 1721 ed.

Johnson, William J. *George Washington, the Christian.* Milford, MI: Mott Media, 1976.

Kirk, Ronald. *Thy Will Be Done: When All Nations Call God Blessed.* Ventura, CA: Nordskog Publishing Inc., 2013.

Kuiper, B. K. *The Church in History.* Grand Rapids, MI: The National Union of Christian Schools and Eerdmans, 1978.

Kurtz, Paul. *Humanist Manifestos I and II.* Buffalo, NY: Prometheus Books, 1977.

Latourette, Kenneth Scott. *A History of Christianity.* Vol II: *Reformation to the Present.* San Francisco: Harper & Row, 1975.

Locke, John. *The Reasonableness of Christianity As Delivered in the Scriptures.* Edited and introduced by George W. Ewing. A Gateway Edition. Chicago: Henry Regnery Company, 1965.

Locke, John. *Two Treatises of Government. A Critical Edition with Introduction and Criticus Apparatus by Peter Laslett.* Cambridge University Press, 1960; New York and Toronto: The New American Library, 1965.

Marshall, Peter, and David Manuel. *The Light and the Glory.* Old Tappan, NJ: Fleming H. Revell Co, 1977.

Mason, George. *The Papers of George Mason.* 3 vols. Edited by Robert A. Rutland. Chapel Hill, NC: The University of North Carolina Press, 1970.

McLaughlin, Andrew C. *The Foundations of American Constitutionalism.* New York: New York University Press, 1932; Greenwich, CT: Fawcett World Library, 1961.

Miller, Perry. *The New England Mind: The Seventeenth Century.* New York: The MacMillan Company, 1939; Beacon Press, 1968.

Montesquieu, Baron. *The Spirit of Laws* (1742). London and New York: The Colonial Press, 1900. Available in many publications.

Morgan, Edmund S. *The Puritan Family.* New York: Harper & Row, 1966.

Morison, Samuel Eliot, *Builders of the Bay Colony.* 2nd ed., rev. and enl. Boston: Houghton, Mifflin Co., 1958.

Neal, Daniel. *The History of the Puritans.* 5 vols. London: Richard Hett, 1732.

Neill, Edward D. *History of the Virginia Company of London.* Albany, NY: Joel Munsell, 1869.

Newcombe, Jerry. *American Amnesia: Is America Paying the Price for Forgetting God, the Source of Our Liberty?* Ventura, CA: Nordskog Publishing Inc., 2018.

———. *The Book that Made America: How the Bible Formed Our Nation.* Ventura: CA: Nordskog Publishing Inc., 2009.

Oberholtzer, Ellis Paxson. *Robert Morris, Patriot and Financier.* New York: The Macmillan Company, 1903.

Powell, Edward A., and Rousas John Rushdoony. *Tithing and Dominion.* Vallecito, CA: Ross House Books, 1979.

Prince, Thomas. *The Salvations of God in 1746.* Boston: D. Henchman, 1746.

Robinson, John. *The Works of John Robinson.* 3 vols. London: John Snow, 1851.

Rushdoony, Rousas John. *Institutes of Biblical Law.* Phillipsburg, NJ: Presbyterian & Reformed Publishing Company, 1973.

Rutland, Robert A. *George Mason: Reluctant Statesman.* Williamsburg, VA: Colonial Williamsburg, Inc.; Holt, Rinehart & Winston, 1961.

Rutherford, Samuel. *Lex Rex: The Law and the Prince.* London: John Field, 1644. Available in many publications.

Schaff, Philip. *History of the Christian Church.* 8 vols. Grand Rapids, MI: Eerdmans, 1978.

Schaeffer, Francis A. *A Christian Manifesto.* Westchester, IL: Crossway Books, 1982.

———. *Escape from Reason.* Downer's Grove, IL: InterVarsity Press, 1968.

Schroeder, John Frederick, D.D., ed. *Maxims of Washington.* 5th ed. Mount Vernon, VA: The Mount Vernon Ladies' Association, 1974.

Selby, John. *The Road to Yorktown.* New York: St. Martin's Press, 1976.

Shafer, Paul W., and John Howland Snow. *The Turning of the Tides.* New Canaan, CT: The Long House, 1962.

Slater, Rosalie J. *Teaching and Learning America's Christian History.* American Revolution Bicentennial edition. San Francisco, CA: Foundation for American Christian Education, 1975.

Smith, Bradford. *Bradford of Plymouth.* Philadelphia and New York: J. B. Lippincott Co., 1951.

Smith, Bradford. *Captain John Smith, His Life and Legend.* Philadelphia and New York: J. B. Lippincott Company, 1953.

Smith, H. Sheldon, Robert T. Handy, and Lefferts A. Loetscher. *American Christianity: An Historical Interpretation with Representative Documents.* Vol. 1: *1607–1820.* New York: Charles Scribner's Sons, 1960.

Smith, James Ward, and A. Leland Jamison, eds. *Religion in American*

Life. Vol. 1: *The Shaping of American Religion.* Princeton: Princeton University Press, 1961.

Smith, John, Captain. *The General Historie of Virginia, New England and The Summer Isles in Travels and Works of Captain John Smith.* 2 vols. Edited by Edward Arber. Edinburgh: John Grant, 1910.

Smylie, James H. "Madison and Witherspoon: Theological Roots of American Political Thought," *The Princeton University Library Chronicle* 22 (Spring 1981).

Stith, William. *The History of the First Discovery and Settlement of Virginia.* New York: Joseph Sabin repr., 1865, from 1st ed., Williamsburg, VA, 1747.

Swanson, Mary-Elaine. *John Locke: Philosopher of American Liberty.* Ventura, CA: Nordskog Publishing, 2012.

Tanner, J. R. *Constitutional Documents of the Reign of James I, A.D. 1603–1625.* Cambridge, England: Cambridge University Press, 1930.

Tocqueville, Alexis de. *Democracy in America.* 2 vols. Translated by Henry Reeve, revised by Francis Bowen, and edited by Phillips Bradley. New York: Alfred A. Knopf, Inc., 1945; New York: Vintage Books, Inc., 1955.

Washington, George. *Farewell Address.* New York: Duffield & Company, 1907.

Webster, Noah. *An American Dictionary of the English Language, 1828.* San Francisco: Foundation for American Christian Education, 1967.

Whitehead, John W. *The Second American Revolution.* Elgin, IL: David C. Cook, 1982.

———. *The Separation Illusion.* Milford, MI: Mott Media, 1977.

Wrong, George M. *The Conquest of New France.* New Haven: University Press, 1918.

Young, Alexander. *Chronicles of The Pilgrim Fathers of The Colony of Plymouth: 1602–1625.* Boston: Charles C. Little & James Brown, 1841.

Acknowledgments

$\mathcal{I}$ am especially grateful to Kirk Cameron and his wonderful family. From the day that I met them, they have stood strong for the Lord and His purpose for America. Kirk is undoubtedly the foremost communicator of America's Christian heritage. His dedication to teach *The American Covenant* live to tens of thousands of Americans every evening for one hundred days at the American Campfire Revival is courageous and without precedent. Kirk exemplifies the "braveheart" spirit of his Scottish Christian ancestors.

An encouraging sign of hope for our nation's future is the rediscovery of America's authentic Christian history over the past few generations. I am deeply indebted to Verna M. Hall and Rosalie J. Slater, who first introduced me to the irrefutable evidence of America's covenant relationship with God. They established the Foundation for American Christian Education (FACE.net). They were early pioneers who spent decades researching, documenting, and teaching the Christian history of the U.S. Constitution. I recommend their books, especially *Christian History of the Constitution: Christian Self-Government* and *Teaching and Learning America's Christian History*.

Mary Elaine Swanson deserves special acknowledgment. Mary Elaine spent years researching in the archives at the University of California at Berkeley. There, she uncovered the nearly "canceled" primary-source evidence of the Christian history of our republic. Mary Elaine was a strategic partner in developing and writing the first *American Covenant* edition as its co-author. She was one of the finest examples I have known of a loving, yet powerfully intelligent,

American patriot. She shall be remembered in coming generations as a hero of liberty.

Special thanks also are due to the team that has been assembled to bring this book to print: Jerry Nordskog, Ron Kirk, Michelle Shelfer, Cherie LaSalla, Andy Jackson, and others who have diligently labored to accomplish this project in record time. I also want to acknowledge the many other individuals and organizations who have been raised up to teach our true American heritage.

My gratitude to my wife, Trish, is beyond measure. She sacrificially works together with me in all of our projects, books, films, seminars, and tours. Her research and editing have been critical in the writing of *The American Covenant: The Untold Story.*

— MARSHALL FOSTER

March 2021

About the Author

*D*r. Marshall Foster is the founder and president of the World History Institute, a non-profit educational foundation. He and his team are dedicated to teaching the lessons of history that have brought freedom and prosperity to individuals and nations worldwide. Marshall is a best-selling author and is a popular keynote speaker at churches, schools, and business conventions in nearly every state in America. Marshall has inspired millions of Americans to remember and help restore America's forgotten covenants with God. He is the Director of Education for ACTS tours. He oversees the training of more than twelve thousand students and families each year on tours of the historic East Coast. Marshall also personally leads historic tours throughout America and the British Isles. Along with Kirk Cameron, Marshall co-produced the classic documentary films *Monumental* and *Unstoppable*.

The World History Institute

Marshall and his wife, Trish, established the World History Institute in 1976. Its mission is to reintroduce the forgotten Biblical and historical foundations of liberty to Americans and others around the world. The World History Institute has become a major force in the movement to restore America to its Judeo-Christian heritage.

The Institute has developed resources, seminars, and tours to benefit Americans of all backgrounds. Marshall Foster has taught our nation's authentic history from primary sources, writings, and the worldview of America's ancestors. Americans have responded with overwhelming enthusiasm and new hope that our republic can be restored. An Army of Compassion is rising up, working to heal the brokenhearted and to peacefully restore our nation.

There is a tidal wave of truth breaking into the mainstream of American thought. That wave is not a "socialist utopia"—it is what C. S. Lewis called the "clean sea breeze of the centuries," which needs to be "blowing through our minds" to help us see beyond our existential moment. The prevailing wave of history is being driven by our loving Creator, whose plan has been the only proven one to bring lasting liberty to any nation. The World History Institute is grateful to be a part—along with other fine organizations—of inspiring a new generation to remember that "blessed is the nation whose God is the Lord."

Kirk Cameron's America's Campfire Revival is an answer to the prayers of millions of Americans. It is lighting the kindling of a new Great Awakening. Kirk's teaching through *The American Covenant: The Untold Story* is providing the hope and the strategy of our forebears needed for the peaceful restoration of our nation.

MY COUNTRY, 'TIS OF THEE

My country, 'tis of thee,
Sweet land of liberty,
Of thee I sing.
Land where my fathers died!
Land of the Pilgrim's pride!
From every mountain side,
Let freedom ring!

My native country, thee,
Land of the noble free,
Thy name I love.
I love thy rocks and rills,
Thy woods and templed hills;
My heart with rapture fills
Like that above.

Let music swell the breeze,
And ring from all the trees
Sweet freedom's song.
Let mortal tongues awake;
Let all that breathe partake;
Let rocks their silence break,
The sound prolong.

Our father's God, to Thee,
Author of liberty,
To Thee we sing.
Long may our land be bright
With freedom's holy light;
Protect us by Thy might,
Great God, our King!

About Nordskog Publishing...

Publishing meaty, tasty, and easily digestible Biblical treasures on Christian theology, American and Church history, and Christ-honoring true stories of men and women of great faith.

NORDSKOG PUBLISHING'S PRIMARY MISSION is to enhance the spiritual growth of Christ's redeemed people through understanding of His Laws, and all Truth, as found in His Holy Scriptures. We seek to illustrate His power in all believers through application of the Bible to every subject and every aspect of life and living.

Nordskog entered Christian book publishing in 2006, specializing in Biblically grounded, *"Meaty, Tasty, and Easily Digestible Biblical Treasures."* Nordskog Publishing has published over fifty titles, exploring various genres. Thus far, we have published children's, devotional, inspirational novels, Christian history, and unique, applied-Biblical-faith categories—over fifty titles, including several translations into Mandarin, Portuguese, Spanish, and Indonesian. Most titles have eBook versions available. The company continues to search for the best in inspiring, stimulating, Christian-growth-inducing themes.

See our full catalog at NordskogPublishing.com.
For ordering, email or call:
staff@NordskogPublishing.com • 805-642-2070

The BELL RINGER

Sign up for our E-Newsletter, *The Bell Ringer*, for timely articles, recent releases, product discounts. NordskogPublishing.com/newsletter/

4562 Westinghouse Street, Suite E, Ventura, CA 93003
staff@NordskogPublishing.com • 805-642-2070